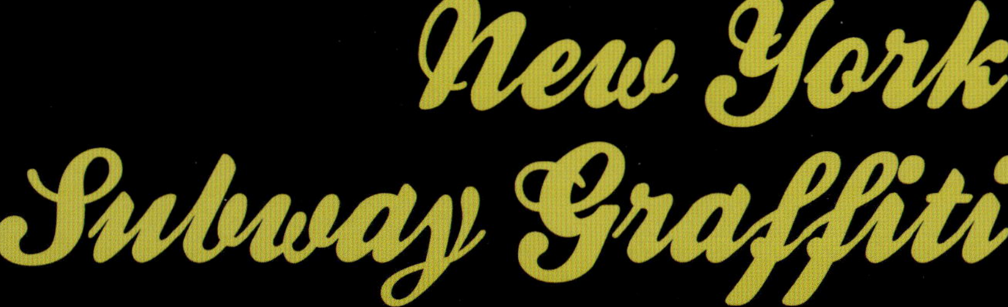

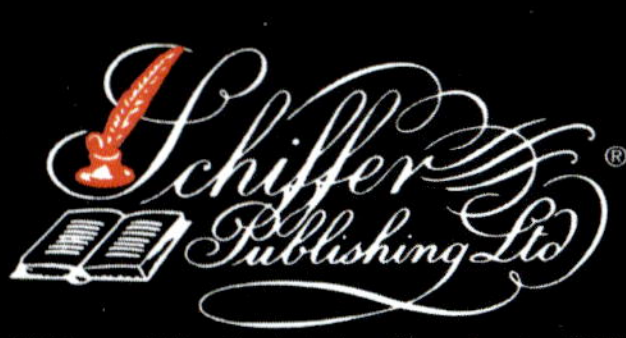

4880 Lower Valley Road Atglen, Pennsylvania 19310

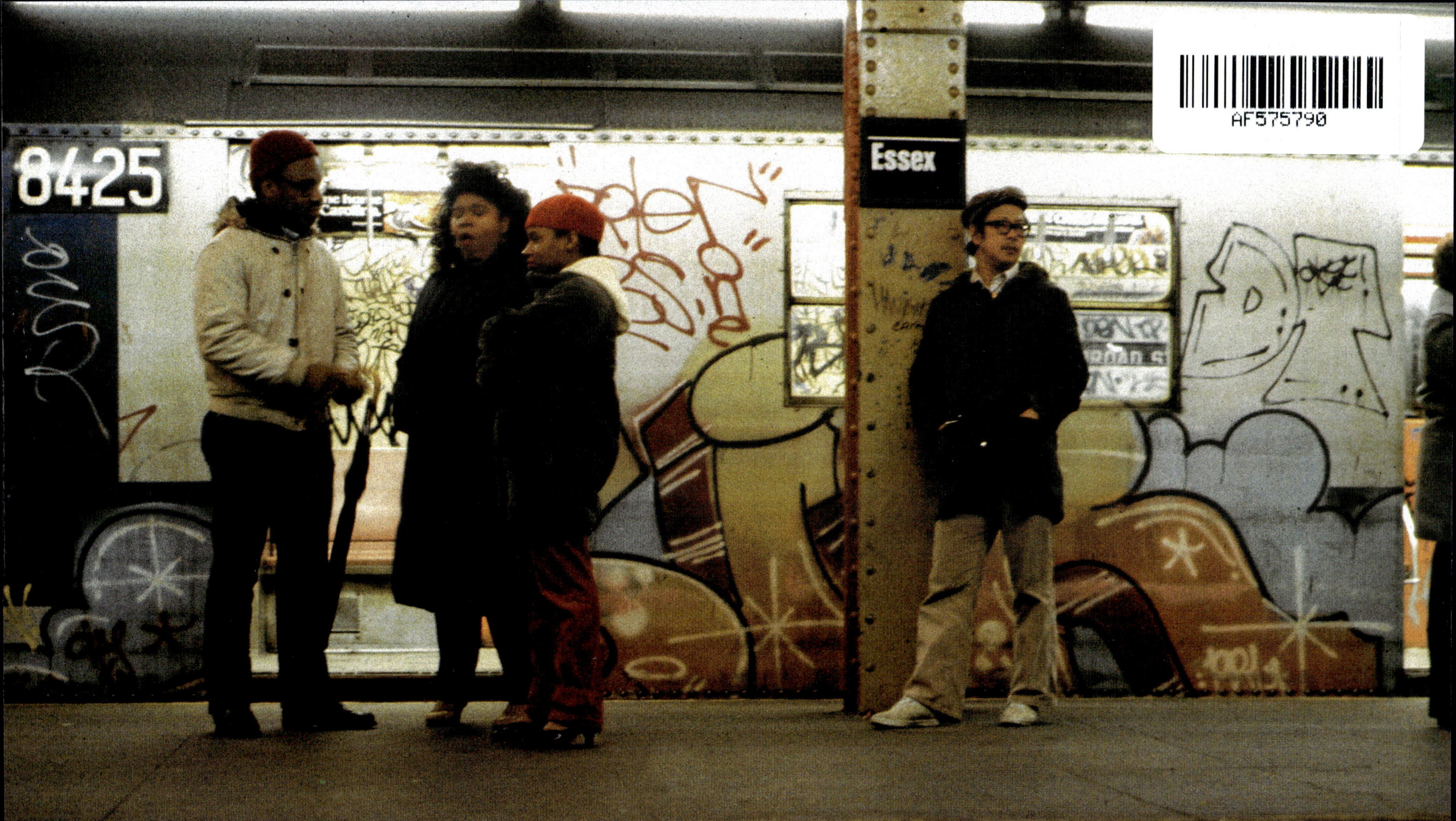

Library of Congress Control Number: 2009926667

Type set in Zurich BT

ISBN: 978-0-7643-3339-2
Printed in China

Schiffer Books are available at special discounts for bulk purchases for sales promotions or premiums. Special editions, including personalized covers, corporate imprints, and excerpts can be created in large quantities for special needs. For more information contact the publisher:

Published by Schiffer Publishing Ltd.
4880 Lower Valley Road
Atglen, PA 19310
Phone: (610) 593-1777; Fax: (610) 593-2002
E-mail: Info@schifferbooks.com

For the largest selection of fine reference books on this and related subjects, please visit our web site at
www.schifferbooks.com
We are always looking for people to write books on new and related subjects. If you have an idea for a book please contact us at the above address.

This book may be purchased from the publisher.
Include $5.00 for shipping.
Please try your bookstore first.
You may write for a free catalog.

In Europe, Schiffer books are distributed by
Bushwood Books
6 Marksbury Ave.
Kew Gardens
Surrey TW9 4JF England
Phone: 44 (0) 20 8392 8585; Fax: 44 (0) 20 8392 9876
E-mail: info@bushwoodbooks.co.uk
Website: www.bushwoodbooks.co.uk

Introduction

This epic time in New York City exists only in memory and photographs. History becomes legend and tales of rails are handed down to another generation. I'm not going to tell you the way it happened. I am going to show you the way I remember it. It is possible to record a historical art phenomenon for the world to see. The photograph documents a moment in time, capturing it for the future.

This book will take you on a journey through time, travelling from the early 1970s through the 1980s and into the 1990s, subway graveyards. The evolution of the art form will become clear. You will see graffiti from its conception to its utter demise. Although the book is only a blink of the eye in the history of graffiti, an enormous amount of work was produced on the subway system during these years. So this book is a piece of the puzzle. It looks at an area of art that is usually misunderstood.

Like most art, it was not appreciated in its time, perhaps because it was ahead of its time. Many would, in fact, argue that it was not art; that it was pure vandalism. Who is qualified to determine what is art and what is not? The trains of the 1970s can be compared to the music of that time. Both were original, creative innovations of the their time.

I believe this phenomenon, known as "writing," could only be formulated in a city like New York. Inspiration comes at you from every angle in New York City. In the 1970s, the city was not the "Disneyland" it is today. New York was the quintessential birth mother of graffiti. It had all the right elements to produce this form of expression. Poverty, crime, and gangs overpowered the streets. The transit system was out of control. It was being run by kids. Kids of the streets. Kids that parents, teachers, and society deemed unteachable, unsuitable, and just plain "animals." They were public animals, with the means and determination to express themselves through their very public art.

Wanted for their late night activities, these young rebels risked it all. With only youth and a bag of paint on their side, they would light up the line with a fresh piece for their peers and the public to see. Watching a graffiti-painted train pull into a station or an elevated train rumbling above is a powerful sight. The colors are like a loud voice that screams out at you to be noticed.

The work produced on the transit system inspired generation of writers all over the world. Chances are, if it is being done today, it was already painted on a train years ago. Every generation likes to believe they hold the mortgage on when graffiti was at its best. Graffiti writing was a kid's game. The best times are your youthful, carefree times. So, if you can trace it back to a time that felt real for you, every generation could be right. This book is for the known and unknown names of subway graffiti. I hope everybody's name is known someday.

The Crews of NYC

In this period there were various crews of writers working around the city, each with their own, uniquely creative name. The following is a list of the crews found in this book, with the abbreviations they used.

AMW	America's Most Wanted
AOK	All Out Kings
BC	Bad Company
BSK	Bad Subway Kings
COD	Children of Destruction
CWK	Craft Work Kings
DSA	Dark Side Artists
KD	Kings Destroy
MPC	Morris Park Crew
NWC	New Wave Crew
RiS	Rocking it Suckers
RTW	Rolling Thunder Writers
SV	Subway Vandals
TAC	The Art Crew
TAT	Tuff Ass Team
TC5	The Crazy Five
TC5	The Cool 5
TDC	The Destiny Children
TDS	The Death Squad
TF	True Fame
TFA	The First Avenue crew
TF5	The Fabulous 5
TFP	The Fantastic Partners
TKC	The Killer Crew
TMB	The Master Blasters
TMC	The Mad Children
TM7	The Magnificent 7
TNR	The Nasty Rebels
TNS	They Never Stop
TOA	Top of All
TPA	The Public Animals
UA	United Artist
VIC	Vandals in Control
WS	Wild Style

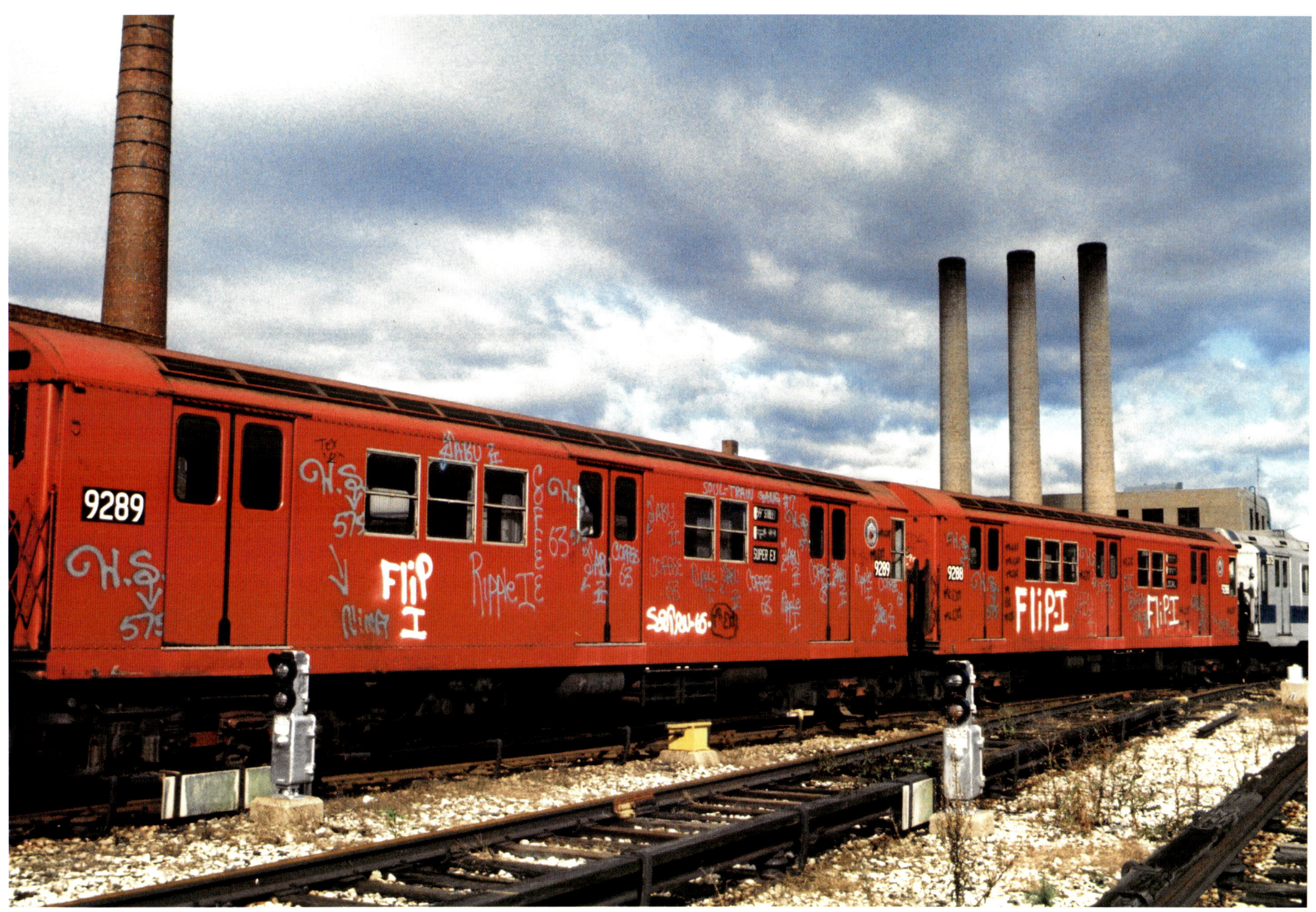

Early 1970s signatures mark the beginnings. The City was not ready for it.

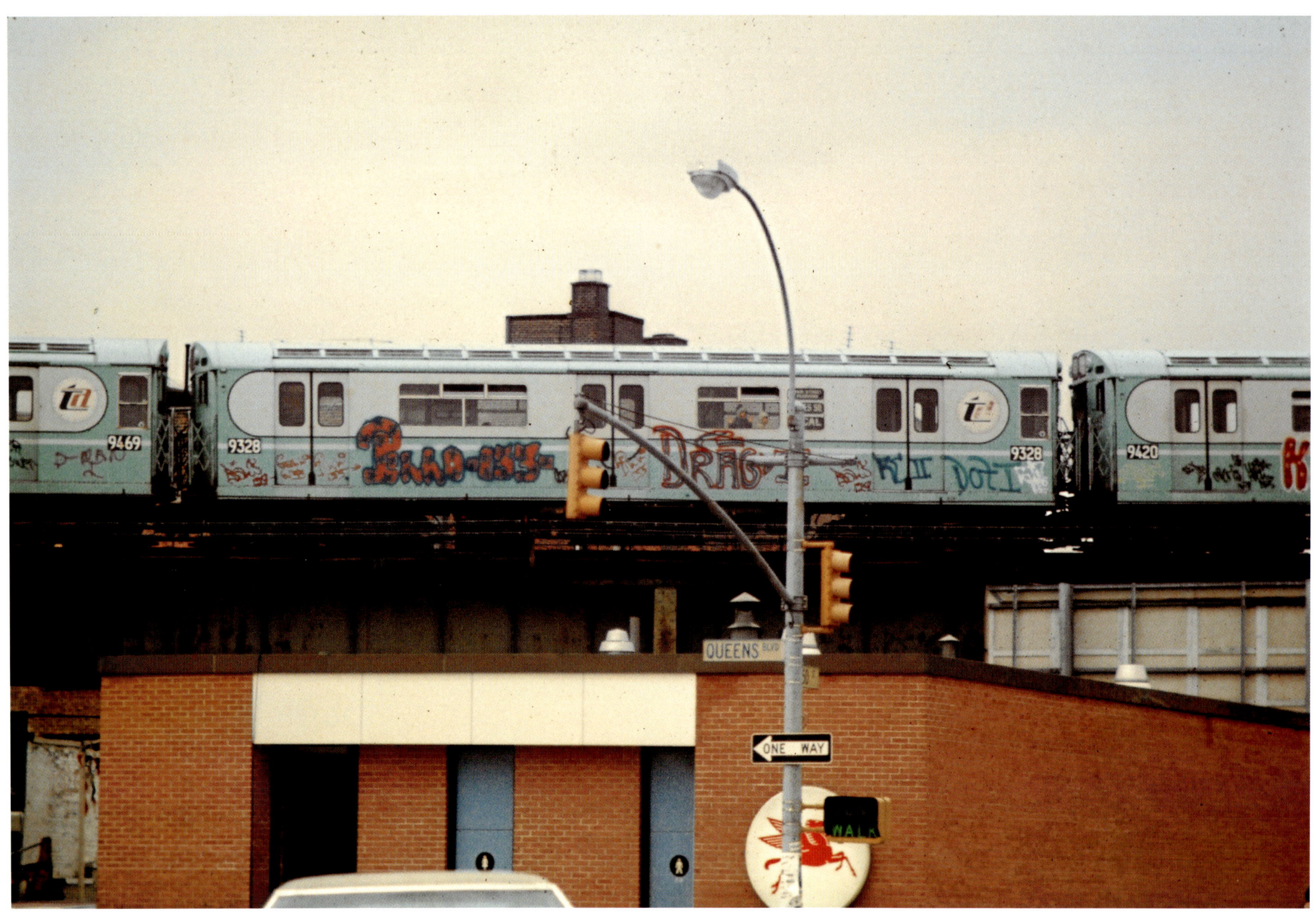

The No. 7 line rumbling by Queens Boulevard, 1973.

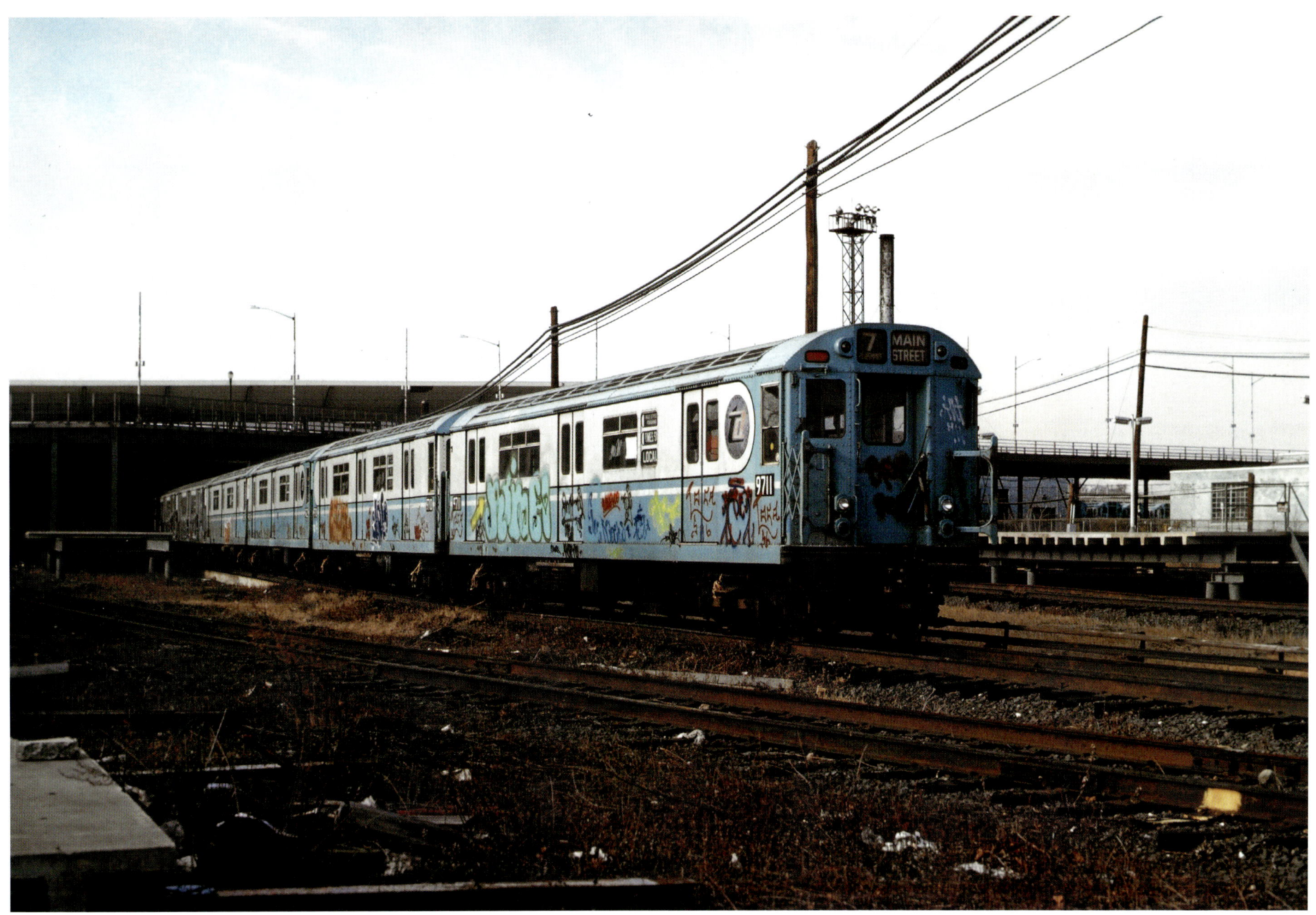

The No. 7 line, 1974

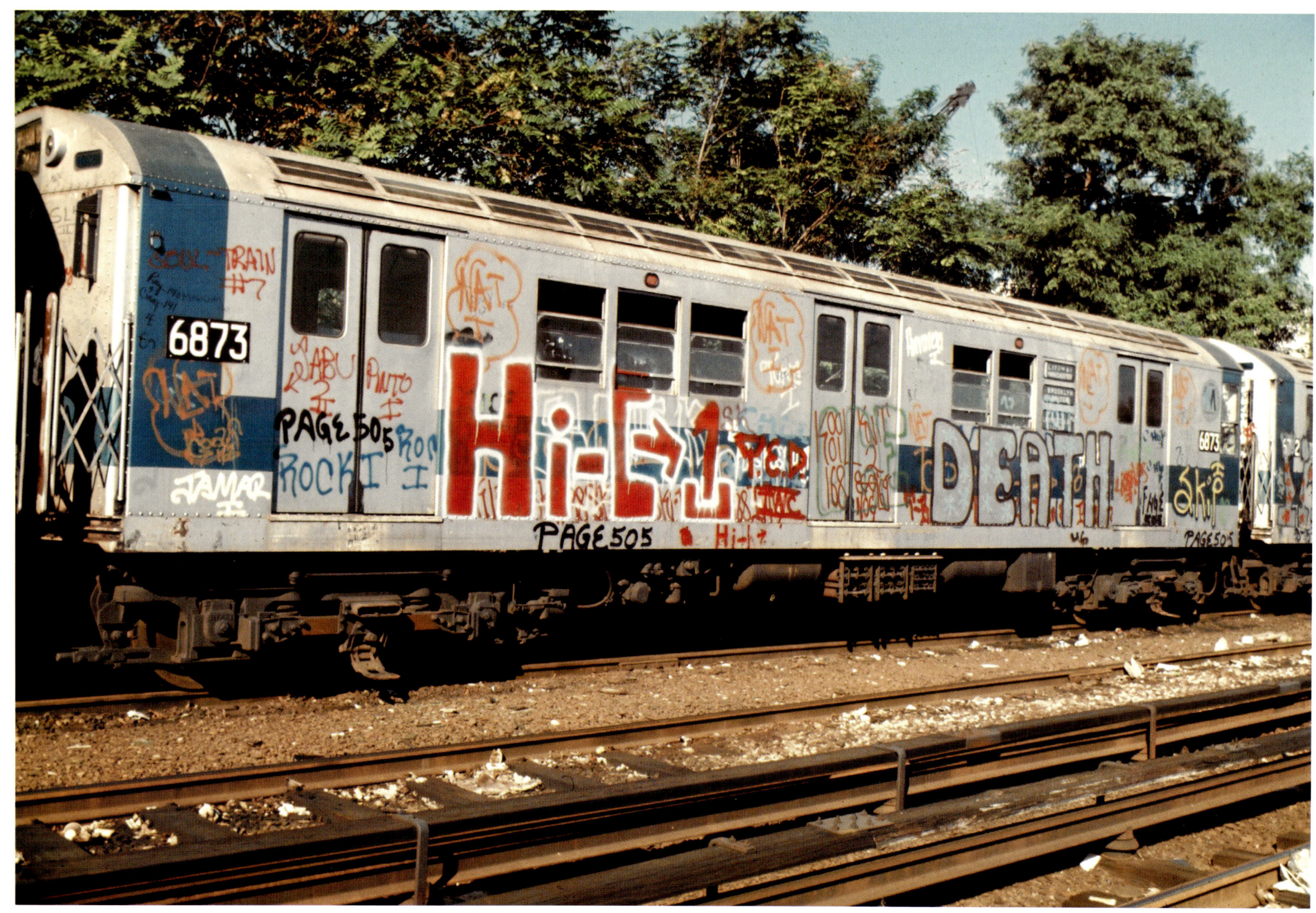

Hi-C-1 and Death, 1972. Death was an original member of The Crazy 5 (TC5).

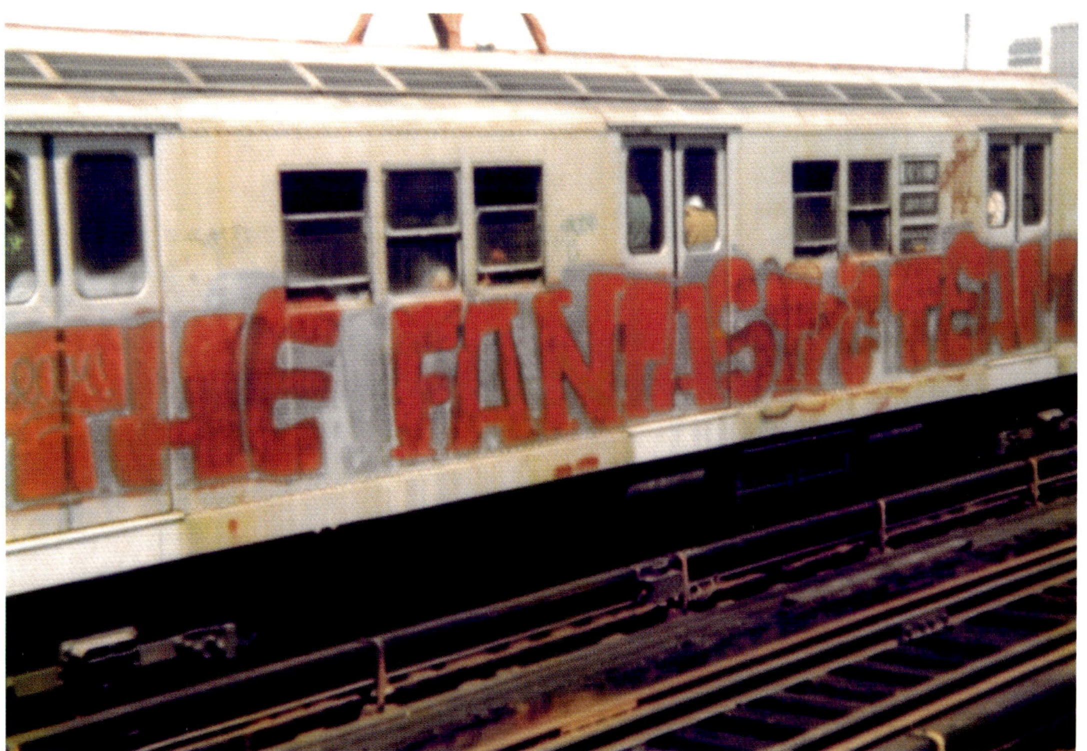

The Fantastic Team, 1975.

I did this window down the whole car on a solo mission. The year was 1975. My partner Max (R.I.P.) used to live on 124th Street and Broadway. I used to stay at his house and we would slip out at night and hit the no. 1 tunnel or various other lay-ups on the Broadway line. One night we saw that, when it snowed, they laid-up trains at the 116th Street station. They kept the trains in the long tunnel that opens up at 120th Street and Broadway. It was possible to jump over the wall from Broadway and go right into the tunnel — or just sneak on at the 116th Street Station, jump down and walk into it.

One night it snowed. I packed a bag of red devil red and silver and snuck out of my house in Greenwich Village. I headed up to 116th Street and "bang" — they were laid up. I jumped out by myself — knowing full well what I wanted to do — and unleashed my spray. I didn't have an outline. I just free-styled with block letters. Even though people could see me from the platform, I didn't care. It was easy enough to run out and hop the wall to the street if I got chased.

Although I barely ever took any flicks back in those days, I did manage to catch a flick of this piece rolling while benching with Max at 125th Street.

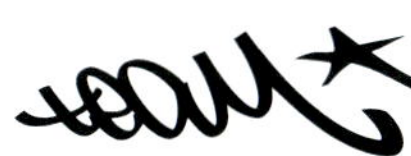

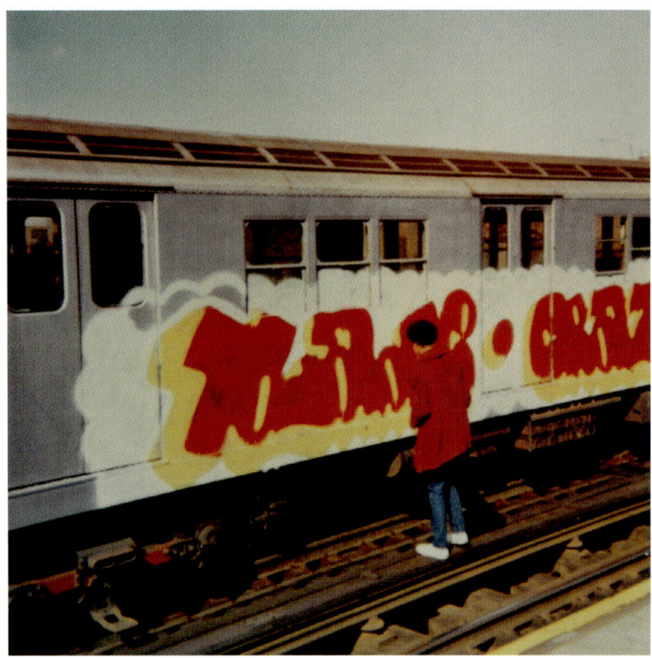

Blade at work.

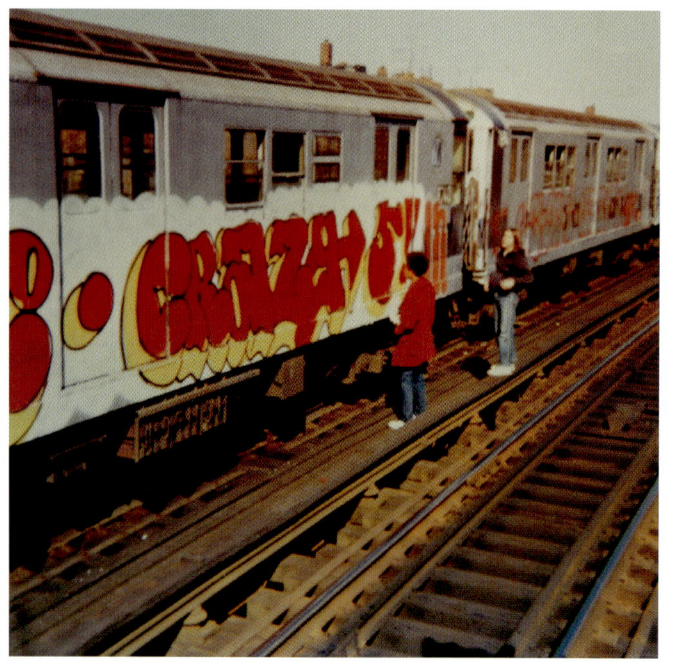

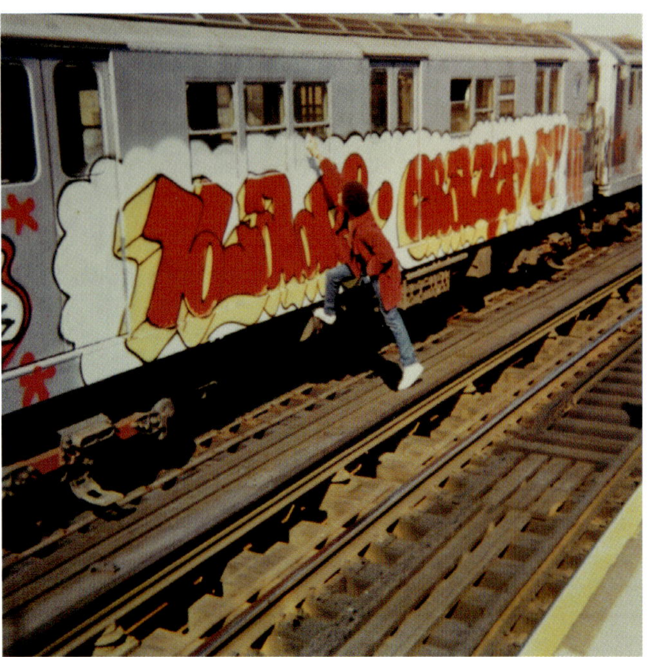

I did this on the Burke Avenue lay-up in the spring of 1975. You see Shorty 5 was also on the lay-up with me. It was all Rustoleum paint from Martin Paints. It's a Blade Crazy 5 end to end. As I was getting toward the end, Hate 168 showed up and took these photos with my camera. As I was finishing the piece, the police showed up on the raid train. I ran the length of the subway platform and as the train pulled out of the station going uptown to Gun Hill Road, I leaped off the end of the platform onto the last car of the moving train and gave the police the finger! If anyone is able to find Hate 168, he will confirm this story. He said it was the coolest thing he ever saw. I was aged 18 in 1975.

—Blade, The Crazy Five

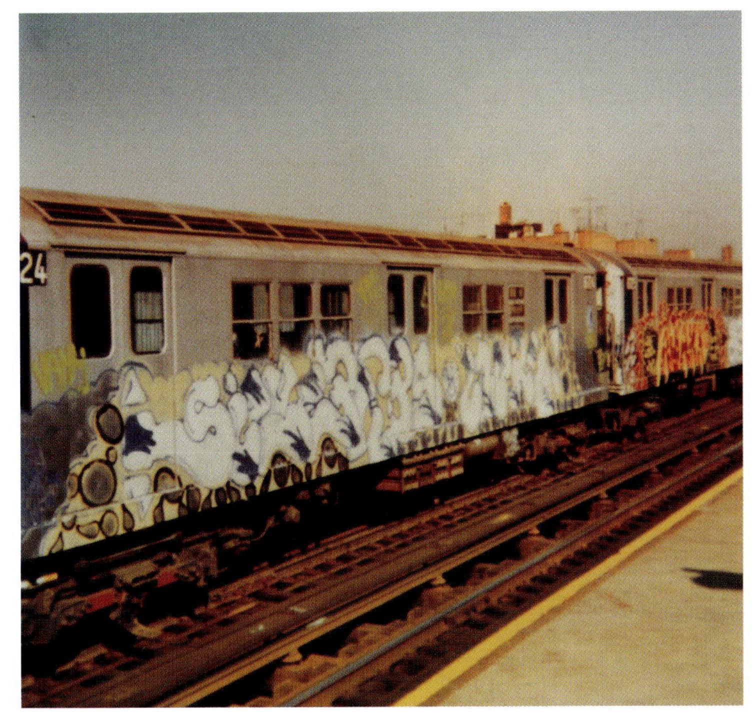

Silvertips, 1975

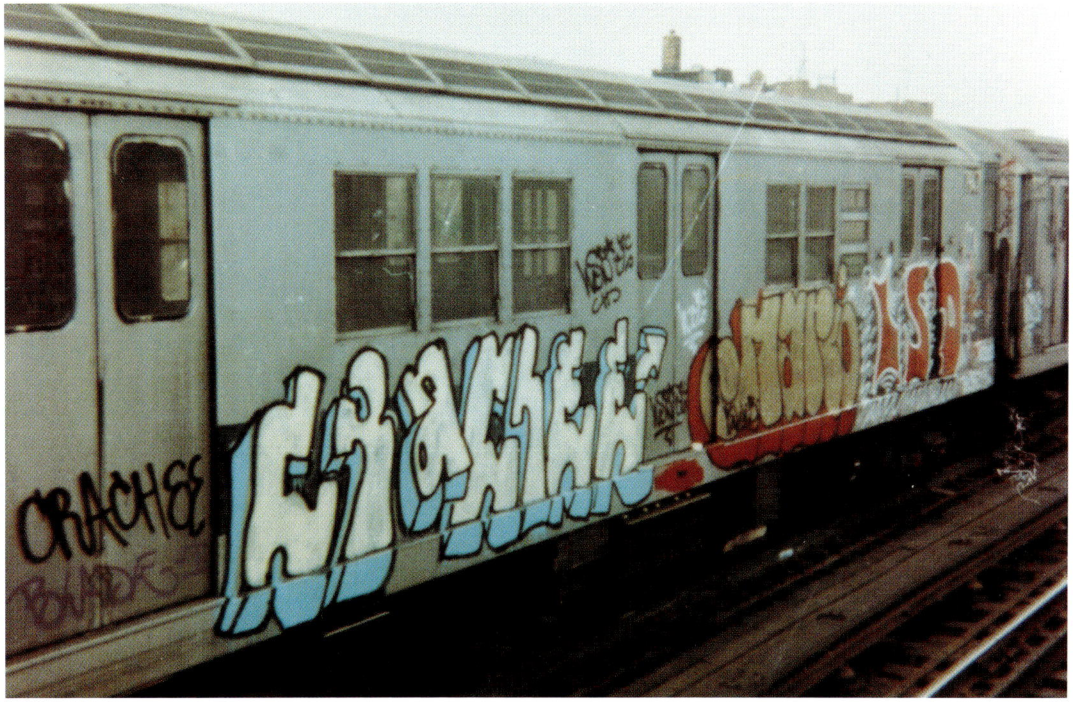

Crachee 11, Mario, & LSD 3, 1975

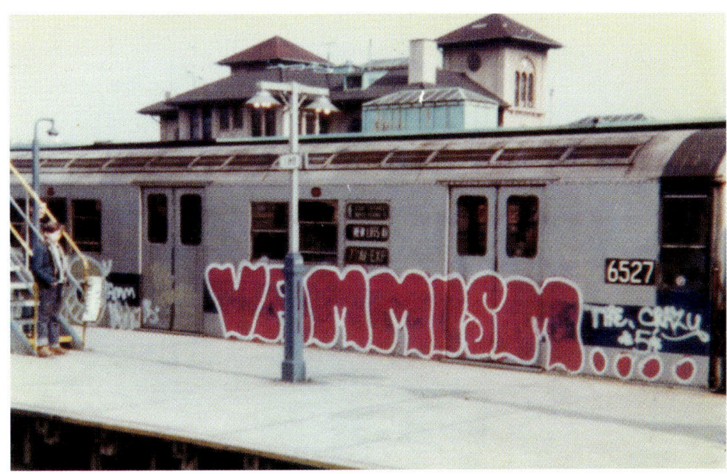

"Vammism" by Vamm (TC5).1974

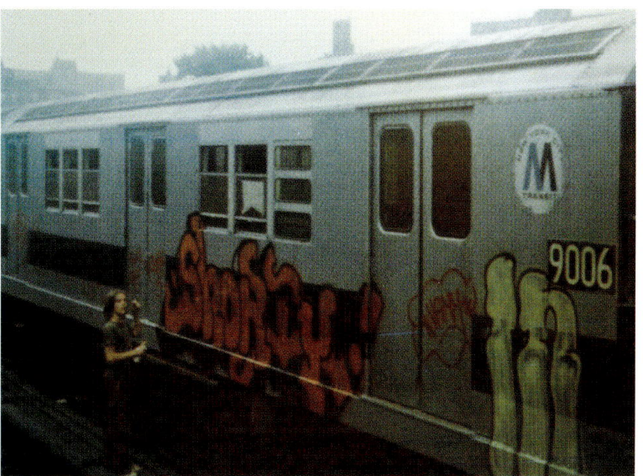

Shorty 5, 1975

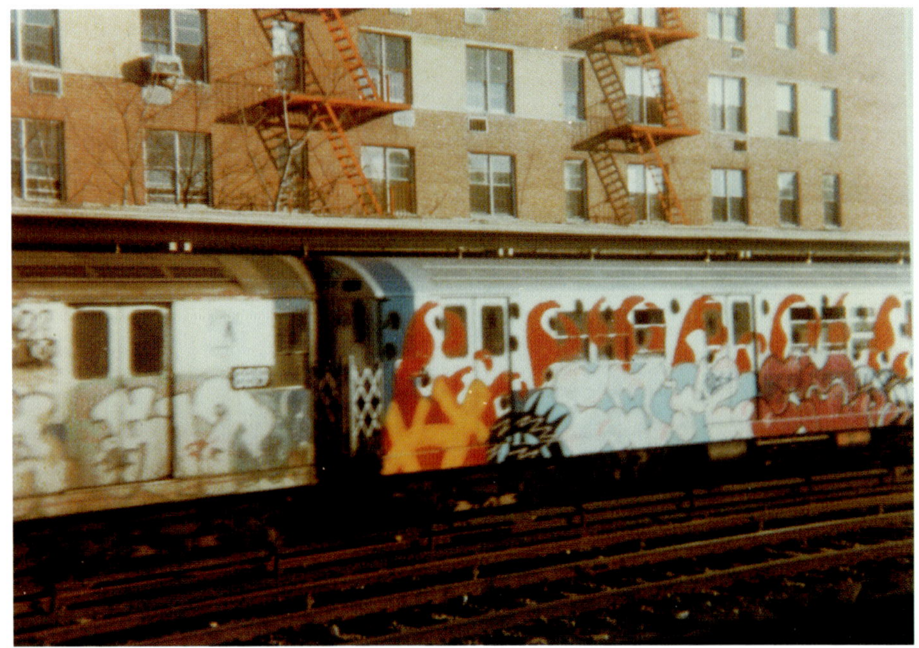

Comet, 1978

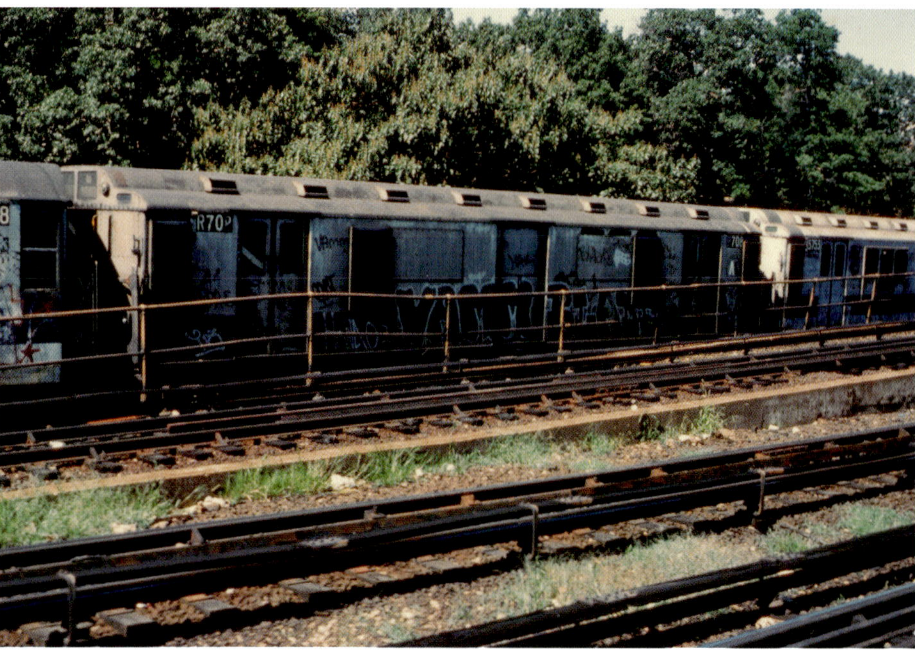

NYCTA money car. Vamm & Blade, 1974

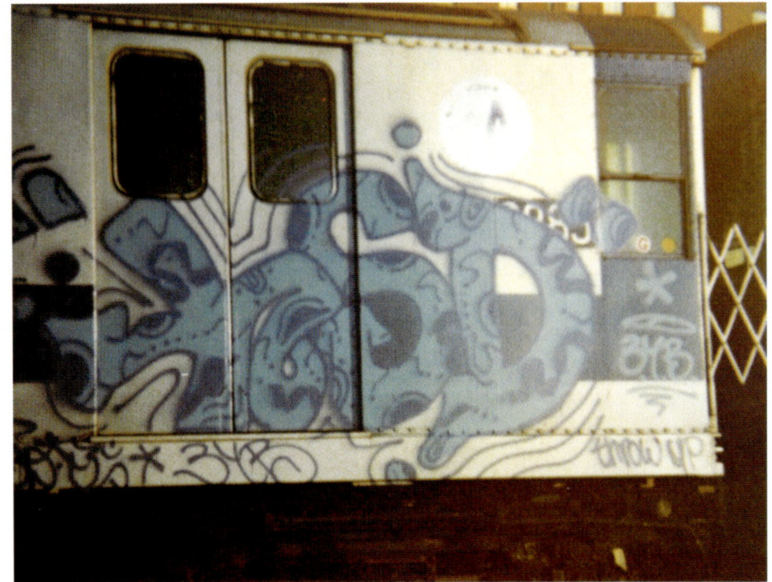

LSD 3, 1975

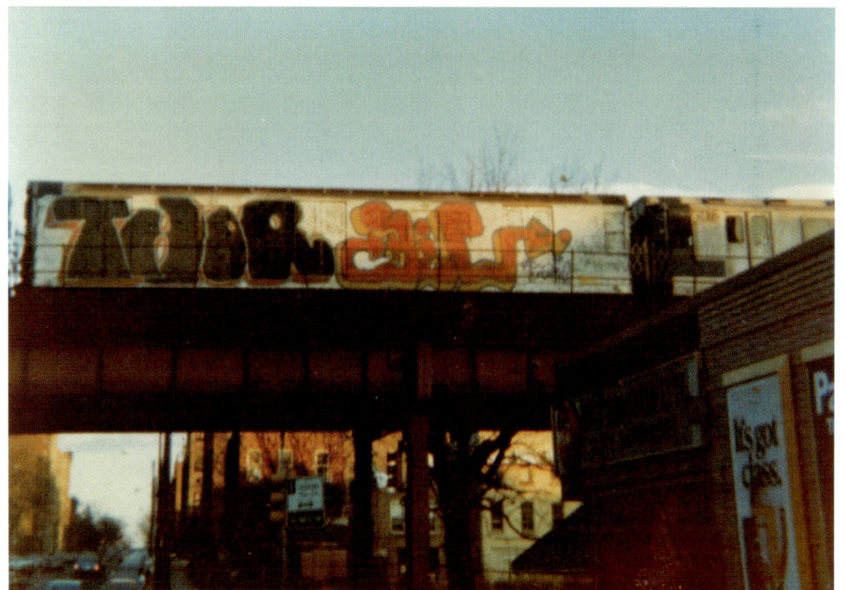

"Thor" by Turk62; Bic 149, 1975

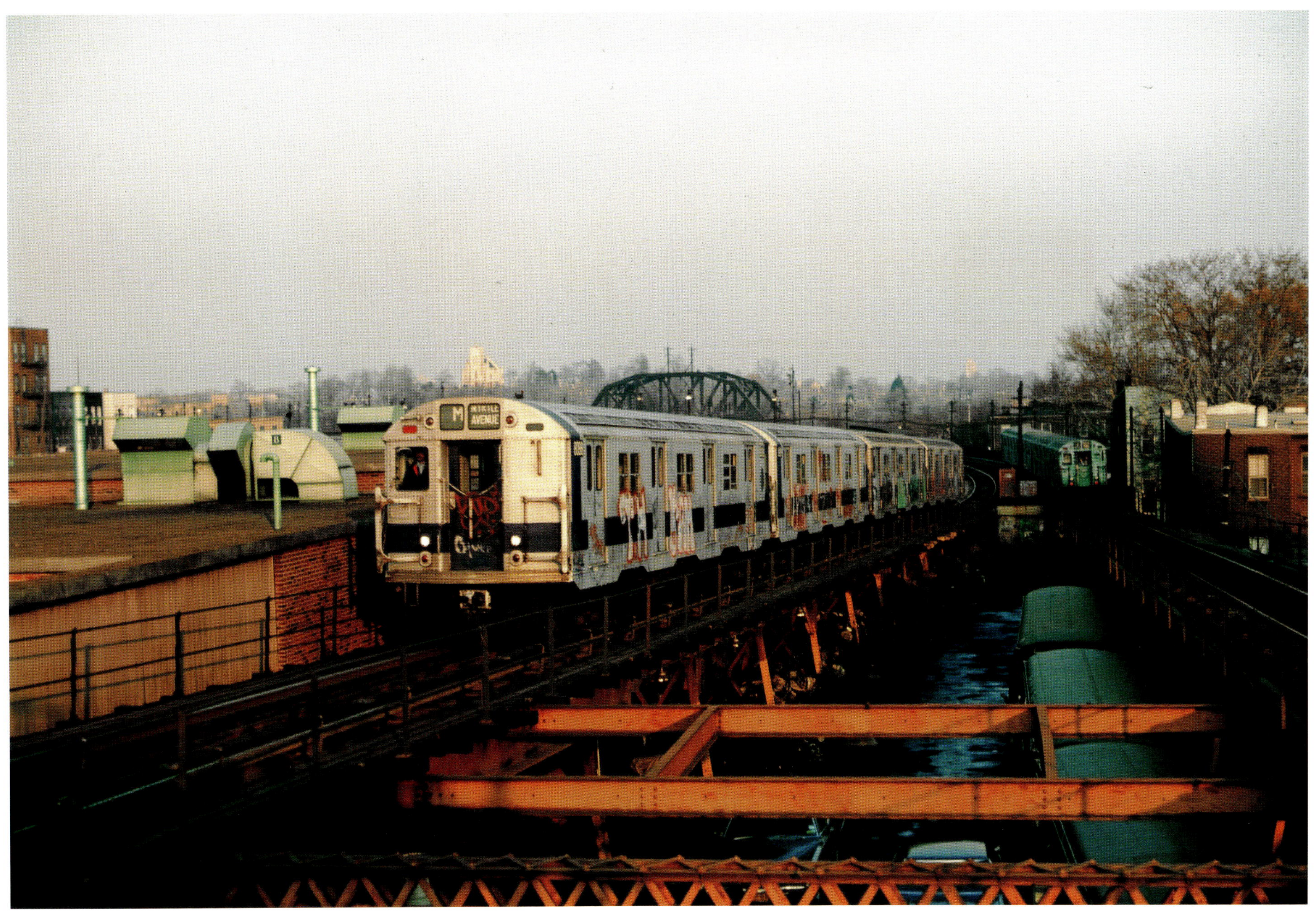

M train puling into Fresh Pond Station, 1976

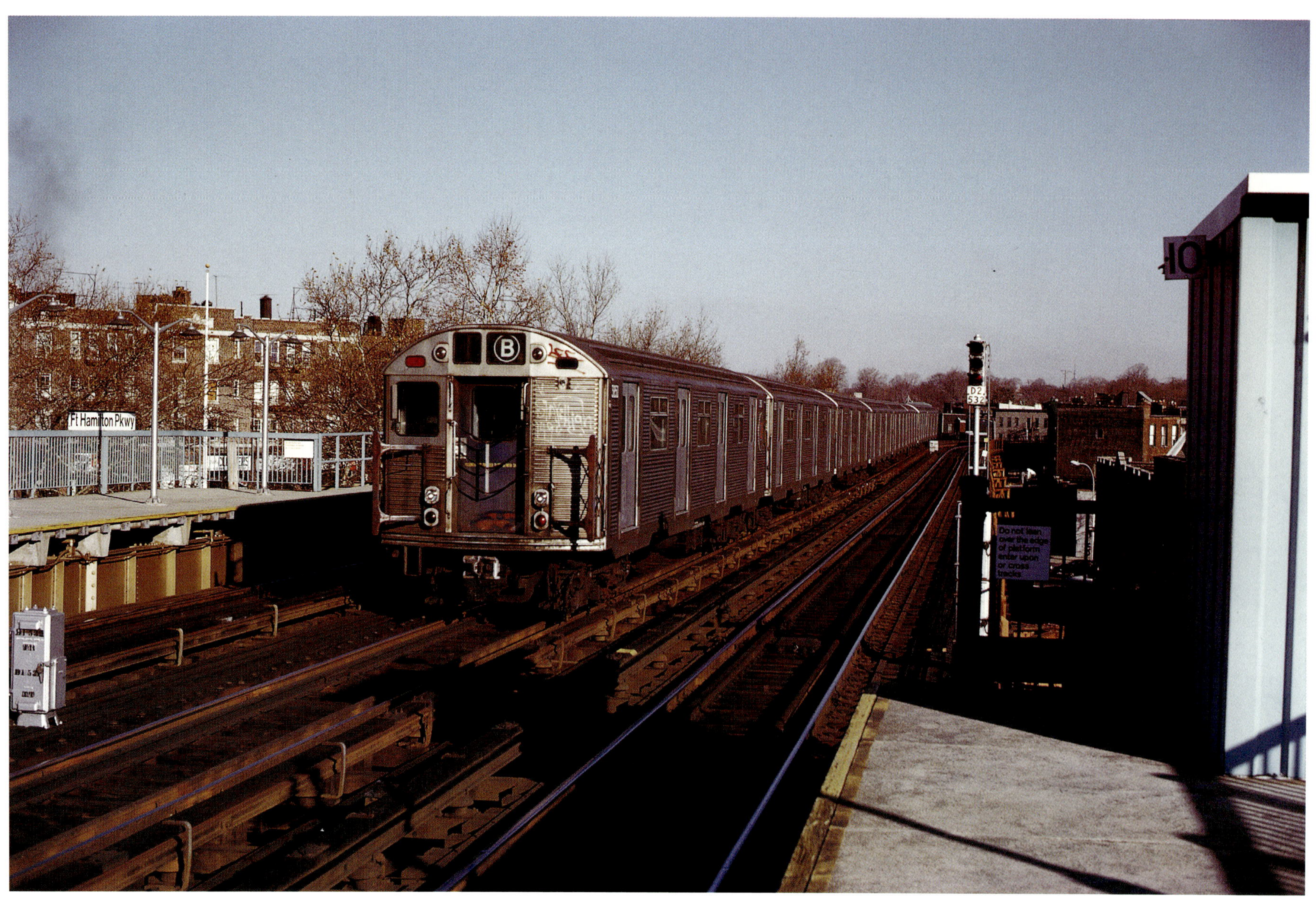

Stay High 149 on a B train, 1973

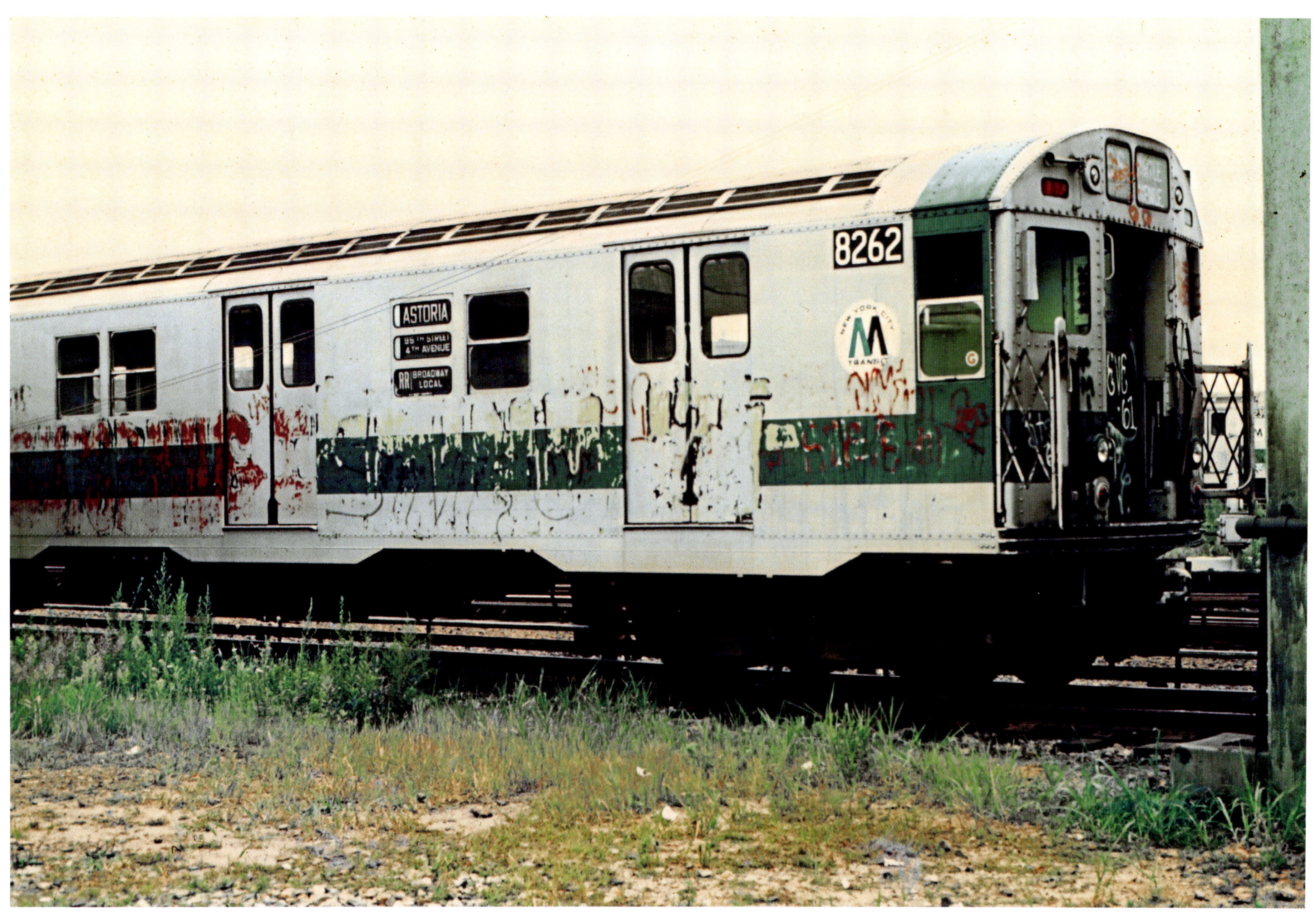

Acid bath for car no. 8262

End of the Line

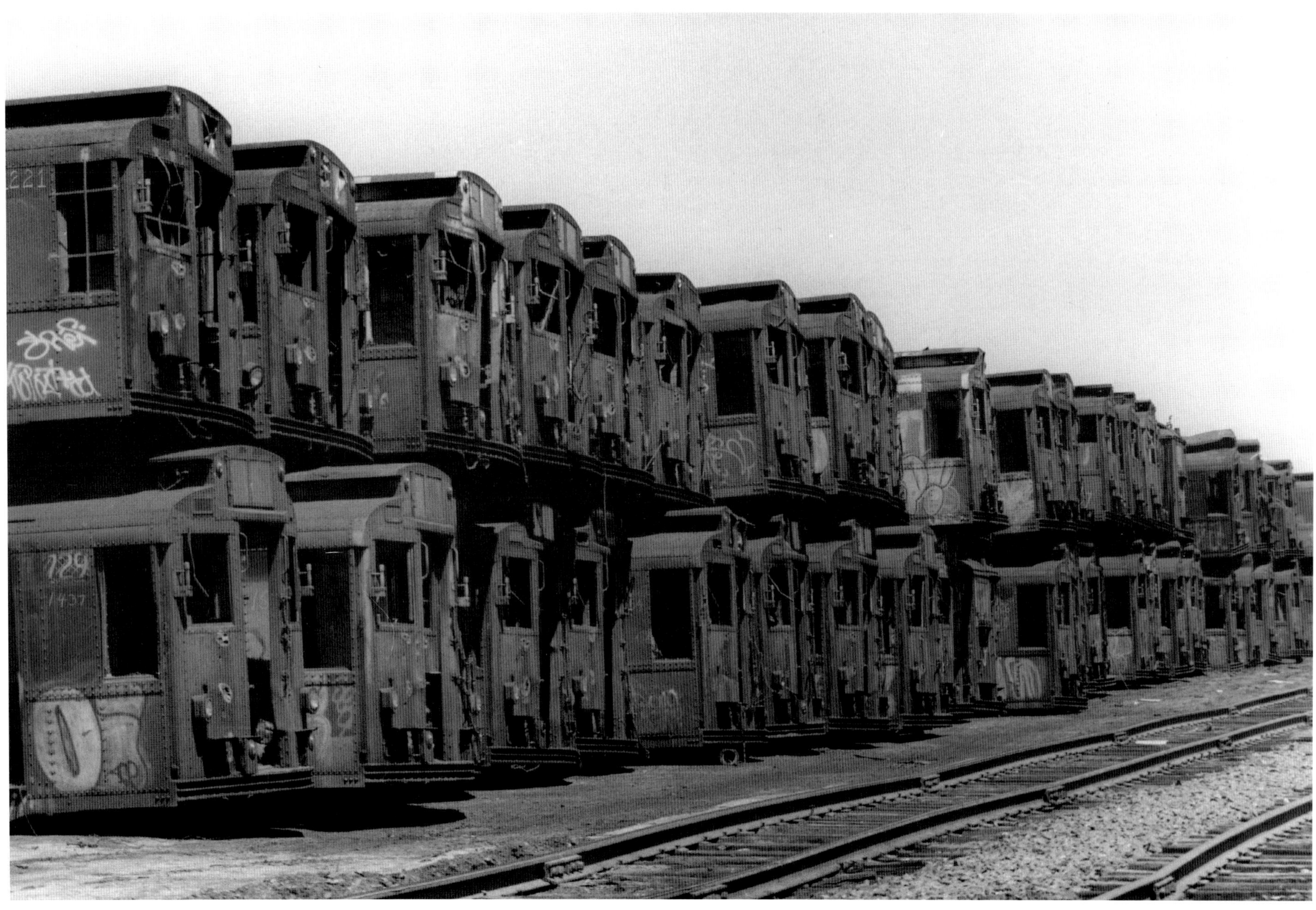

Naparano scrap yard, Newark, New Jersey, 1977 (above and opposite page)

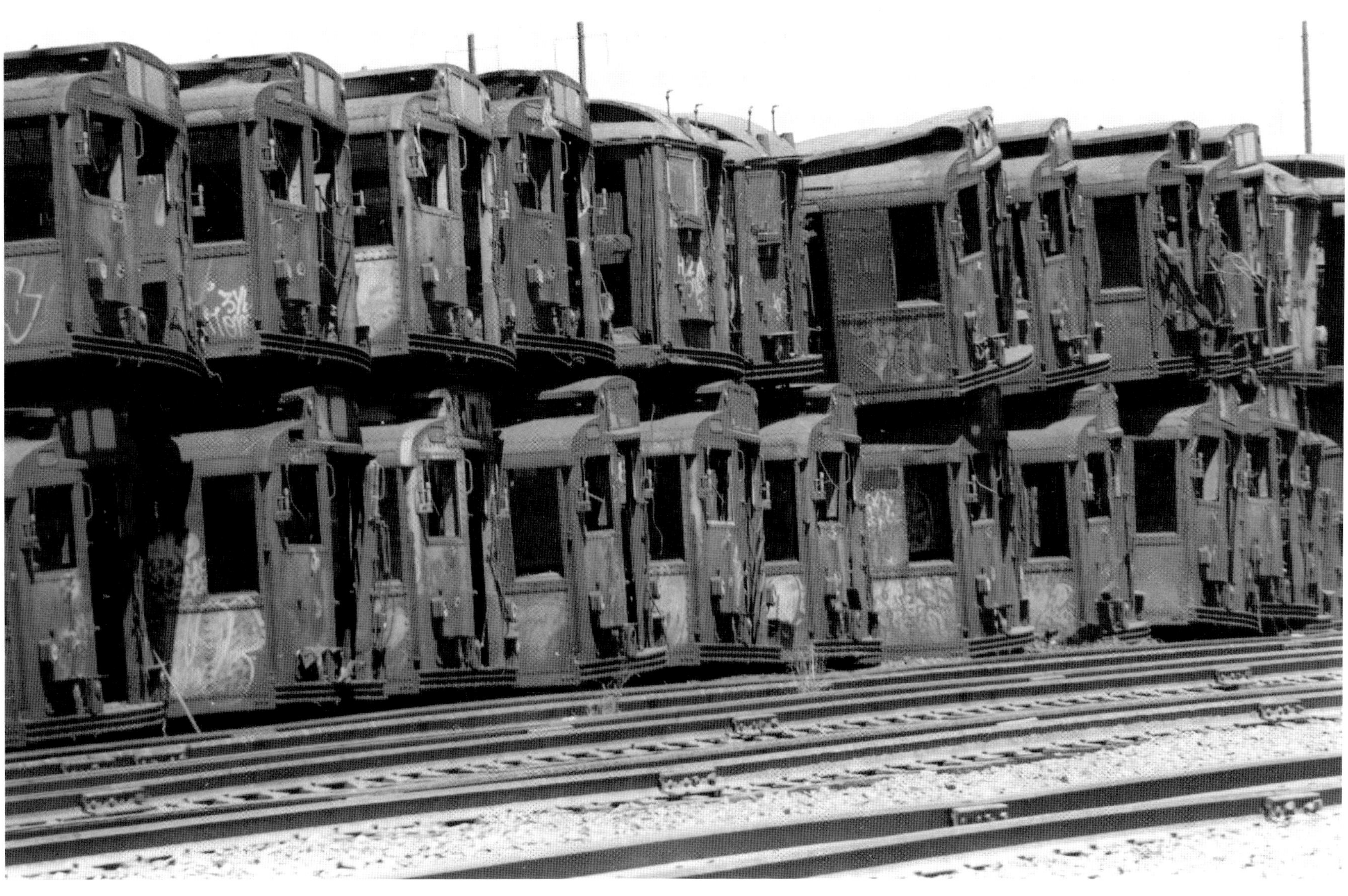

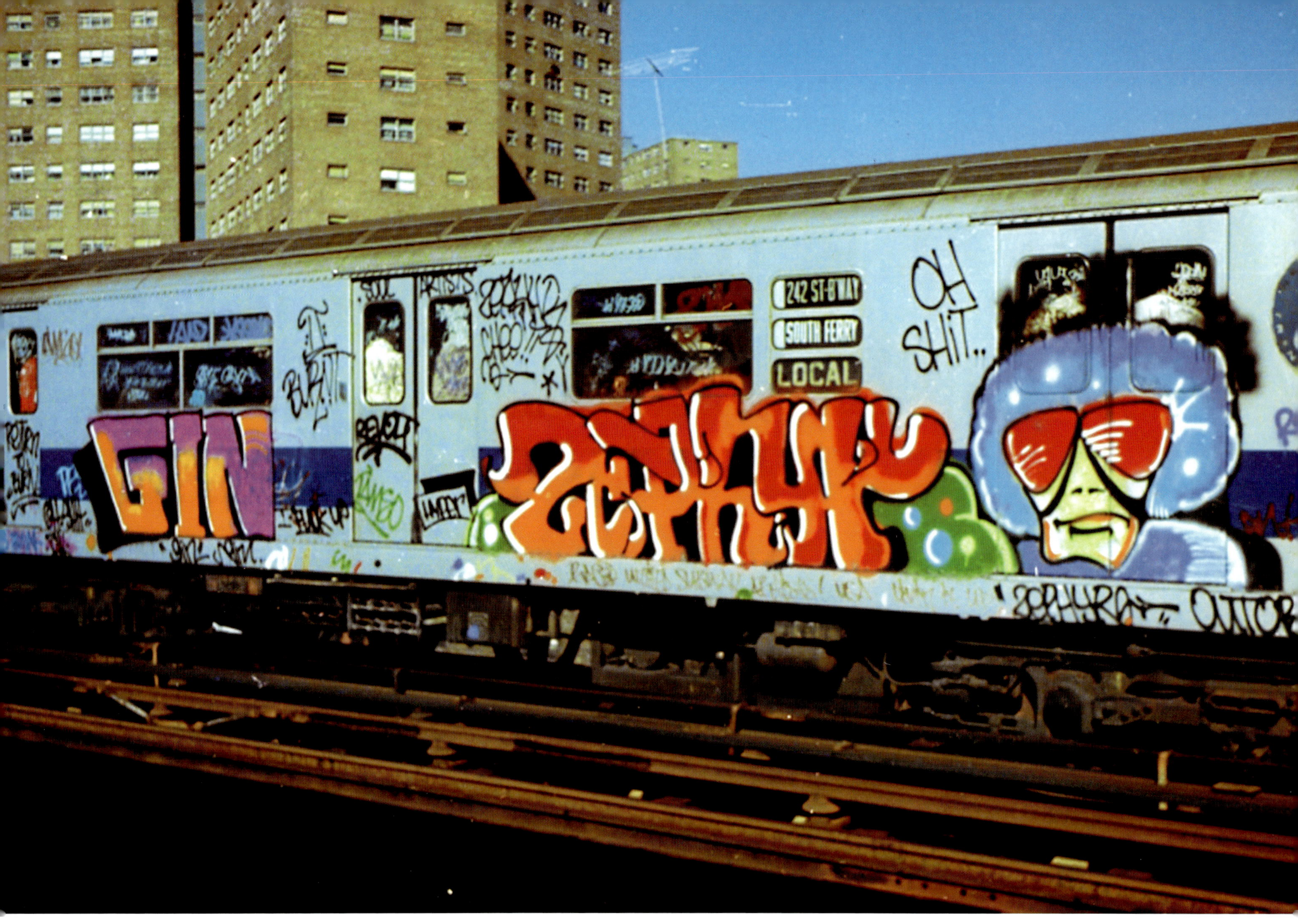

Gin & Zephyr, 1979

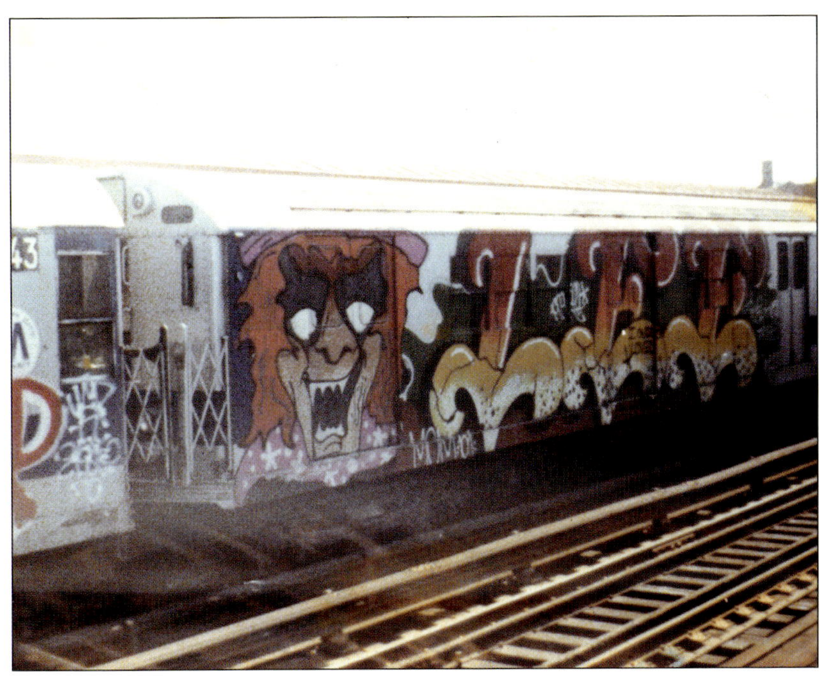
Lee (TF5), 1979

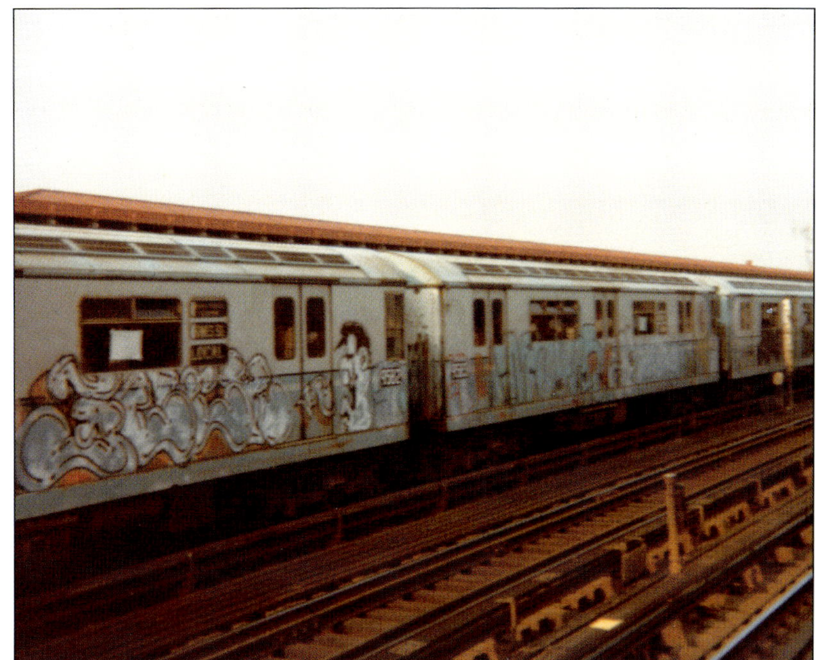
Flick, 1978

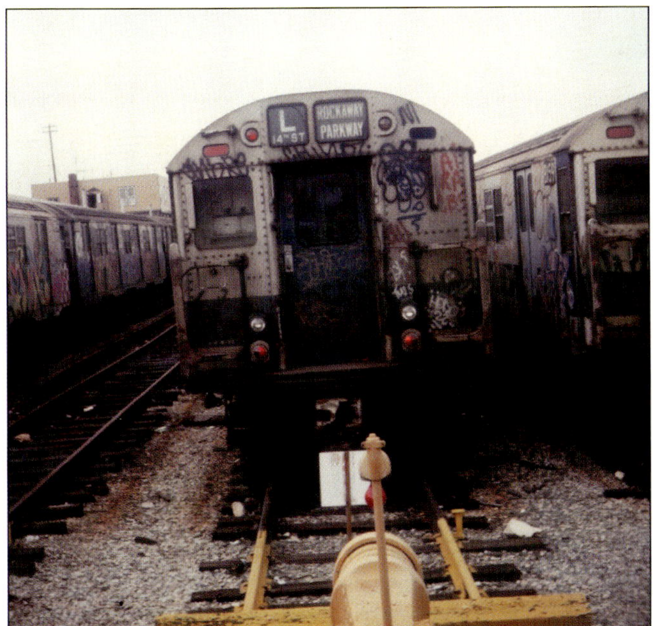

LL train, 1979, Rockaway Parkway yard

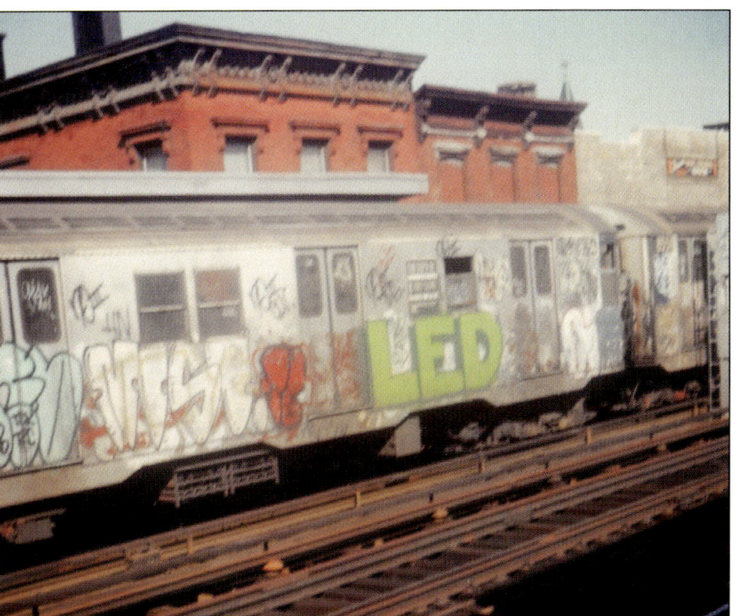

"LED" by Spar (TNS). Painted in 1978, photographed in 1979

Back then, in 1979, I was not just a writer. I was also a rail fan I enjoyed everything that had to do with trains.

—Spar (TNS)

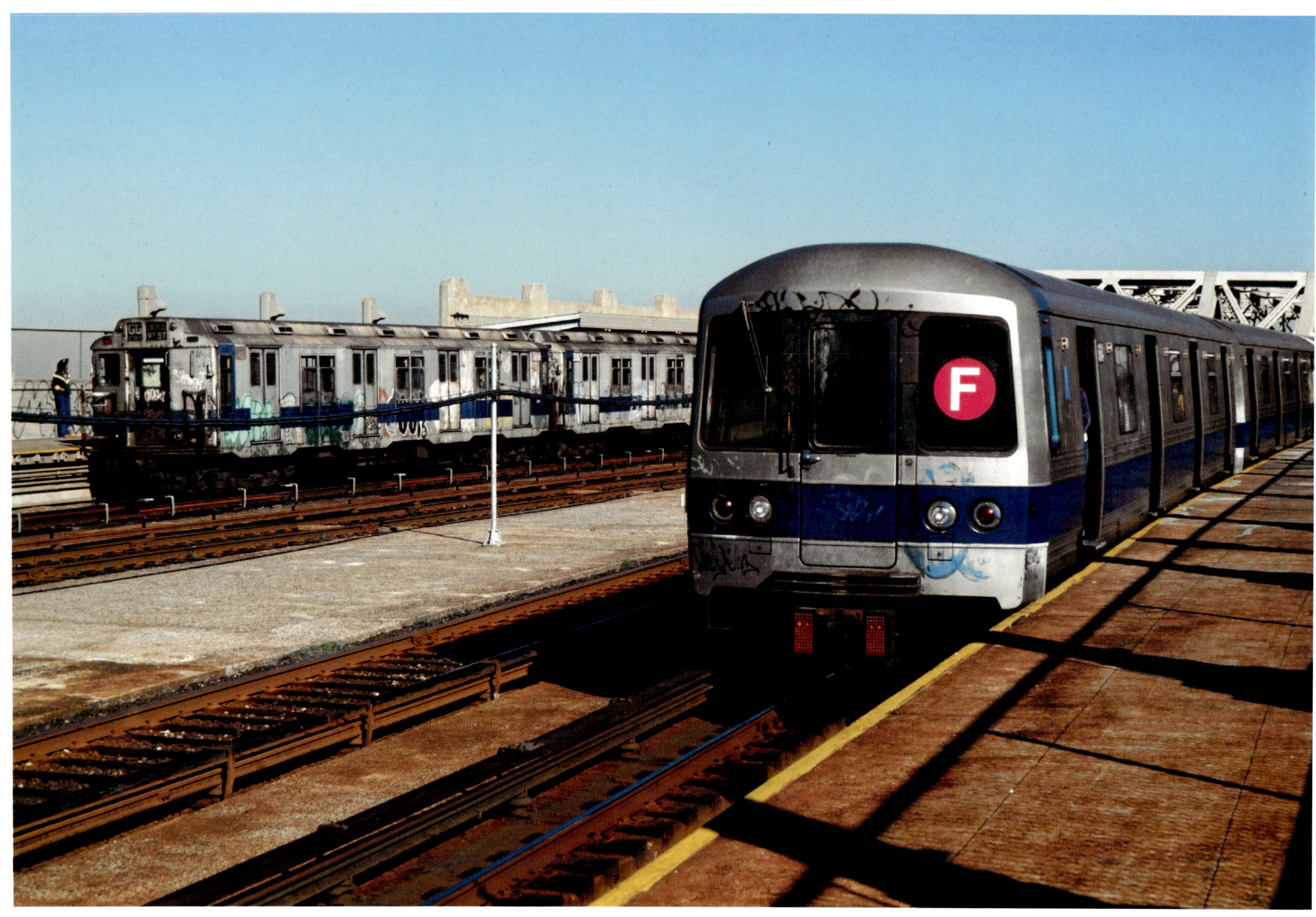

GG and F trains, 1979

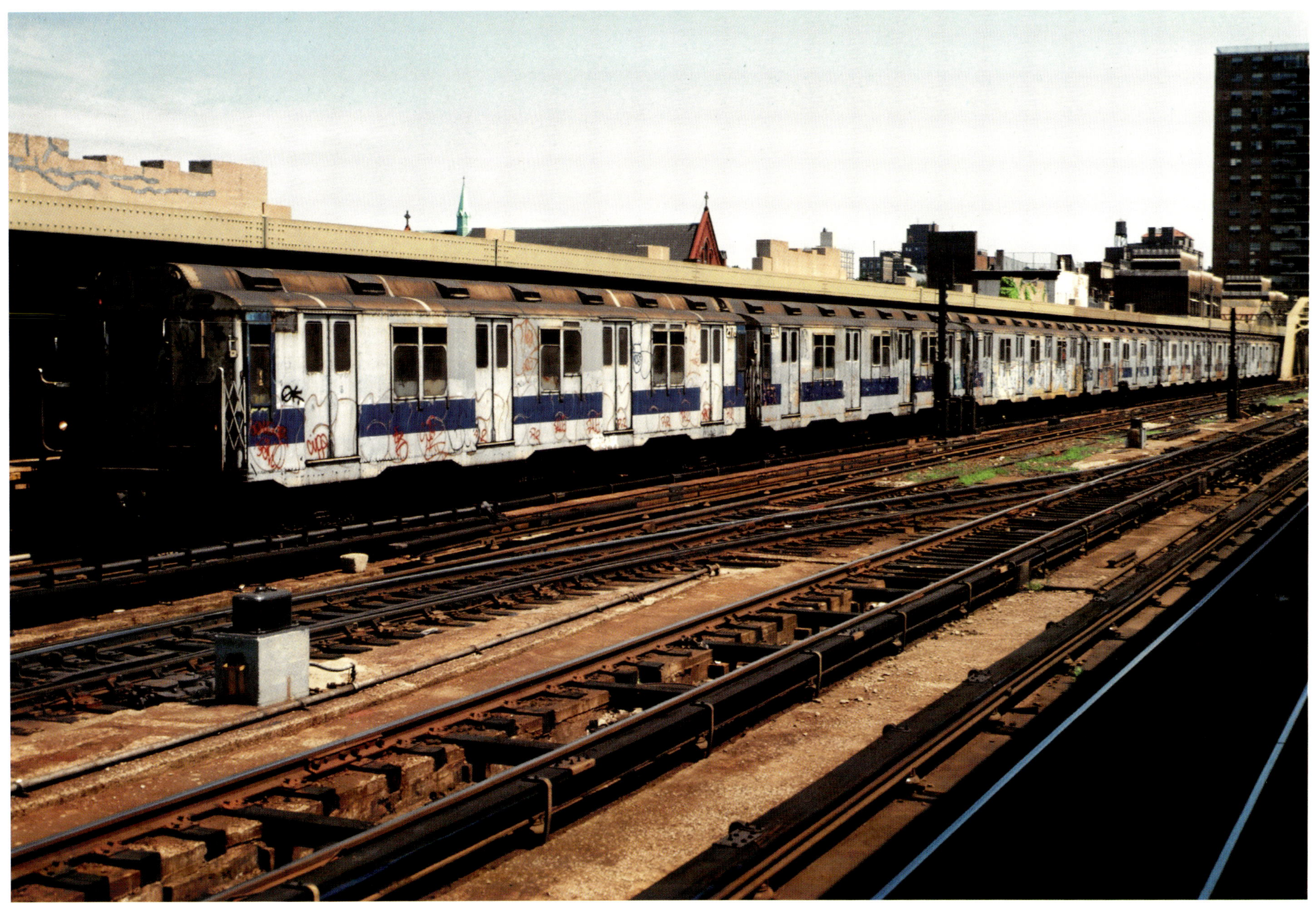

F line, 1980

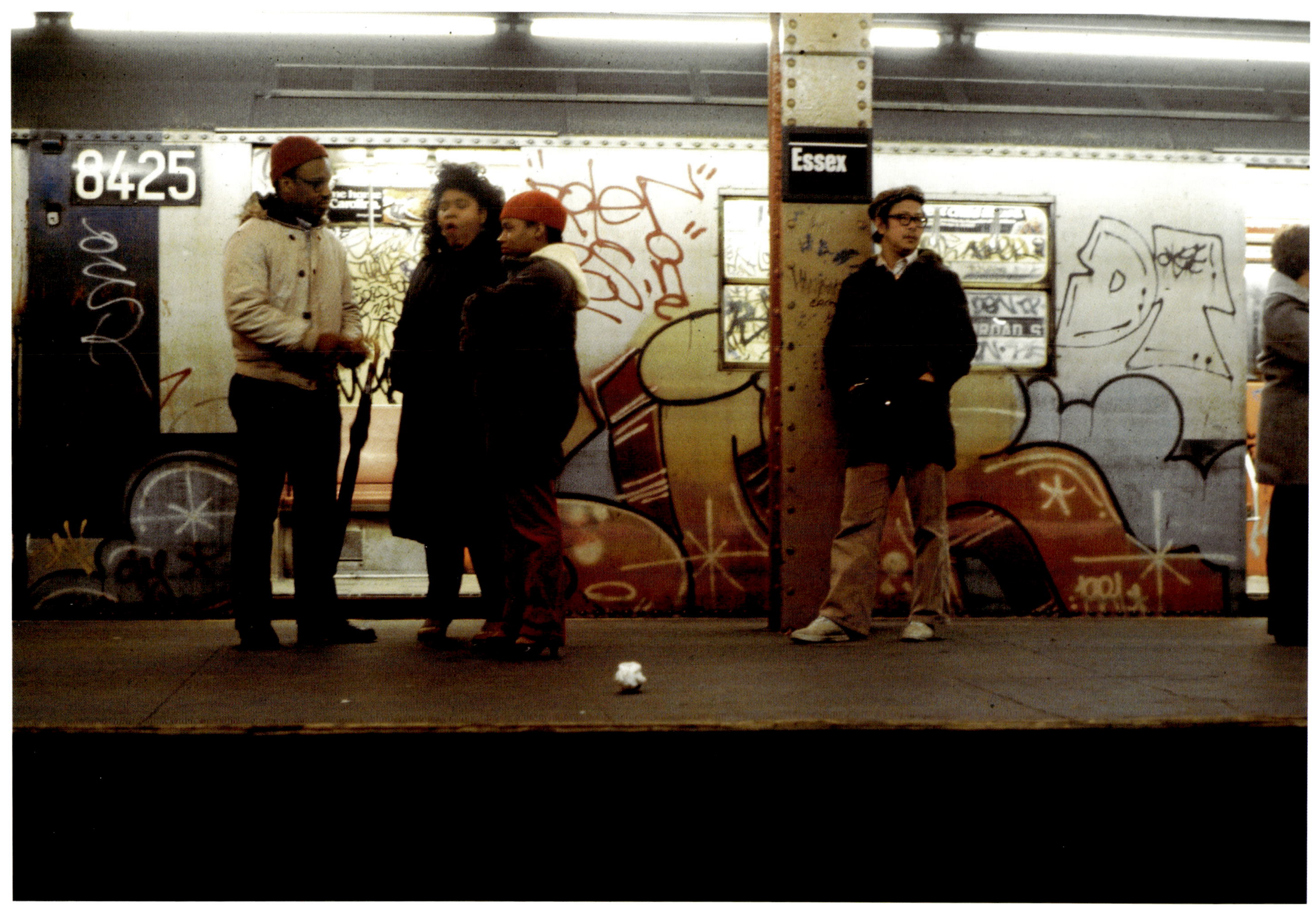

Sir (TKC), dated 1981. Photo taken 1983

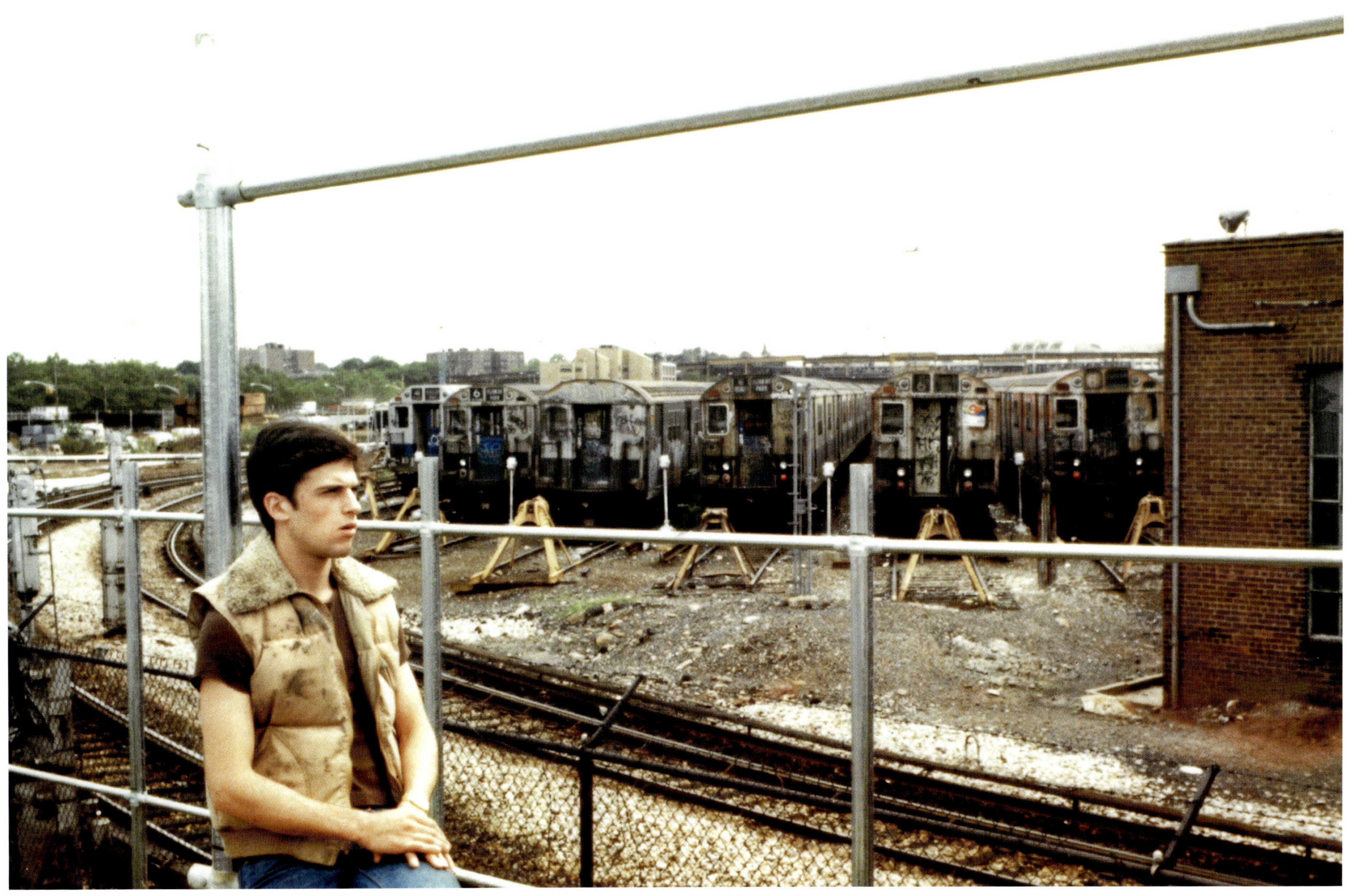

Zephyr, 6 yard, 1982

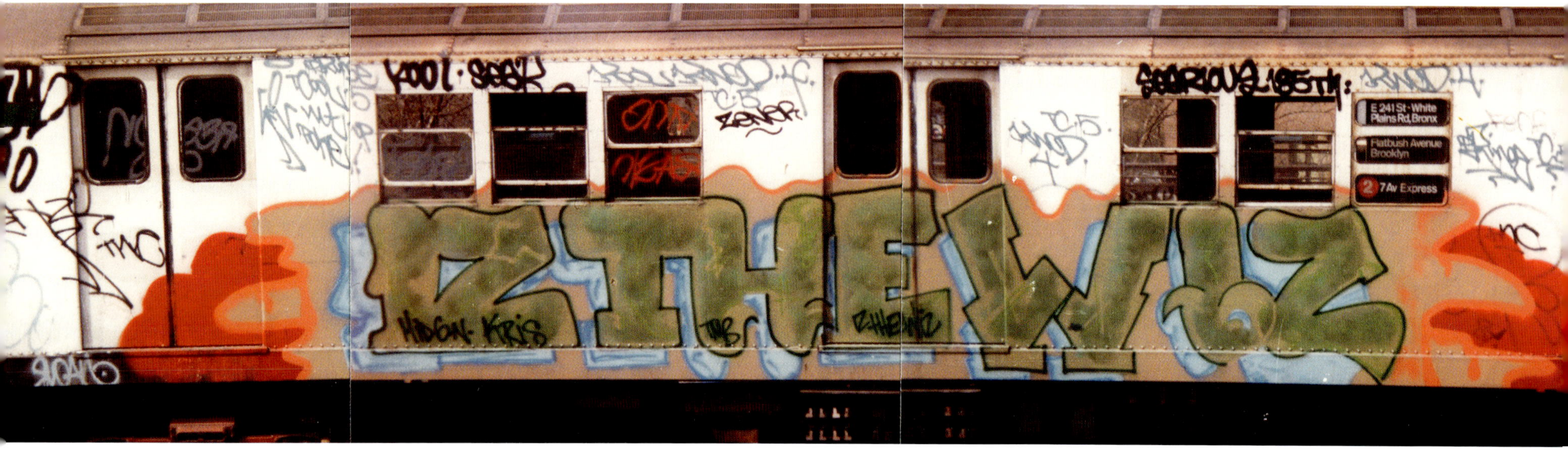

Iz the Wiz (TMB), 1984

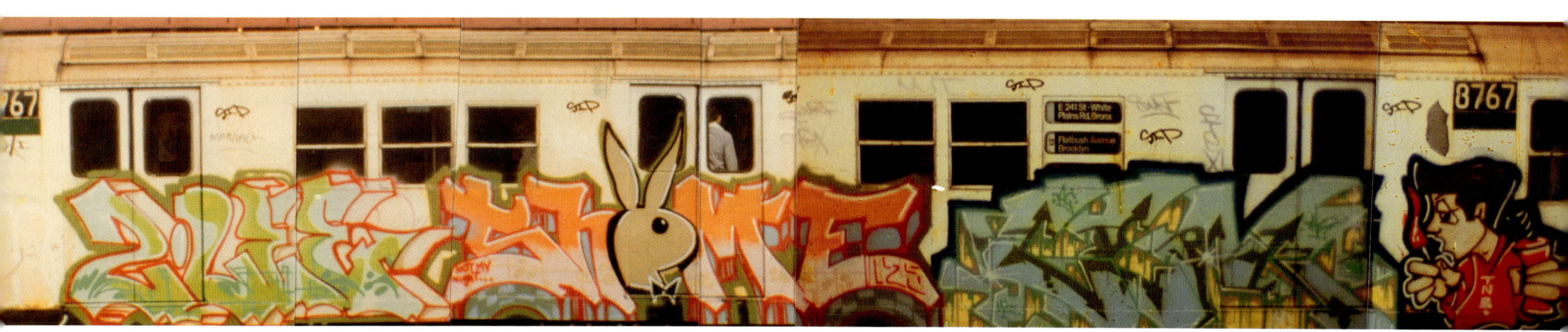

“2Lee,” by Kenn (TAT), Shame125 (TOA), & Cem (TAC), 1984

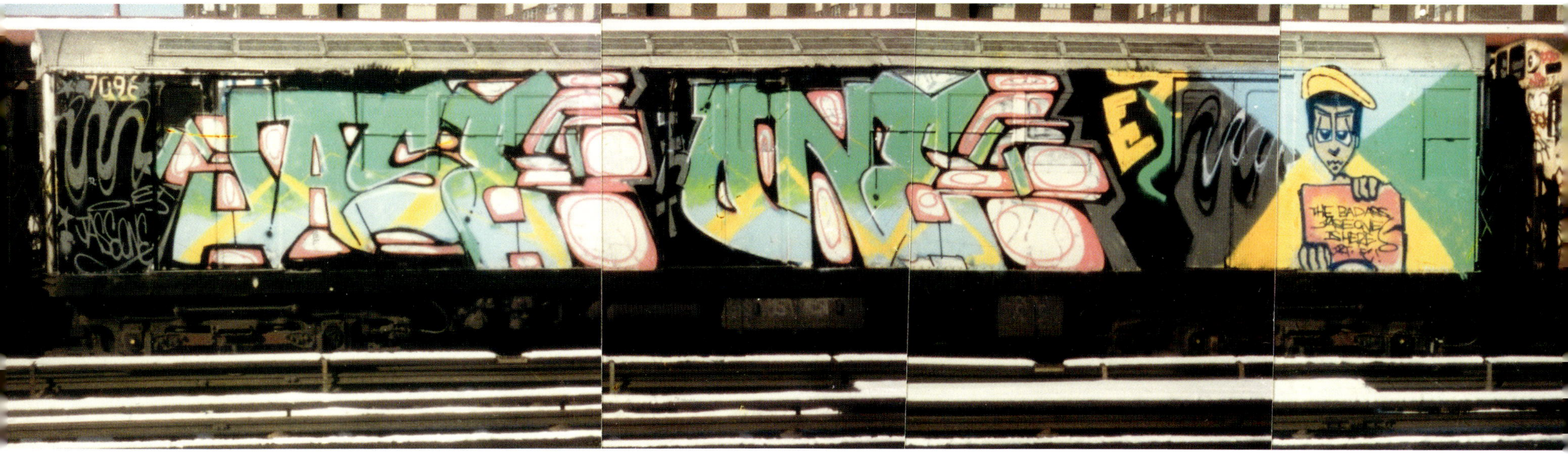

Jase One, 1985

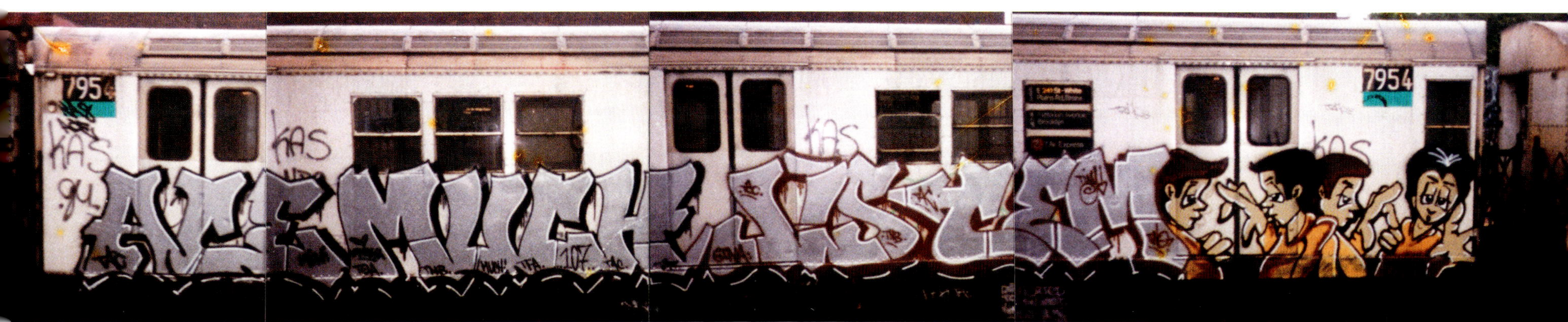

Ace, Much, Jis, & Cem (TAC), 1984

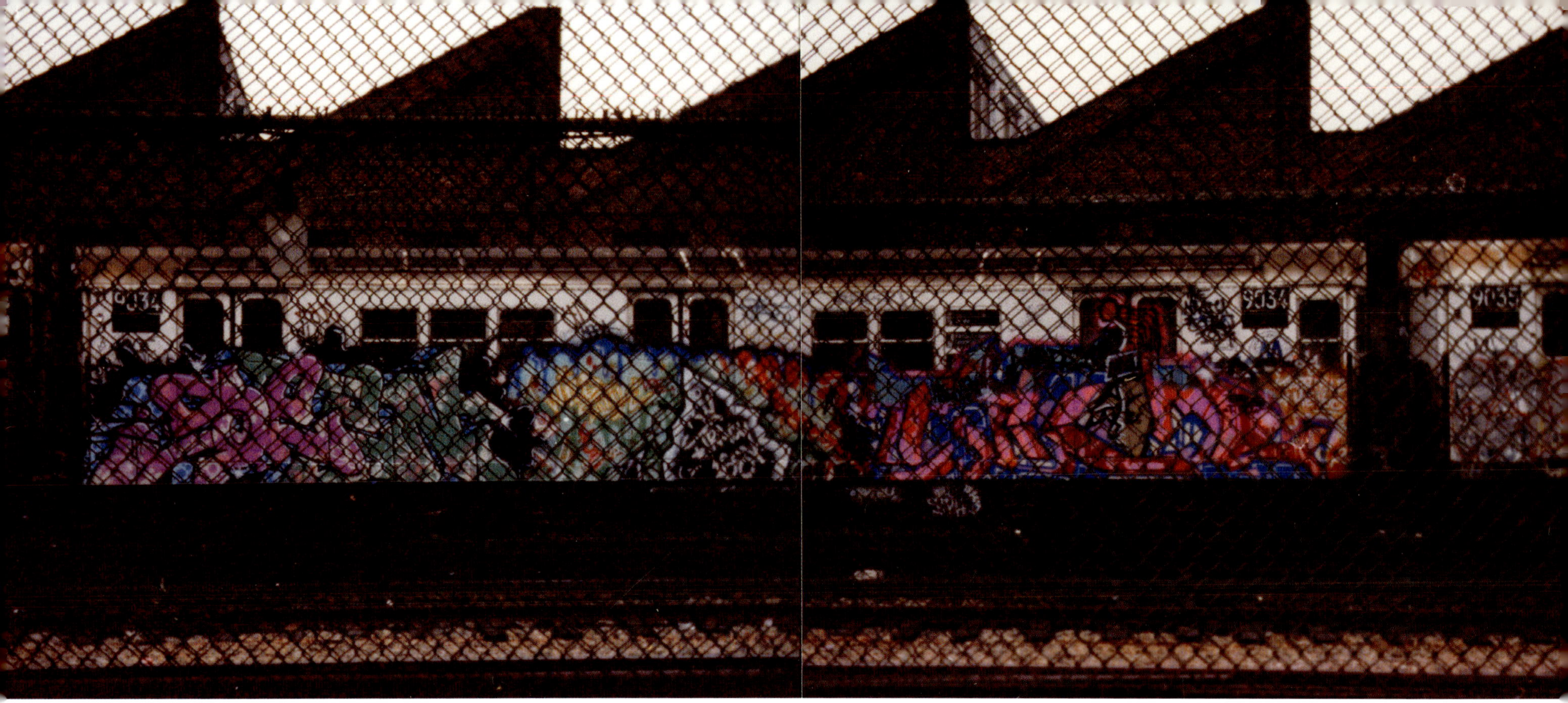

Seen (UA), Tracy168 (WS), & TKID (TNB), 1985

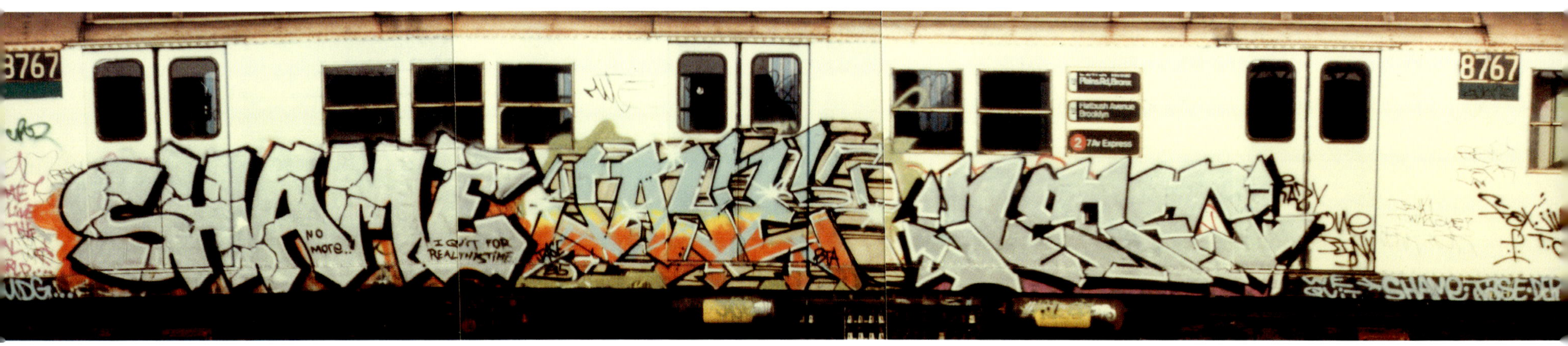

Shame125, Jase, & Dero, 1985

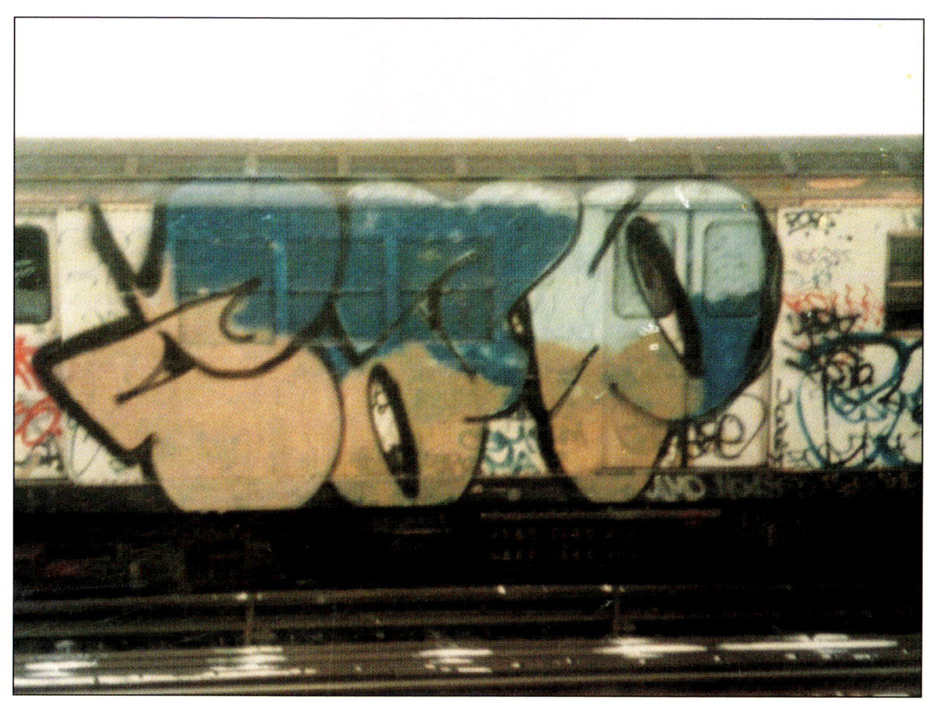

Cap (MPC), 1985

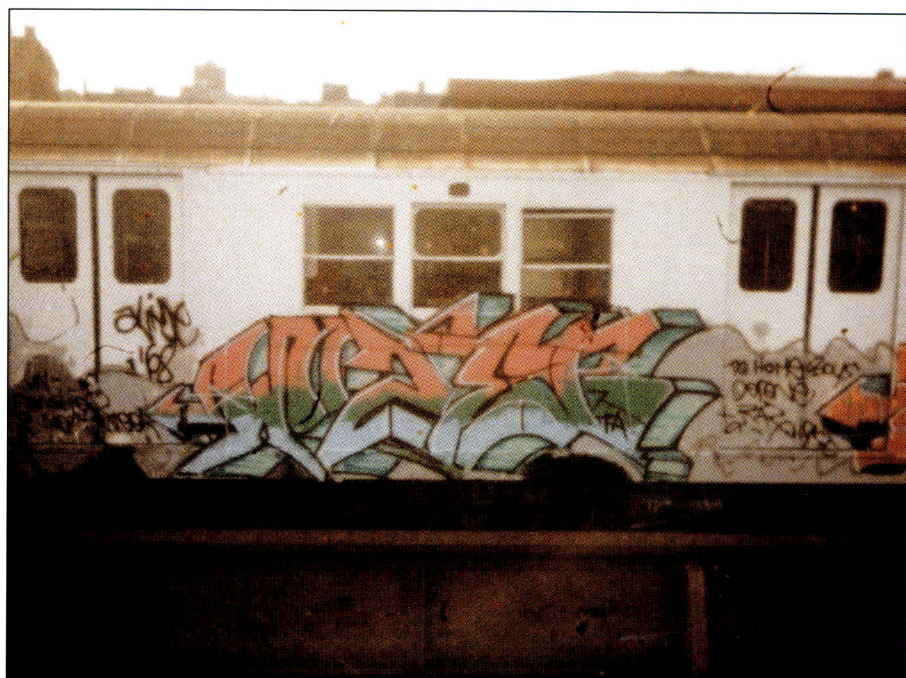

Wuzer, 1985

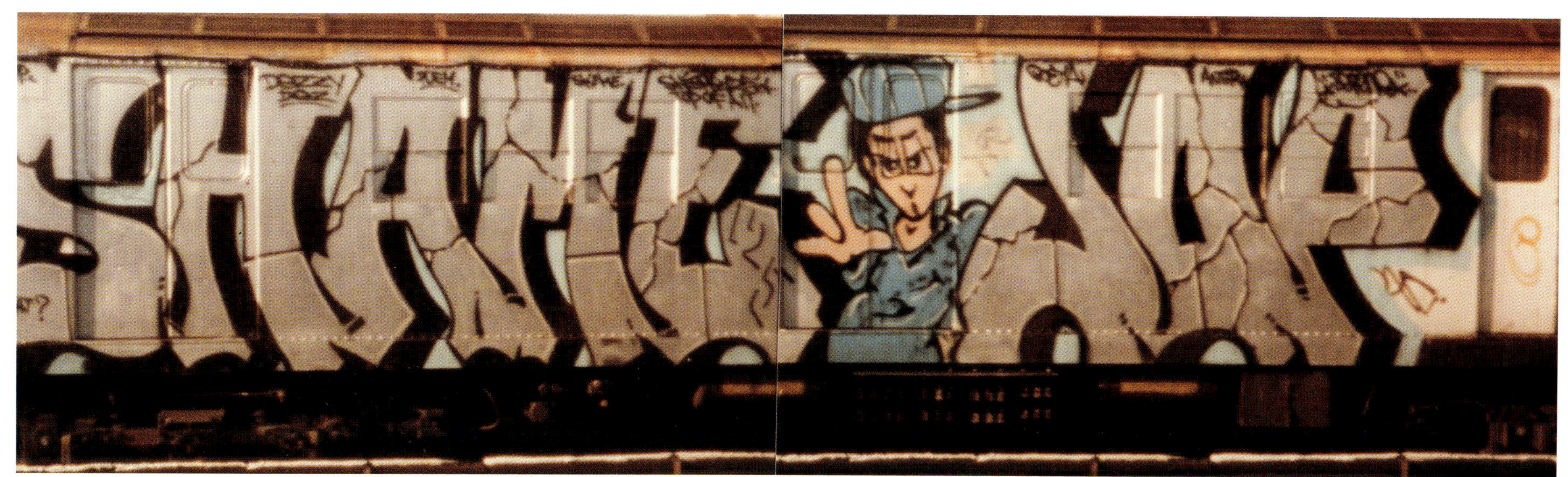

Shame125 & Jop, 1984

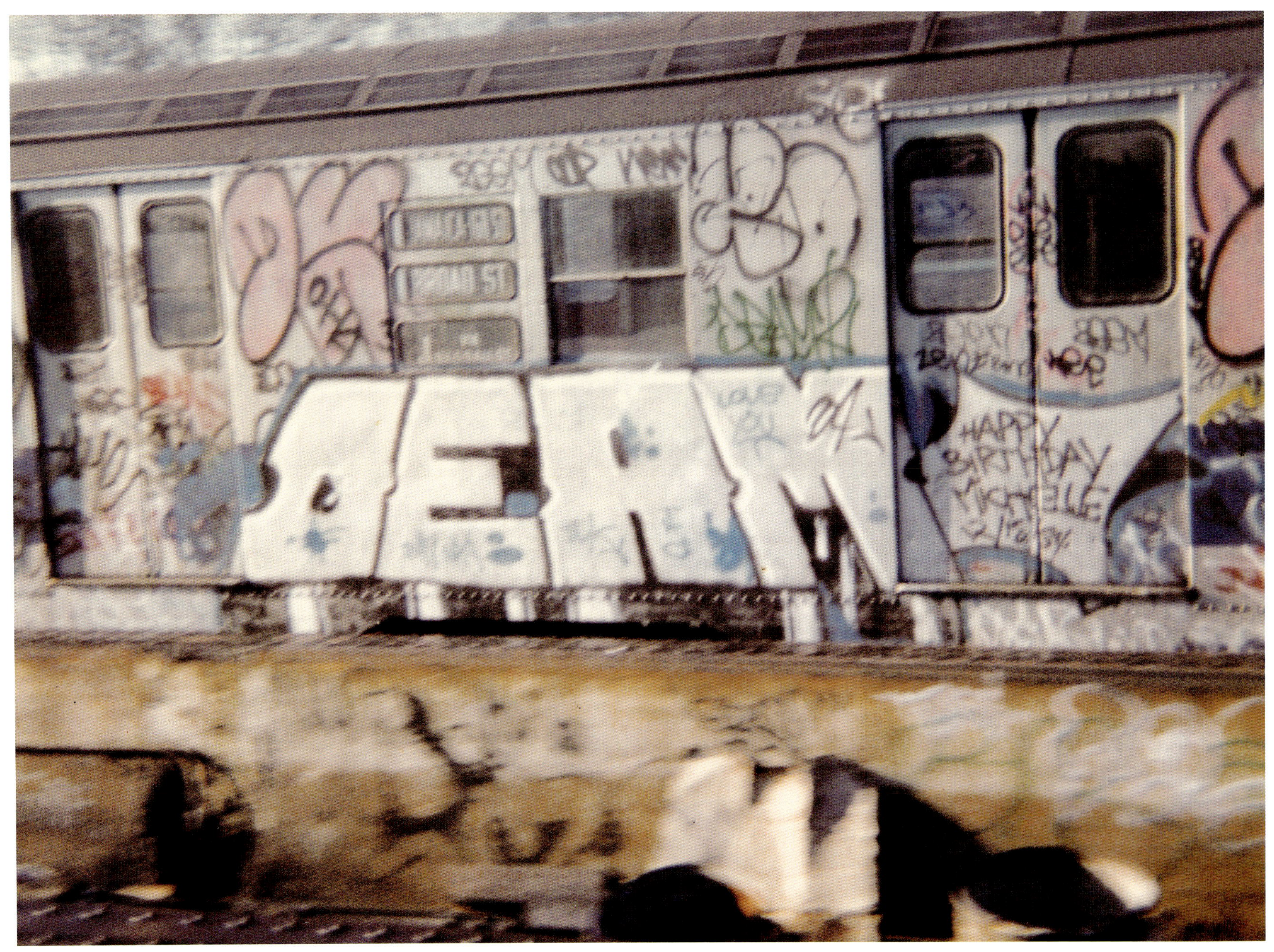

Deam2 (TLK), 1984

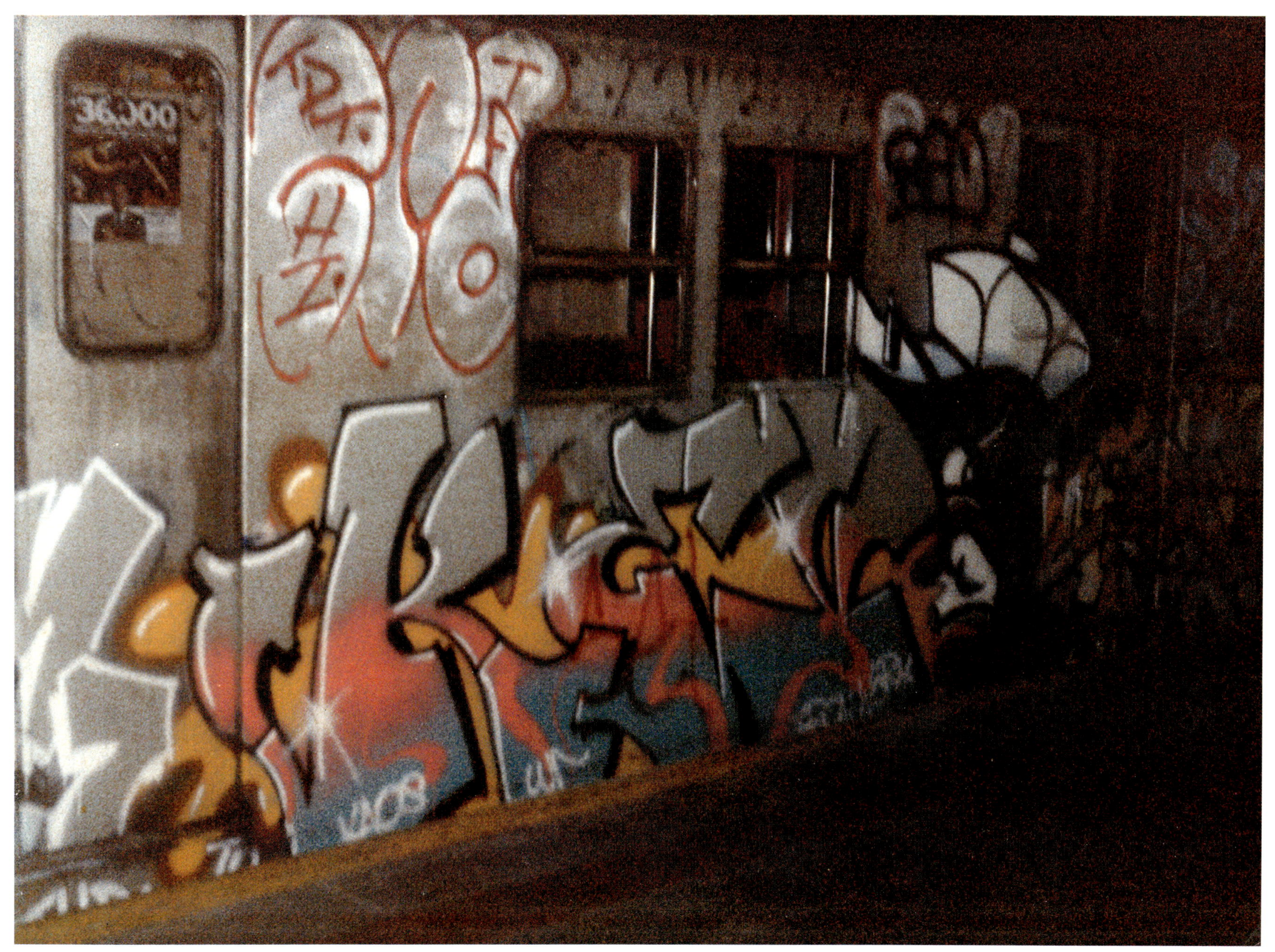

Kev (TM7), 1986, complete with character

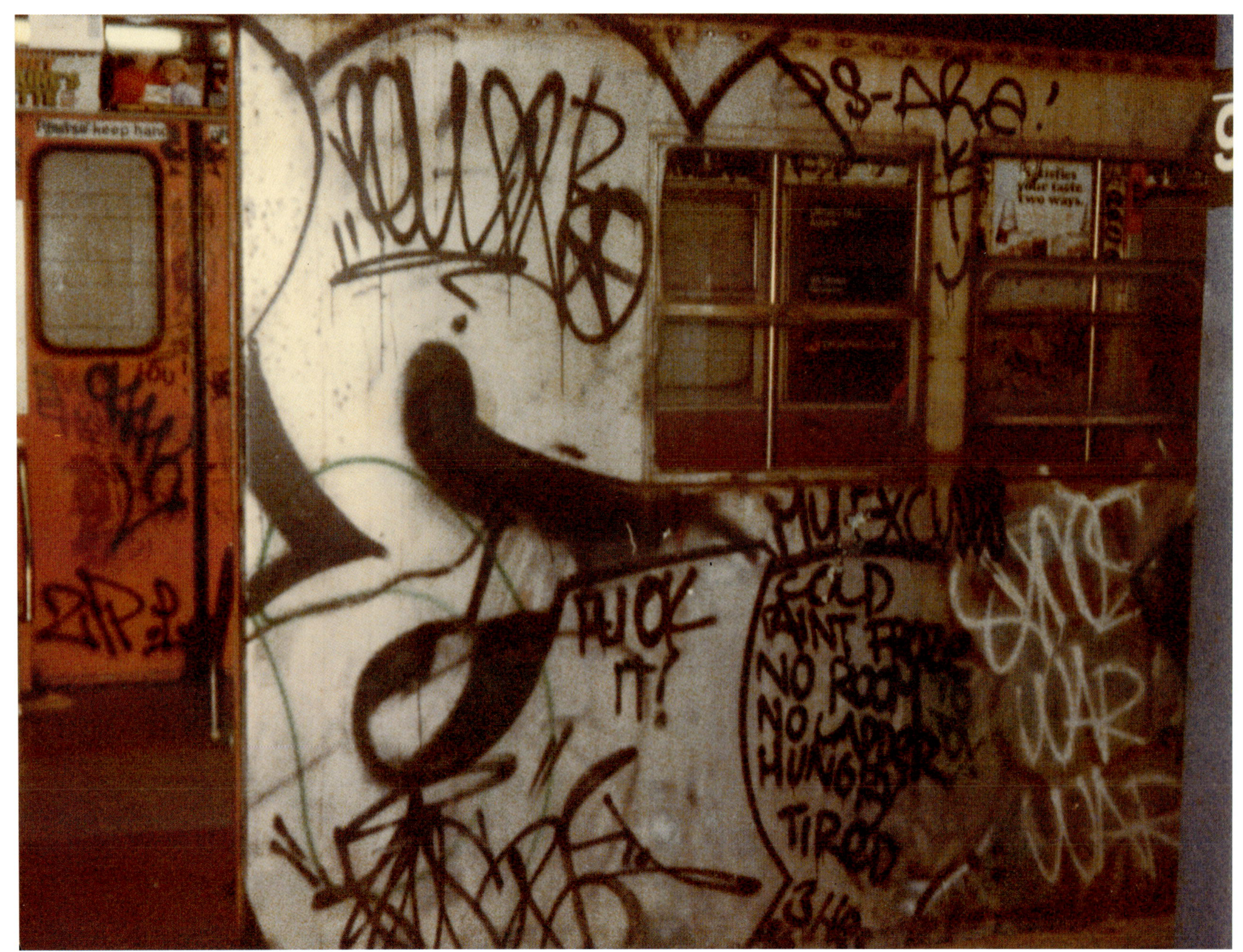

Revlon, unfinished, 1986

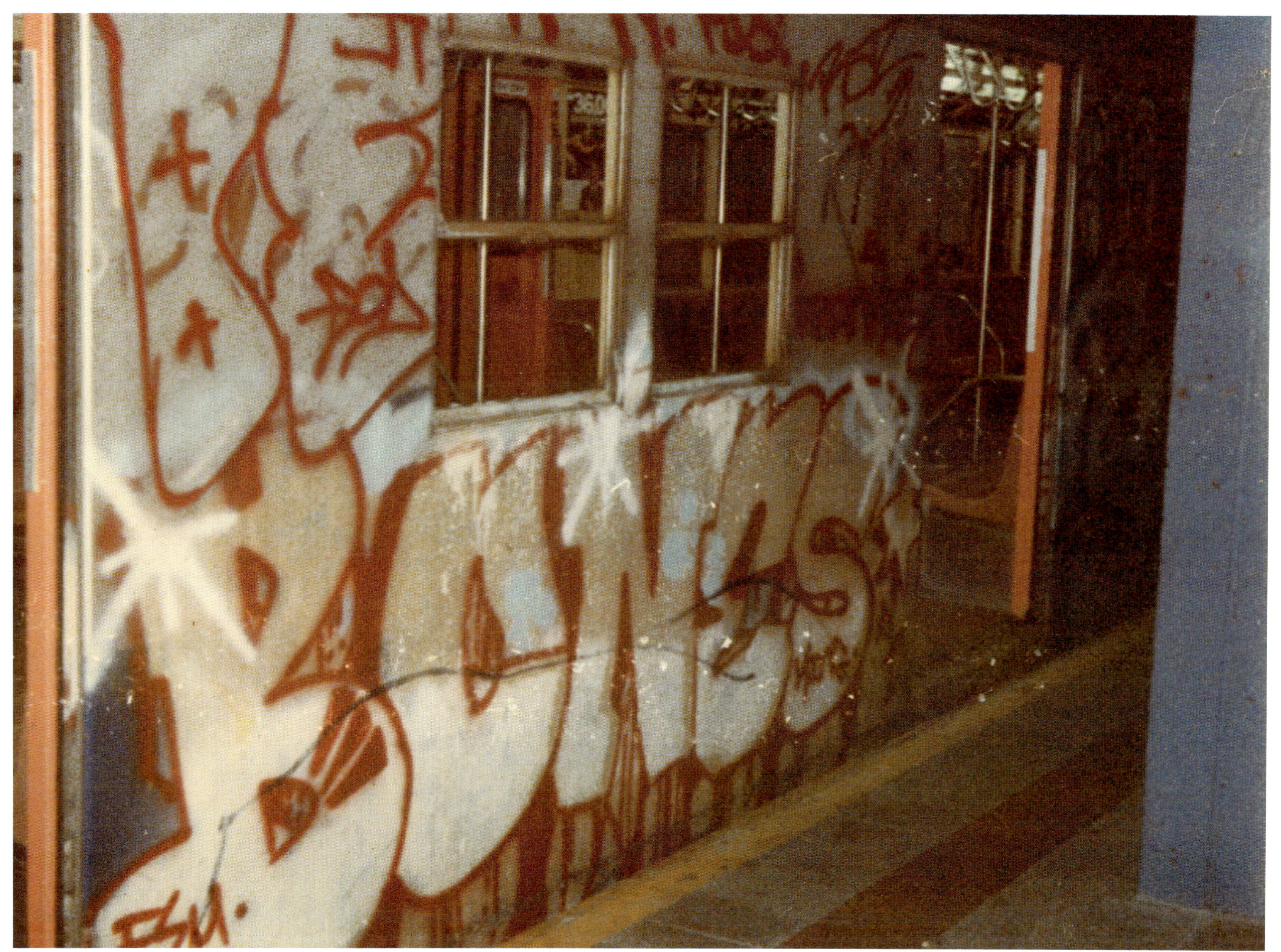

Bones, 1985

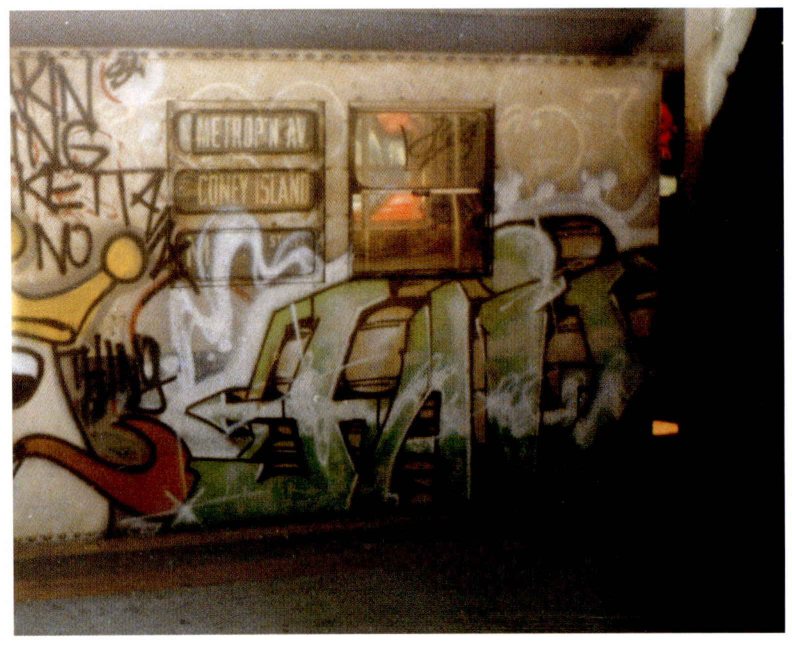

"Jail" by Bind

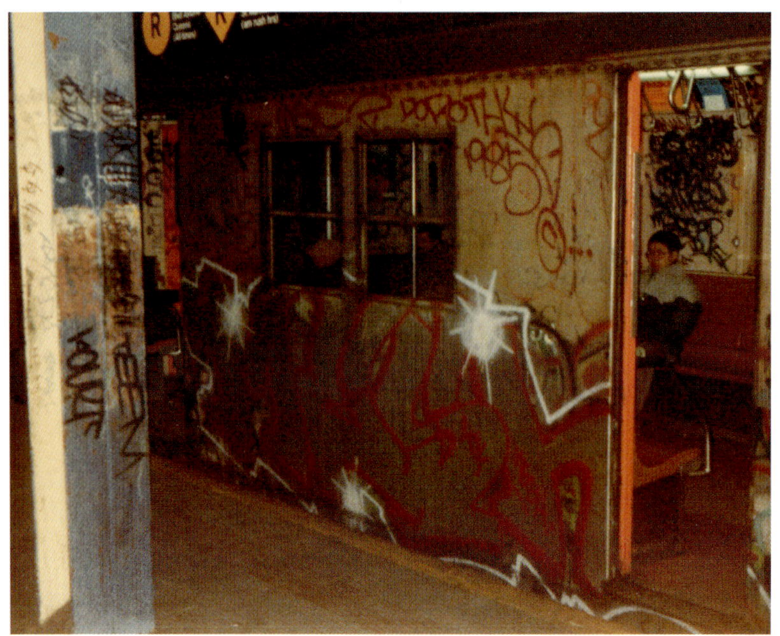
Mesh (AOK), 1986

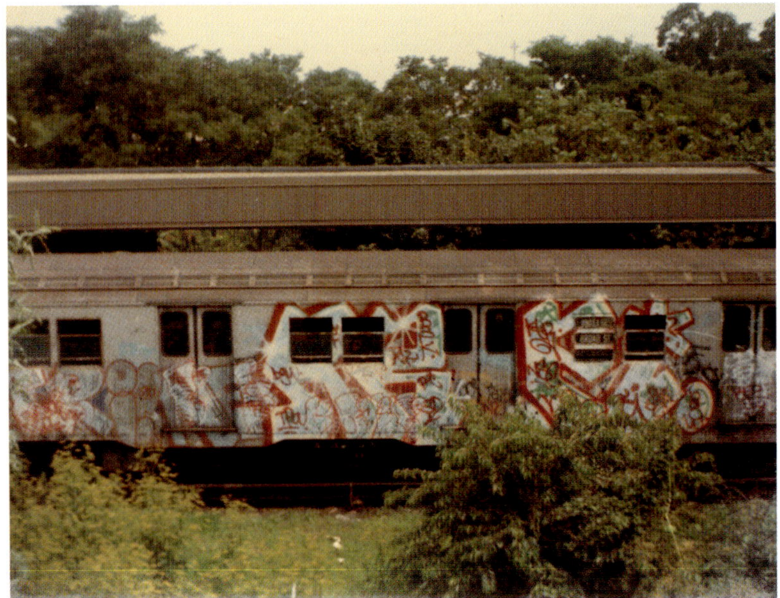
AR & EI (BSK), 1985

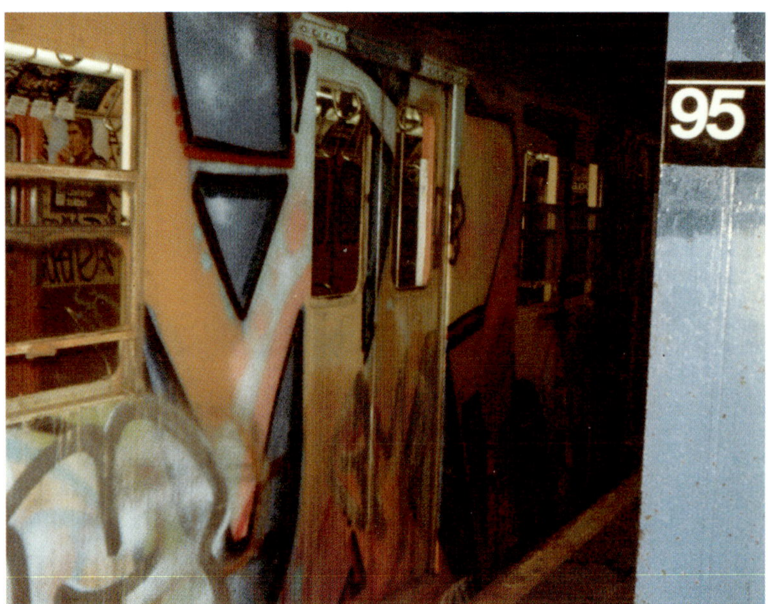

"2 Improve" by Min (RTW)

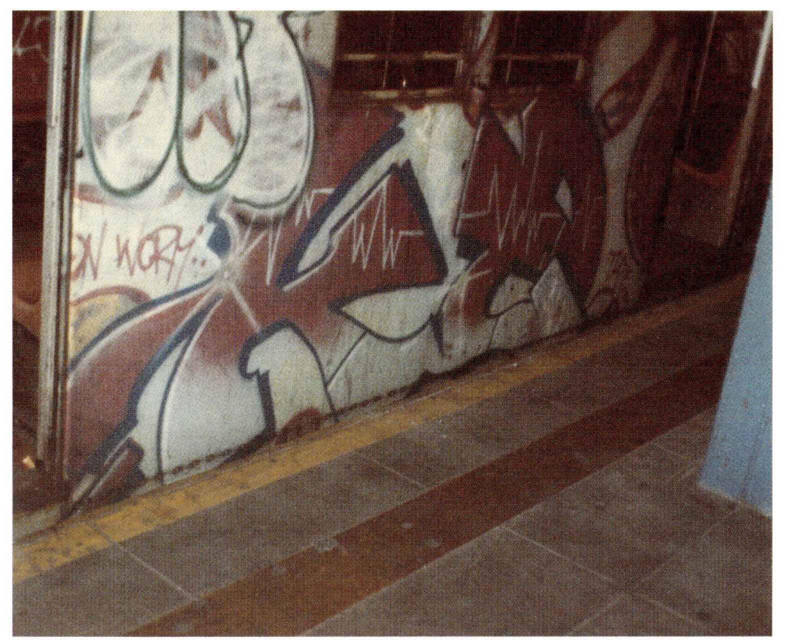

Kev (TM7), 1986

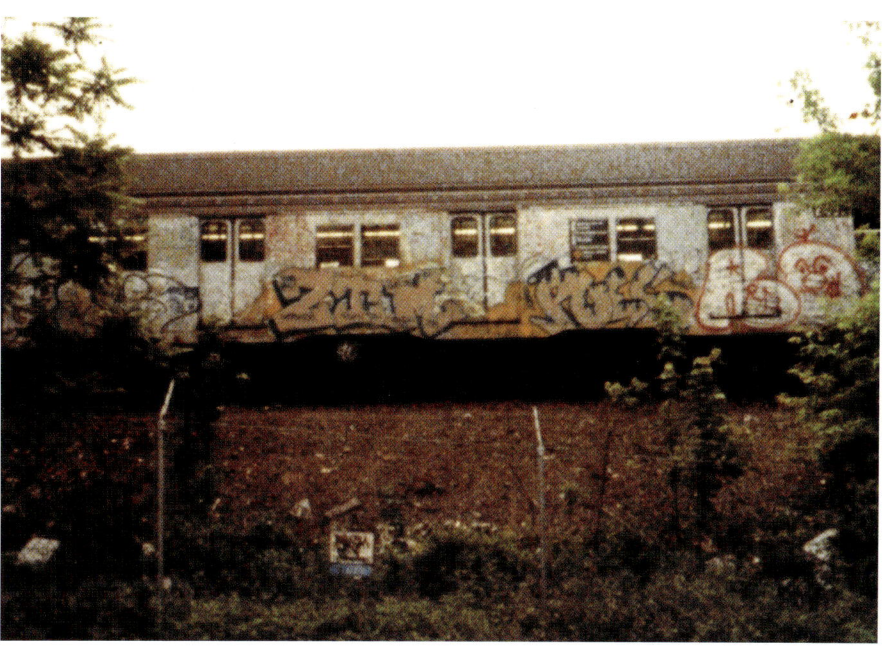

Zim and Poes (TF), 1986

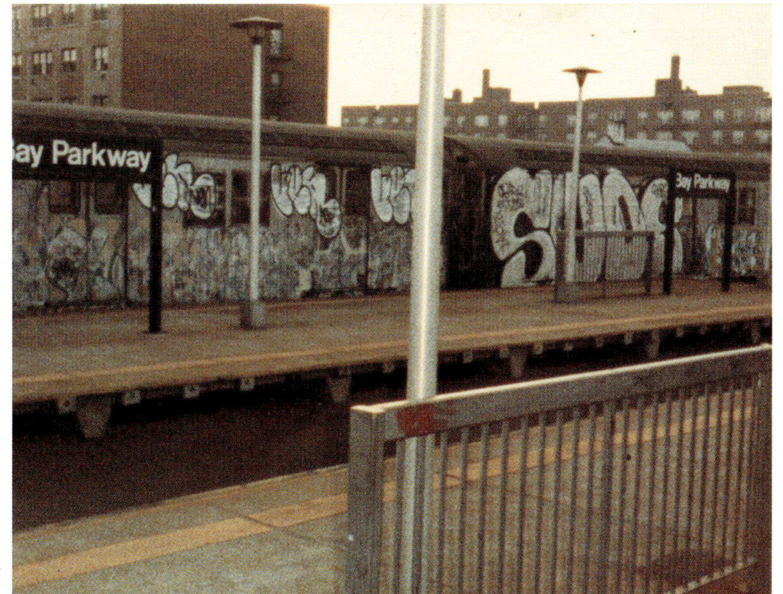

Suds, 1986

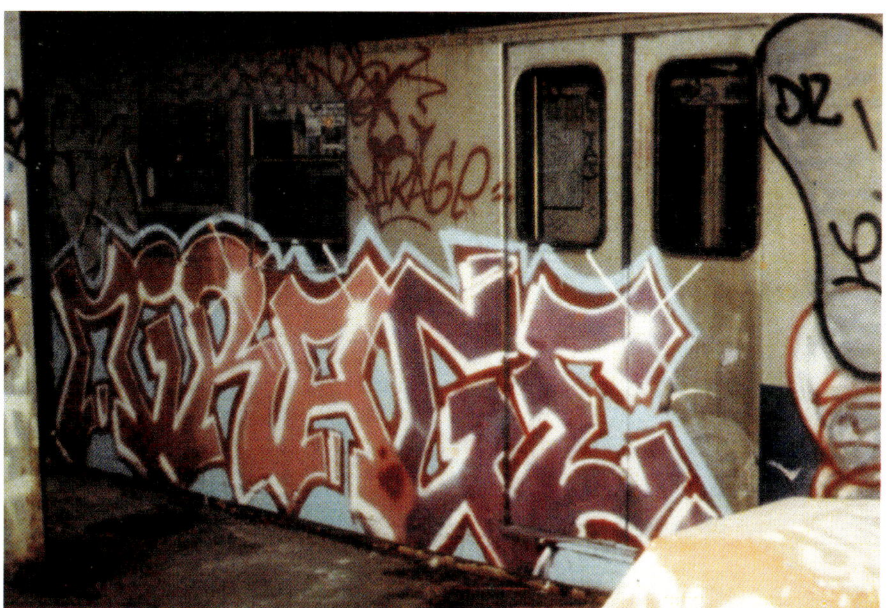

Mirage (BC), 1985

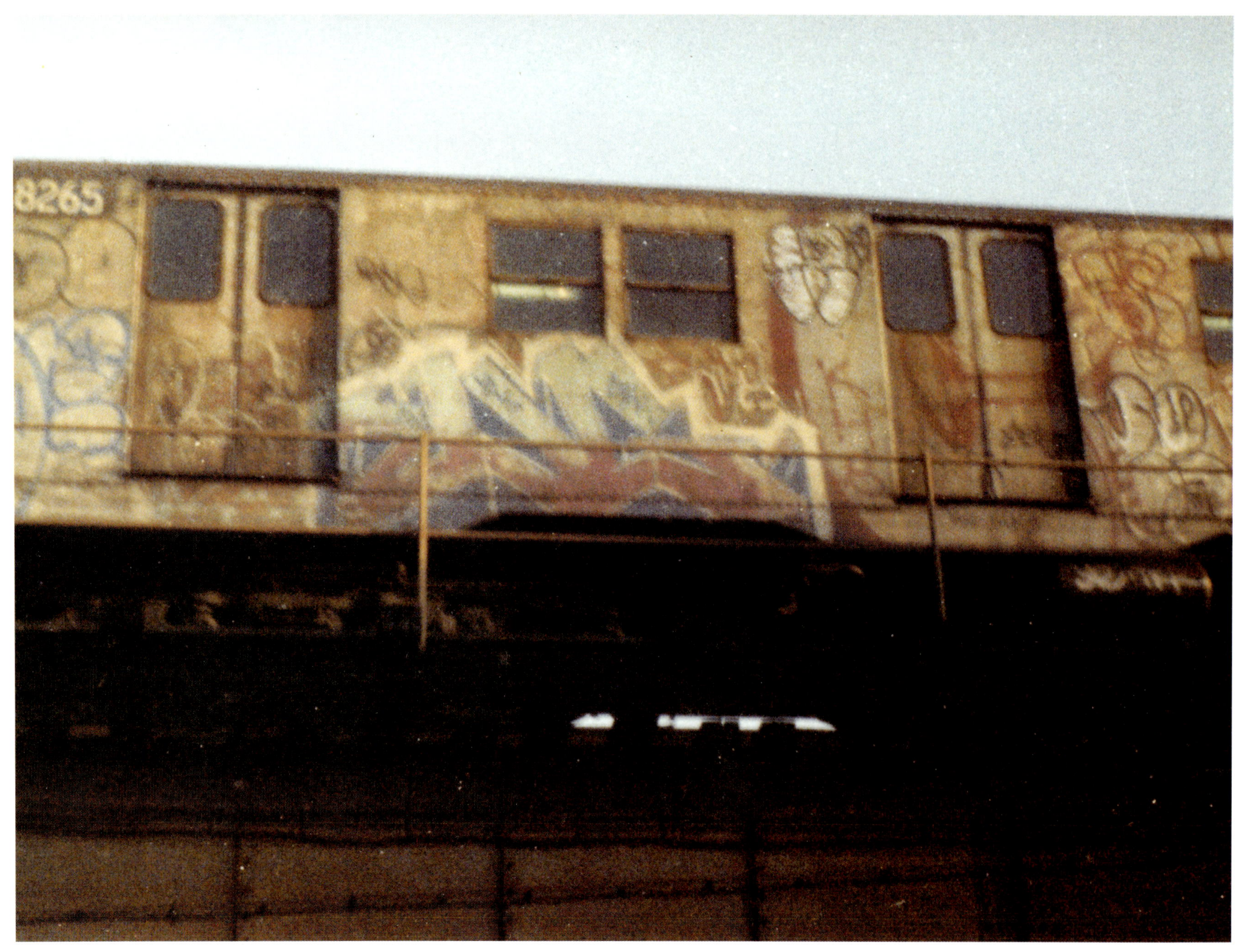

DG (NWC), 1985

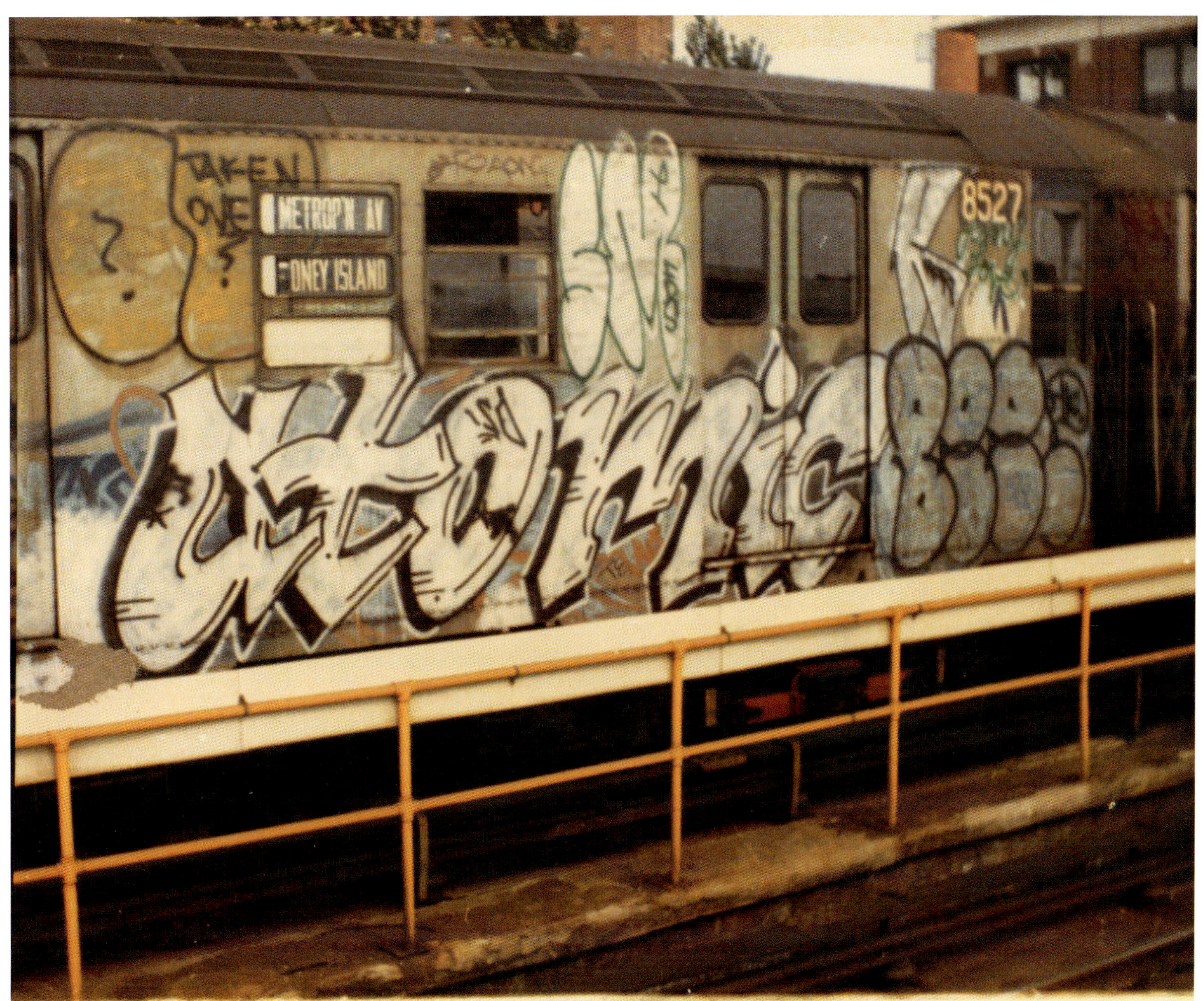

"Atomic" by Atom, 1985

Strider

I moved to NYC from Detroit in 1974. I was 10 years old during the sanitation strike. Garbage was piled high. Litter, rats, roaches, and flies were everywhere. You had to watch your step because of the dogshit.

I loved the subways right away. I was not confined to a backyard or neighborhood. I rode to school on the CC "clunkers." They had ripped red vinyl seats filled with straw. The fans had died years ago. The lights used to blink out and you would fly through the underground in the dark.

I was not really paying attention to graffiti yet. It was just a thought, until I saw an "Iz The Wiz" hunter green window down straight letter with rivets on the CC's. It jumped out so I could read it. Now I was curious.

In junior high school lots of kids had tags, so I got one too. My first tag was "nomad." Later I came up with the name "Strider." After school we would go "motion bombing" on the #1 line at South Ferry loop. The insides were layered with old school tags fading to brown. After a while I started cutting school to watch for pieces on the trains. Me and Chaos started hanging with 2 Japanese kids from school, Saki and Samurai. Chaos was handed his name by the original "Chaos" (3YB). Saki and I started going up to Central Park to hang at the bandshell, which was a writer's spot to get high and skateboard.

I did my first piece at a school yard. I believe that it was orange and black. Fin 2 showed me a "Bad Company" piece on paper with characters that old school "Vane" (Go Club) had done. Being naive, I thought it was the rock and roll band. I found out years later that it was actually Vane's crew. So Vane is the original founder of BC. Months later, I started the new BC crew with Chaos and Brandy.

Entering high school, I met up with the Dark Side Artists (DSA), Delta 7, Sahara, Reflex, Spaced Hate, Dread, Break, DemiGod, and Moxa, a female writer. They dropped DSA and we became "Bad Company" (Burn and Destroy Co.). Wild hand styles were our original trademark. I got more into piecing.

Finally, I went to the AA 175th Street lay-up with Sahara and Chaos in 1979. I did my first piece on a "ridge." It was two-tone and dripped like shit, but I was hooked. I did my second piece on a 2 train at Esplanade lay-up in the Bronx. That place was insane. 50 writers at a time. Partying with radios, smashing windows, birdcalls, and talking shit.

One night, me, Brandy, and Chaos were walking between trains at Esplanade and bumped into Blade and Comet. I was around 15 and they looked like grown men. Blade stepped up to us and drilled us with the usual fomalities. "What-chew-write?" Intimidating but cool. He knew the original Chaos 3YB and we relaxed. Everything was smooth until he reached in Chaos's jacket and pulled out a steel pipe. "What`s this for?" he asked. Chaos answered a little awkwardly but solid, "You know just in case someone fucks around." Blade slipped it back into his jacket and said, "All right, that's cool." We went and did our thing. I had the innocent idea that I was supposed to use every drop of paint on the "third" train piece (10-15 cans). I did, finishing it off with a giant "delta blue" splash across the whole thing. It was absurdly over burnt. "Silly wack..." Impossible to read, but I was into it. Blade came up later and loked at my piece and said, "Yo! That shit is crazy. I like it." He did one of his "Silver Freak" throw ups next to my "madness" and broke out. That made my whole graffiti career and I got deep into piecing.

I would try to rock any style that was in my head, not trying to "fit in." BC bounced around hitting different lines. I'm not sure, but I think I got sick of the "petty beefs" and pressure, which were getting closer to my family. I got a girl and quit writing for a year or so around 1982. Looking back, I wish I had taken flicks.

While traveling to Staten Island, I met Braze on the boat and connected with a whole new set of writers around 1984 (Trik One, Mirage, Keka, Monie, etc.). BC part 2. We moved around to different lines again. Spaced Hate and Dread were the only "originals" left, destroying the #1s (you remember). I got spoiled doing a few pieces on the RR/N trains. "T-B floaters" on the platform with lights.

I dropped out again around 1988 out of necessity. Rent, bills, wife, son, and the paint was being caged anyway. Tried to maintain a so-called "normal" lifestyle but it didn't work out. I would sneak out and do a piece every once in a while, scope walls and fantasize about trains. All my friends were writers, so I couldn't get out. I watched in the background as some of them made a last run on the trains (Ghost, Reas, Web, etc.). Sub 5, Age, and Eros did some nice pieces out on the Island while I was sleeping.

Nowadays, I piece when I can afford it. Even when I can't afford it, I constantly search for the original feeling I got from graffiti and fight the annoying urge for fame. Which irritates me now. I just like the mission of it and styling letters. I like when it comes out looking like graffiti not "advertisement." It's a drag when I hear some bullshit philosophy about a "true" writer. That's "baby food" Just do your thing whenever and as often as you want. "Fame" is what you learned from TV. If that's what you want, move to Hollywood. Graffiti will leave you broke and invisible. The true soul of graffiti is when you went out for the first time to do you're possible wack, masterpiece. "Who cares if it drips?"

—Strider BC

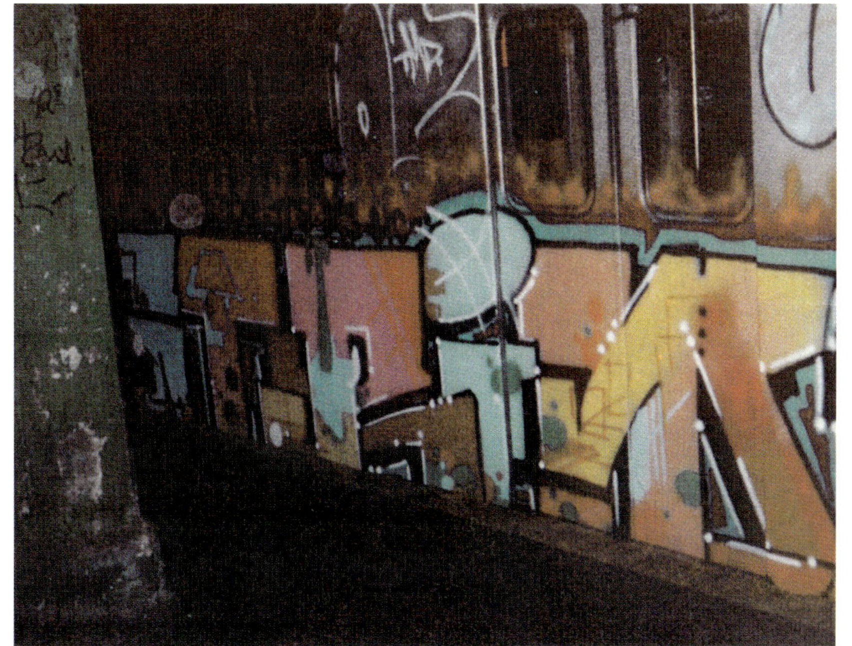

Strider, 1985

Grant Avenue lay-up, 1984

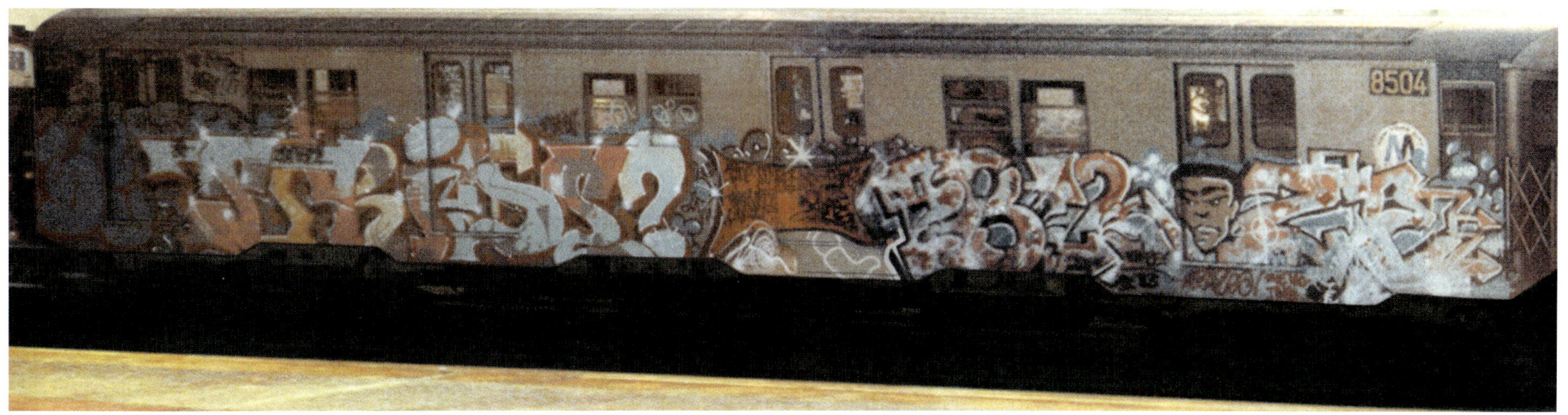

Strider & Braze, 1983

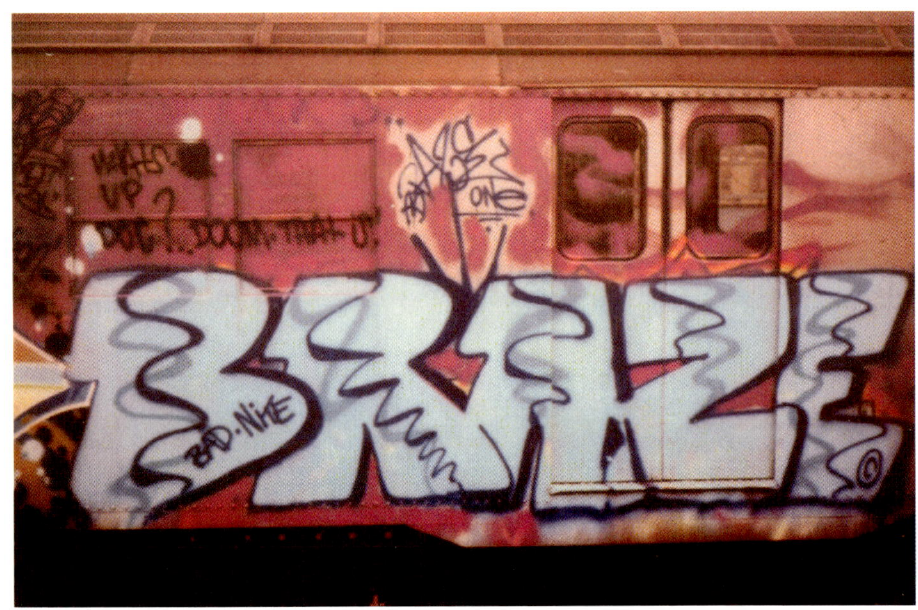

Braze, 1985

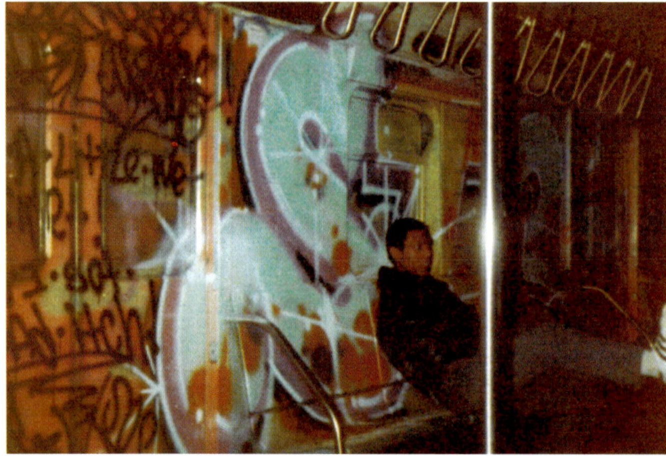

Braze, 1985

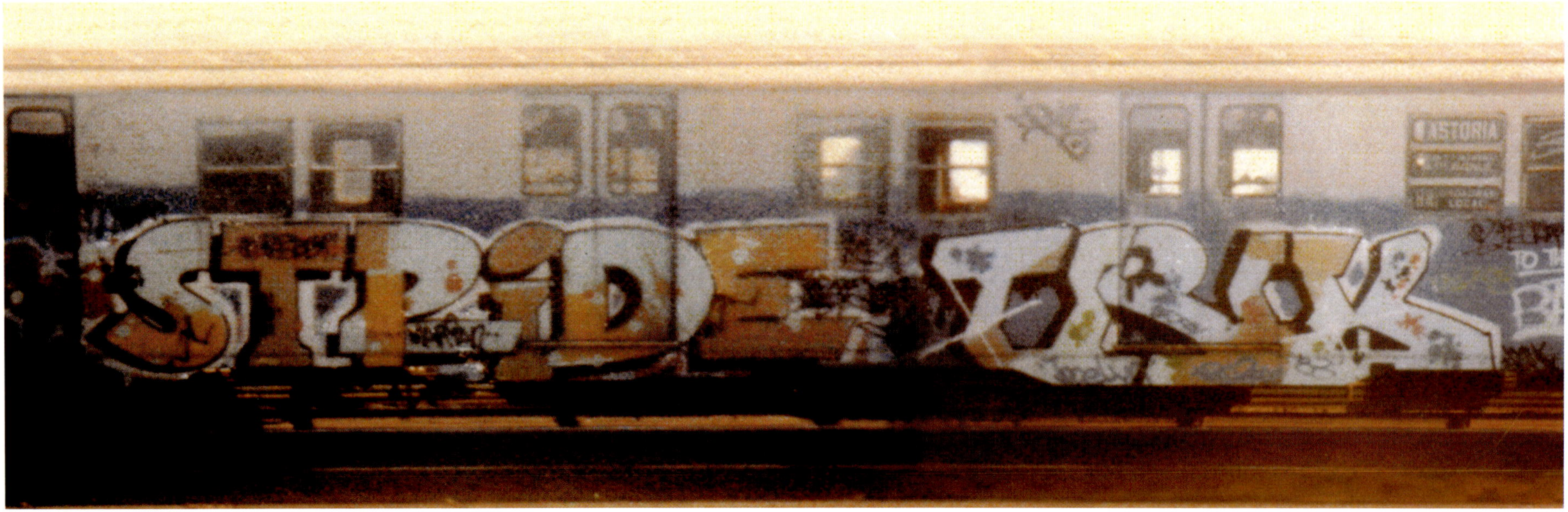

Stride & Trik, 1983

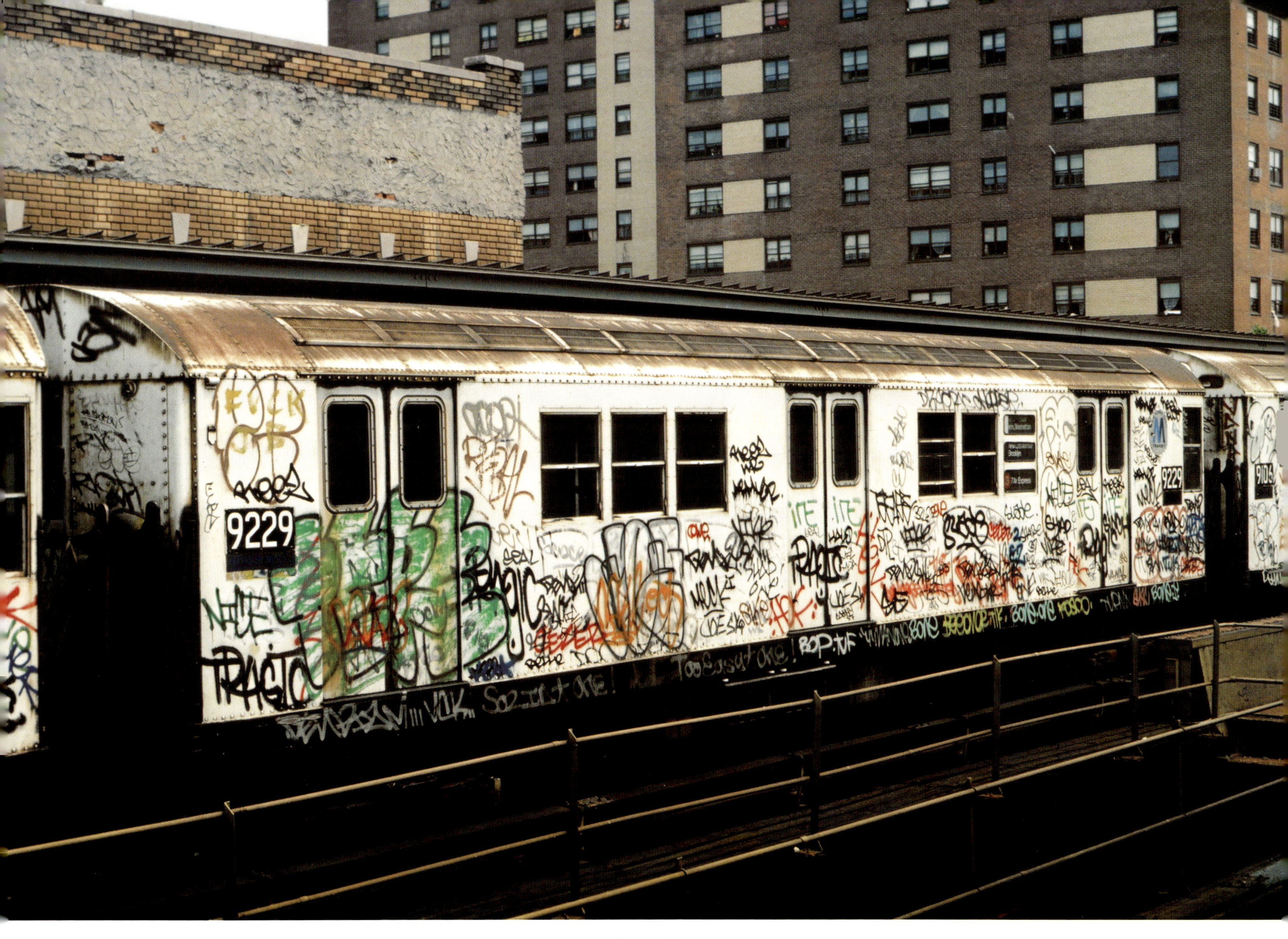

3 line, 1987

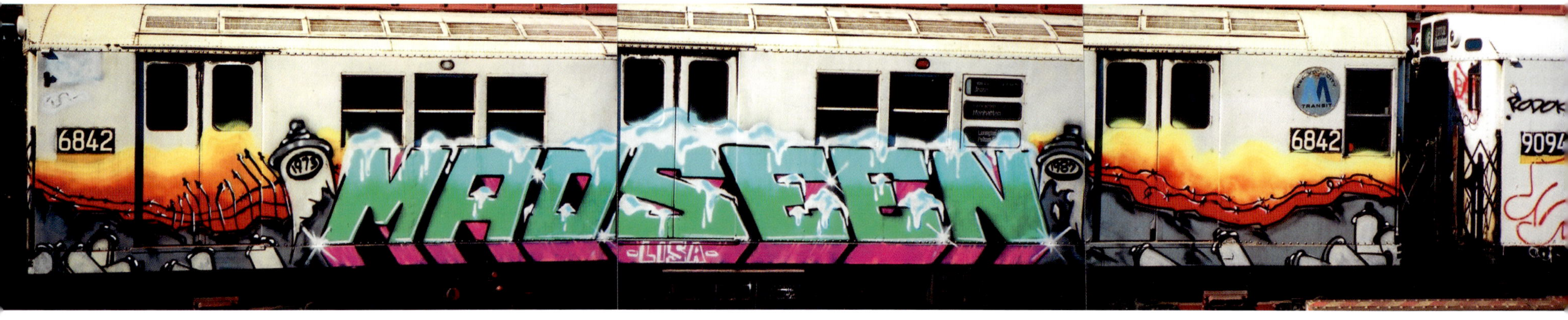

"Madseen" by Seen (UA), 1987

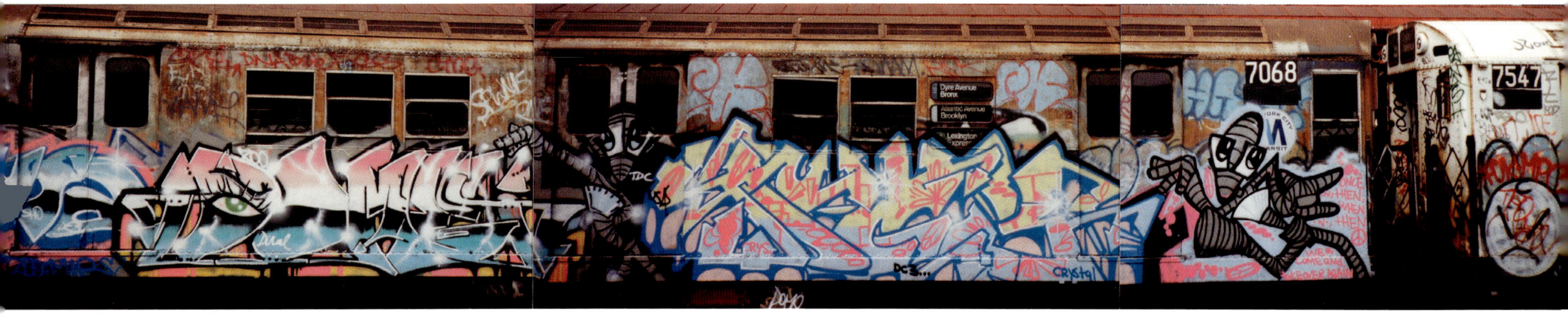

Dome & DC3 (TDC), 1987

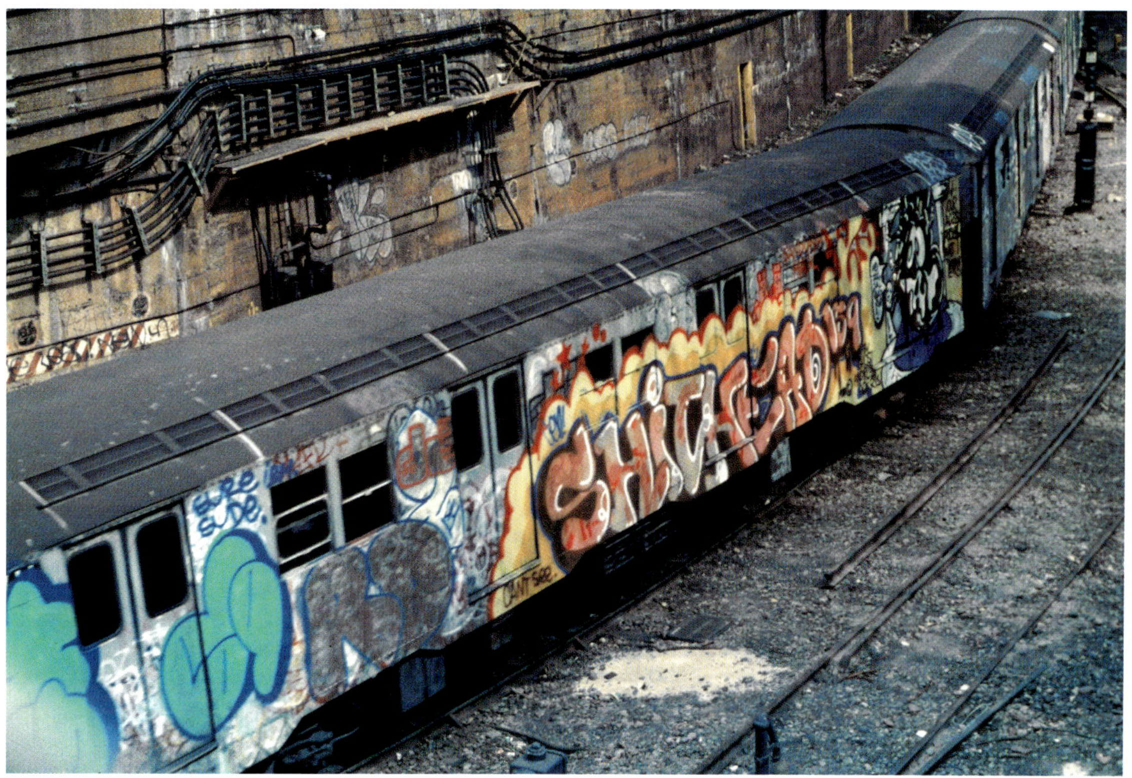

"Shit Head 159" by Ghost & Reas.

I remember planning the Shit Head car in my mom's living room with Ghost the day we decided to go paint it. We were doing all kinds of crazy pieces at that time, like the frying pan car, and he was doing these upside down whole cars. I had done the Eat Shit car and he had done the Ghost in the boat car. We had gotten to a point where we didn't care about our names as much and were going for ideas.

So what started as a joke became a reality about 12 hours later. We went to the Franklin Avenue shuttle. I remember how dark it was because I had two browns for the turd character, but in the dark it got confusing and became a real mess and nothing like I planned it. It's supposed to be a turd cop either coming out of a toilet or ready to be flushed down it. Ghost obviously did the piece, and I think we both filled it in. I love it and it's probably good that it wasn't perfect and clean. I think it was a good piece of graffiti in every way.

—Reas (AOK)

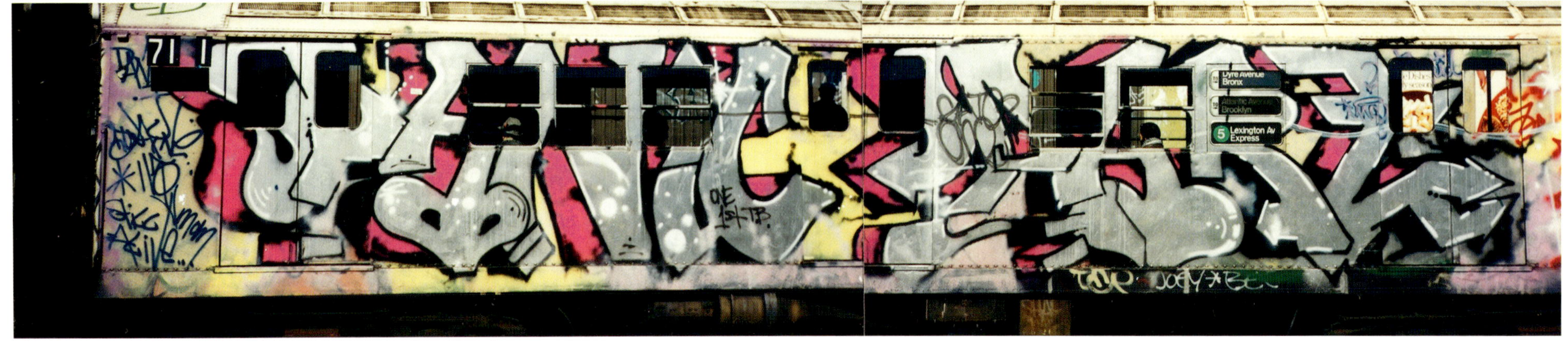

Panic & Part, (TDS), 1987

The best playgrounds in New York City were provided by the MTA, from exploring miles and depths of tunnels stretching from Queens, Brooklyn, Manhattan, and the Bronx, to painting in yards. Flashbacks of hearing the roar of a train being reved up while hiding next to the motor as the great raids terminated, to painting the aisles of steel, and ending a night's bombing by blowing particles of paint fermented with train dust out of my system.

—Neo

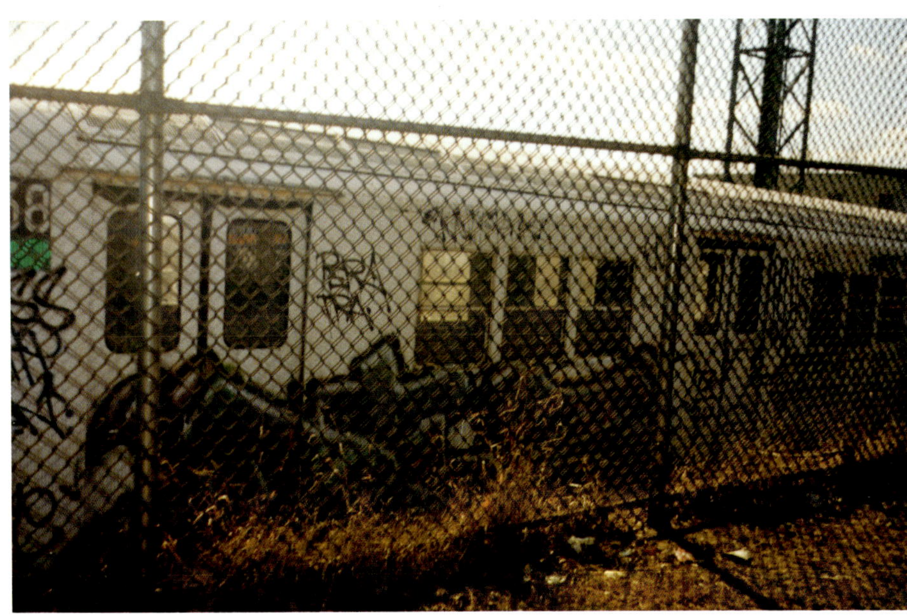

Dez (TFA), 1988

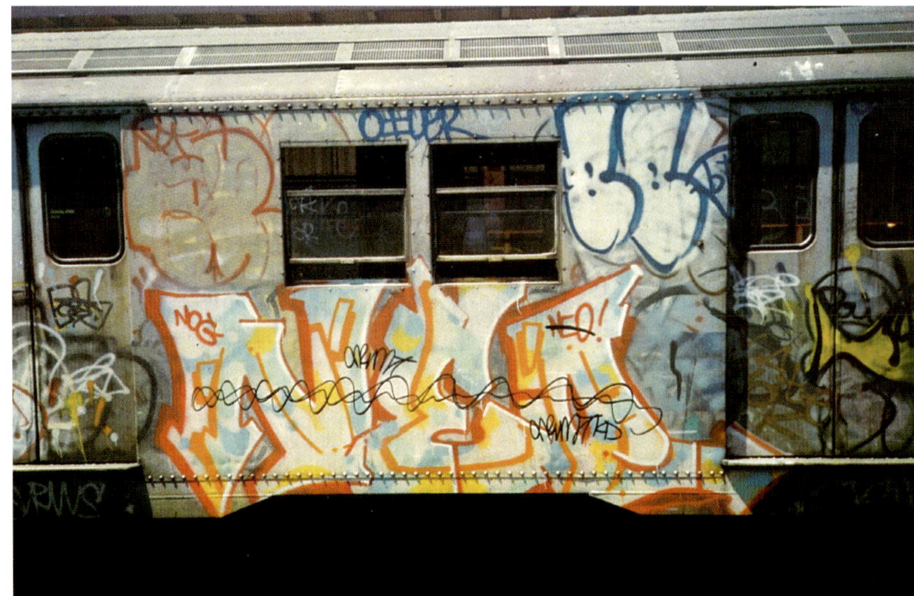

Neo (RIS), 1987

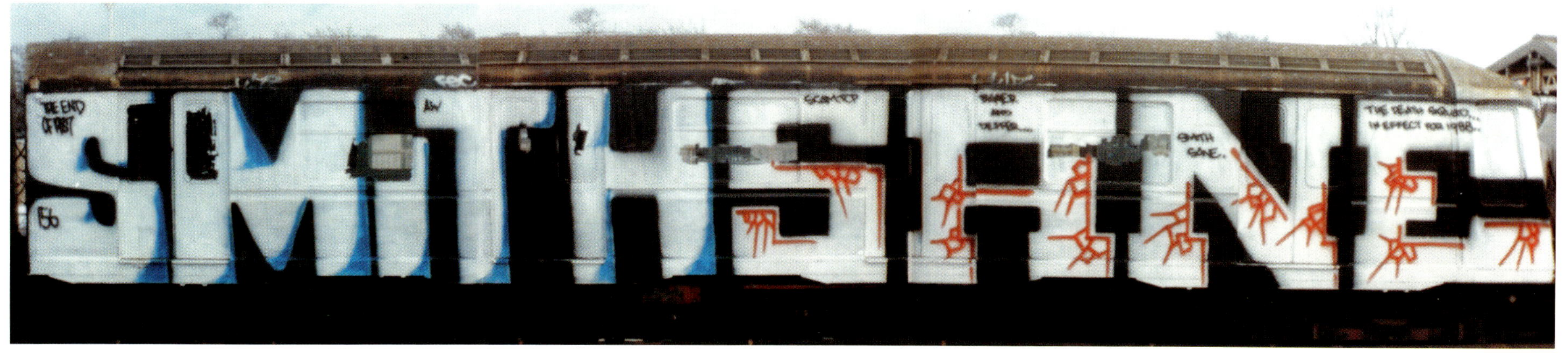

Smith & Sane, 1987

The only whole car done by SaneSmith was done on the B line in the 57th Street lay-up. We were into doing end-to-ends, not really whole cars, but when we got to the lay-up and the side we had planned to do was mostly taken, we wound up on the side with a catwalk so we went bigger. We had done over 50 end-to-ends in our favorite haunt, the 175 lay-up, but we were trying to expand to other areas of the city.

That night there were a few other writers running around and that was when we met the RIS crew at the time, Ghost, Reas, and Ven. Ven was tearing shit up at the time and Reas had some nice pieces out there, but Ghost we hardly knew. So when he threw us down with RIS we didn't know what to make of it. Being from Washington Heights, little did we know what legends these guys were. As we were looking for a spot to paint, Stane came up and asked us not to go over his stuff. As soon as he left, though, we wound up going over one of his throw-ups, since there wasn't any other space. Sorry Bro!

As we were half way through filling in, I could hear the commotion of the other guys in the train bugging out on us using bucket paint. We were using 4" brushes, since we hadn't got the hang of rollers completely, practically attacking the side of the train. Ven even came over to see for himself and said, "You guys are using buckets? Now I've seen everything."

—Smith

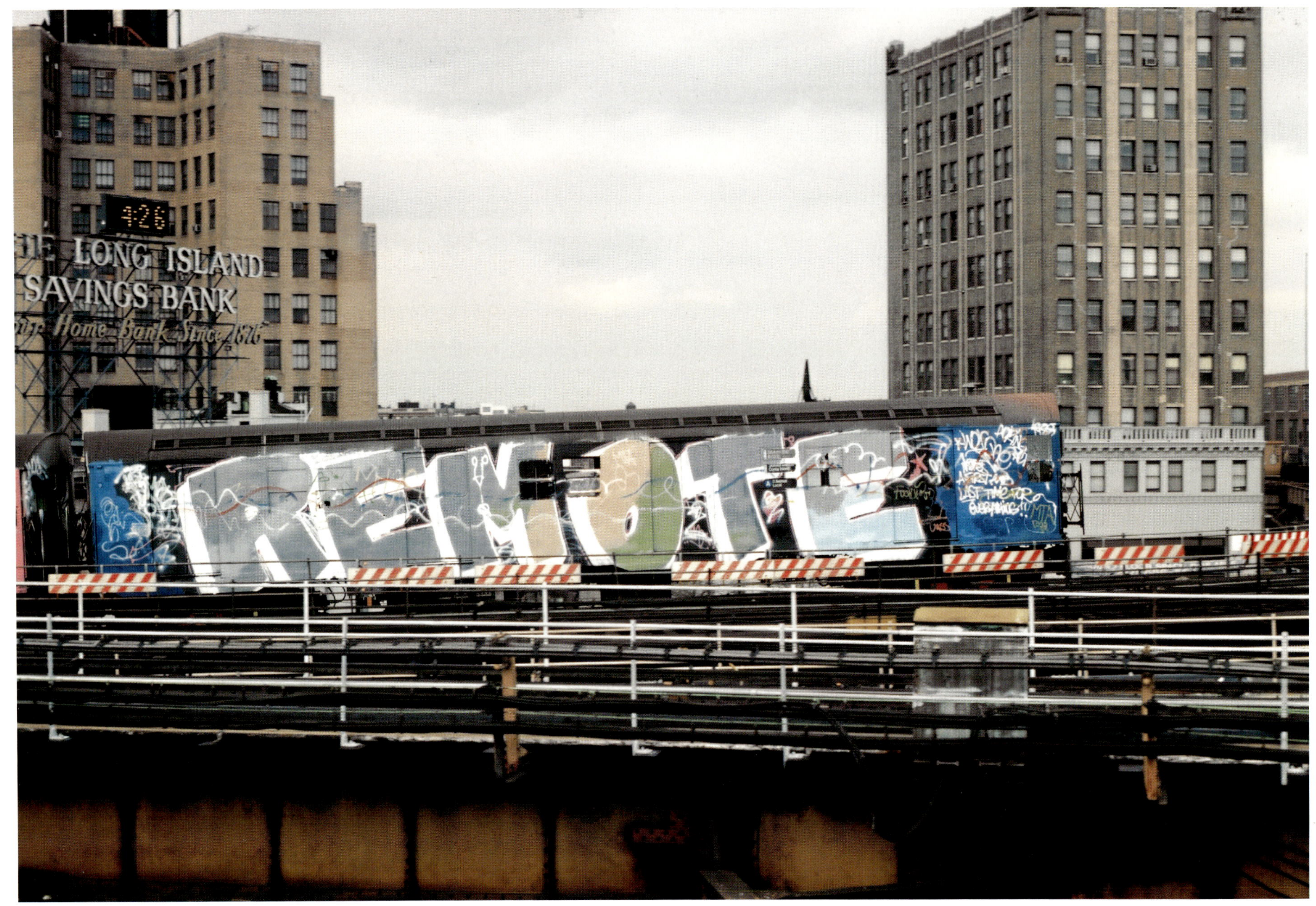

Remote, 1988

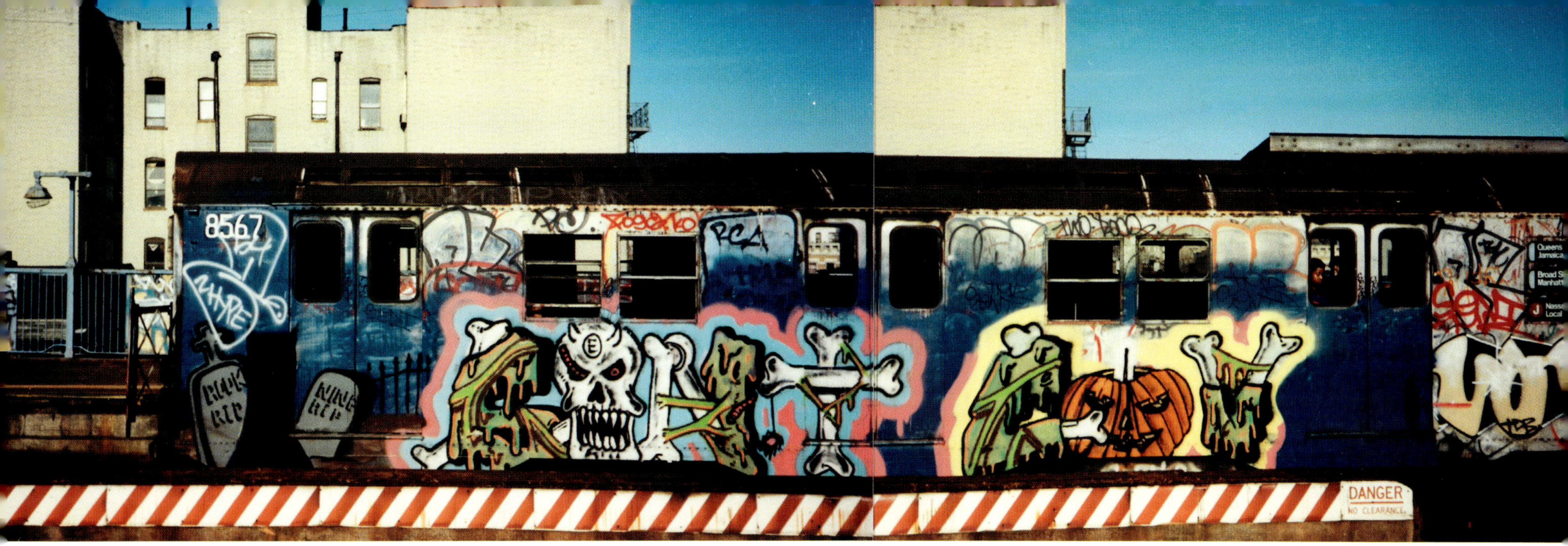

Sent & Cav, 1988

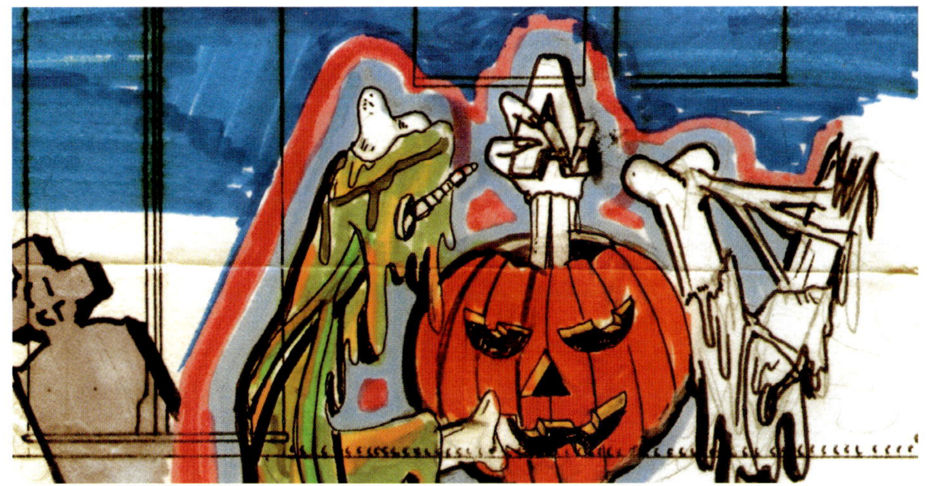
The original outline on paper

The year was 1988. Sent and I planned a Halloween car in Brooklyn at the Franklin Avenue shuttle lay-up. As we worked on our car we were pelted with bottles from a nearby building, causing some unwanted attention. We had to hide underneath the train until things calmed down. Time was not on our side that night. We never got to finish that car. It was daylight savings time. We only had a few hours left before the sun came up and the train pulled out. Then our journey back to the Bronx began.

—Cavs (SV)

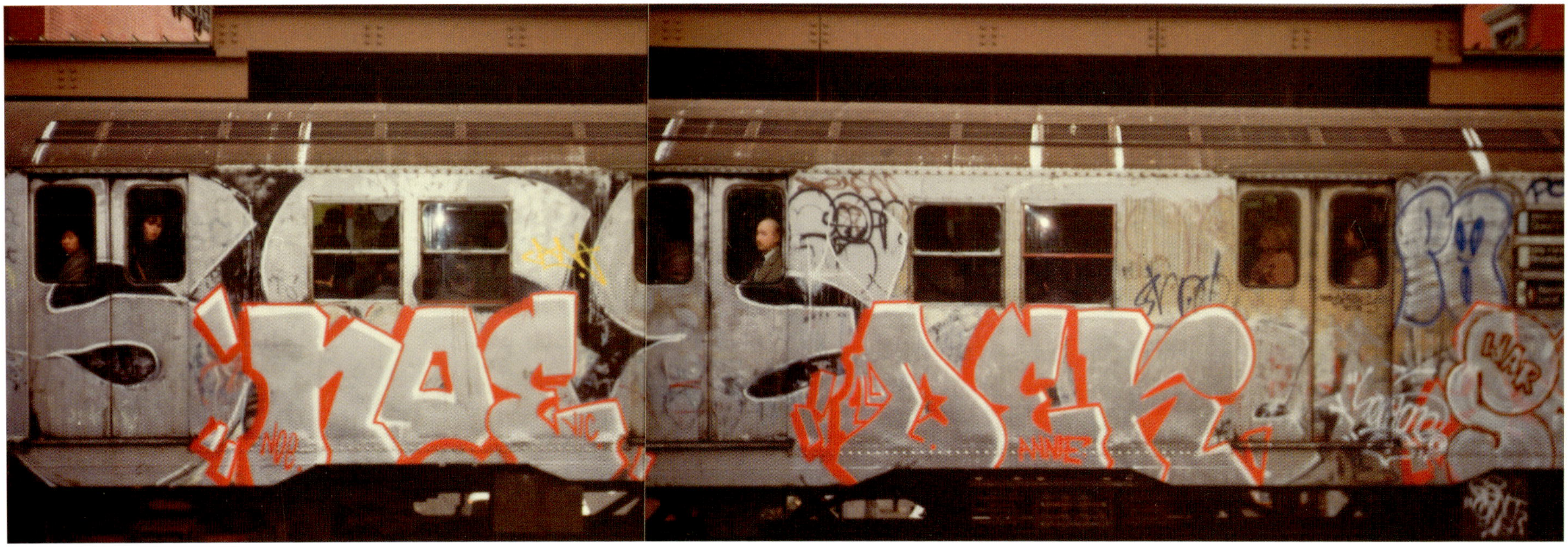

Noe & Dek (Vic), 1988

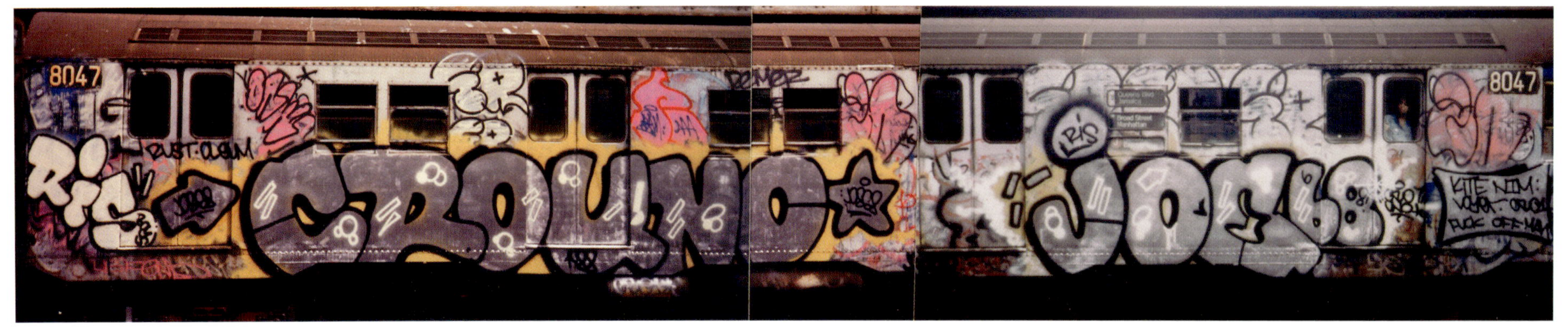

Cro, Joe68 (Ris), 1988

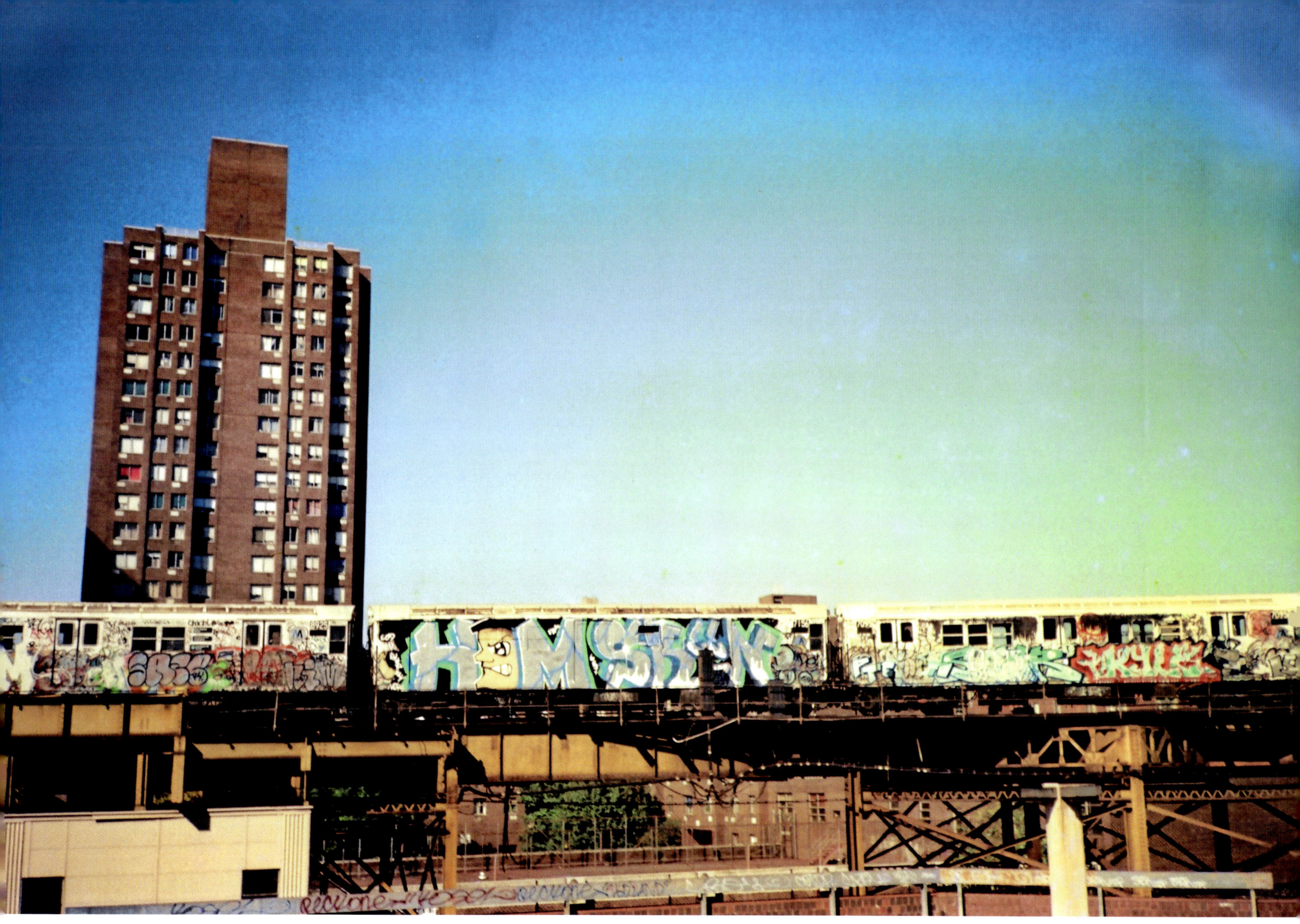

Him & Skeen (COD), 1987

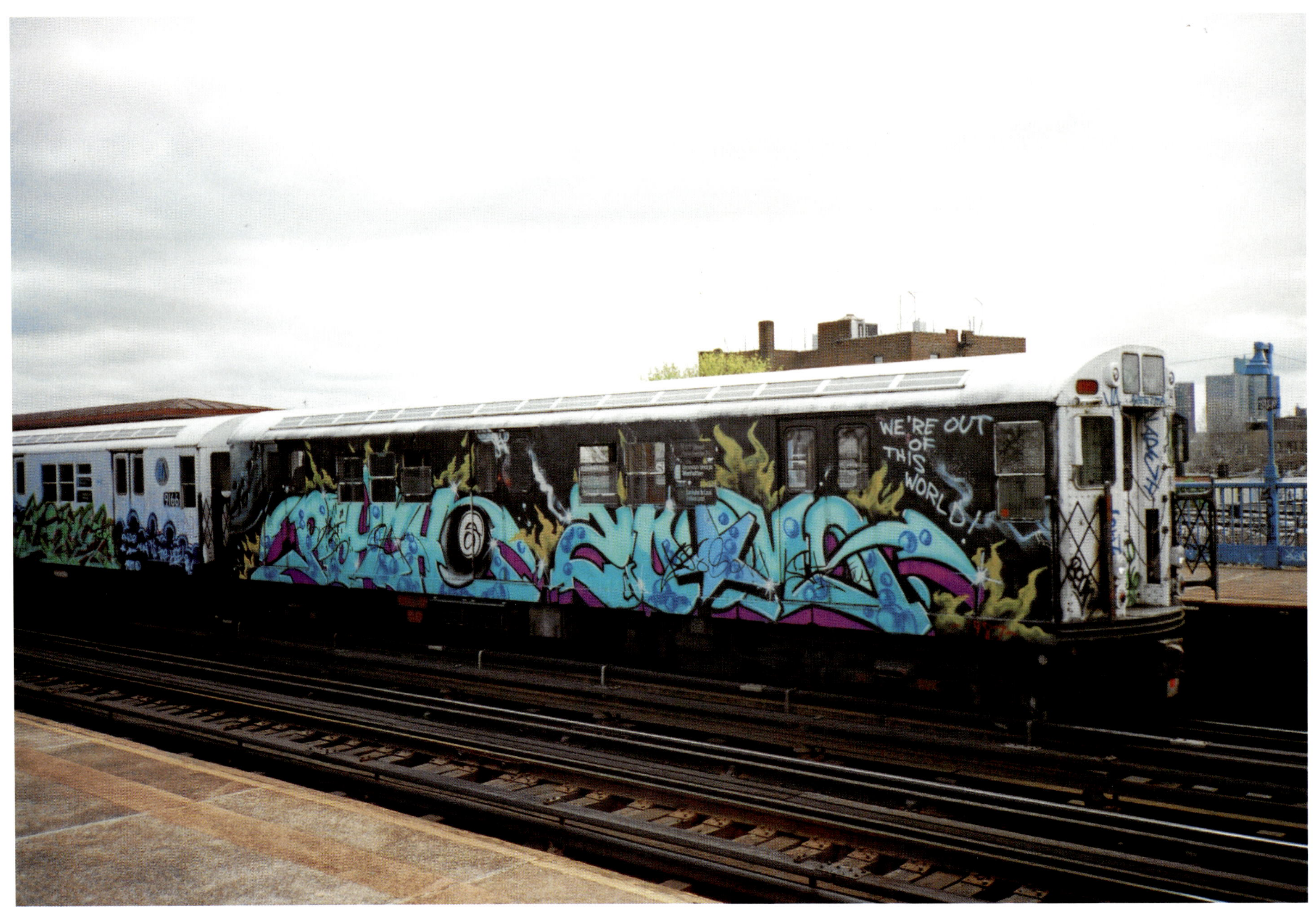

"Psycho" by Seen; Zoom (UA), 1987

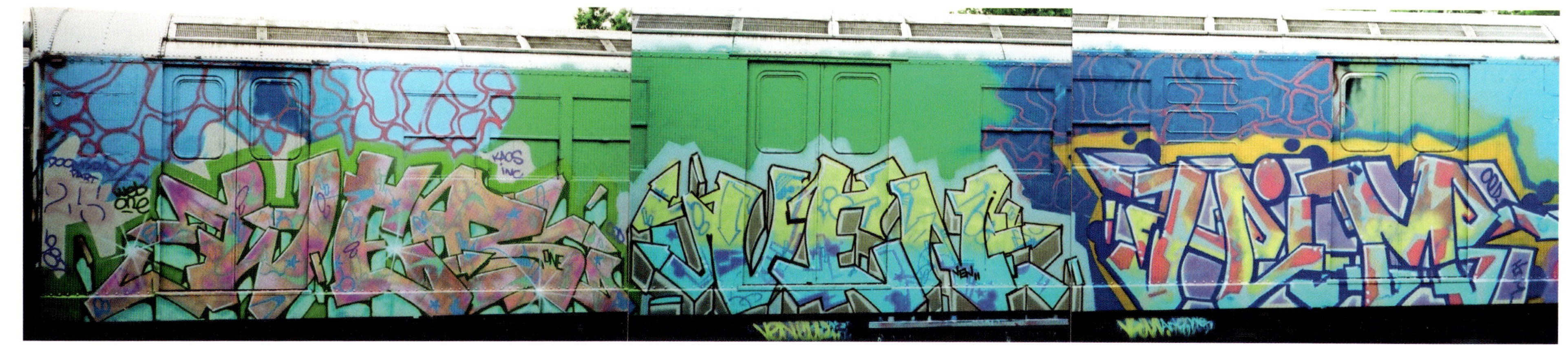

Web, Ven, & Him, 1987

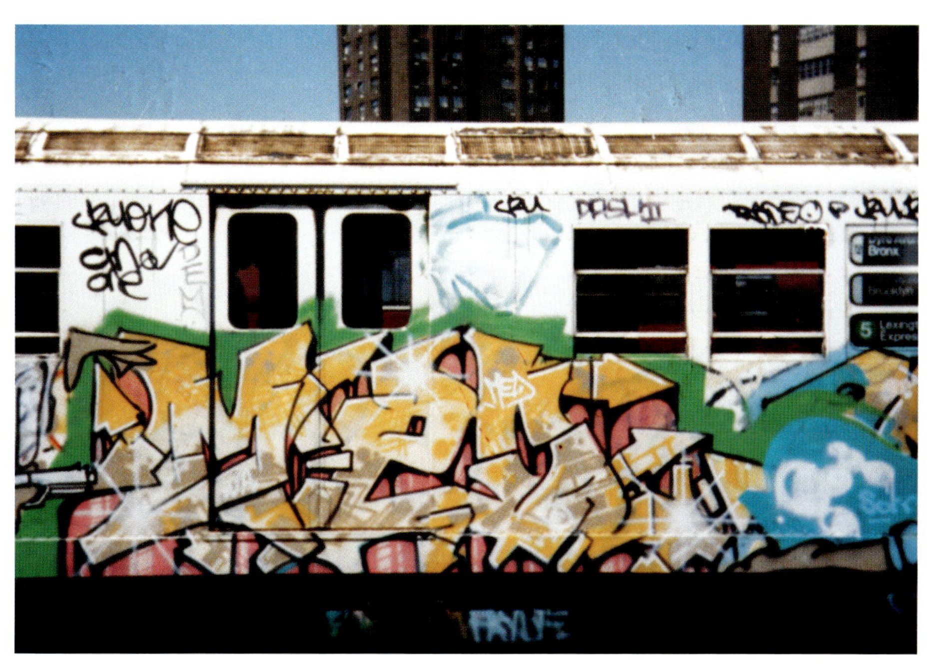

Med, 1985

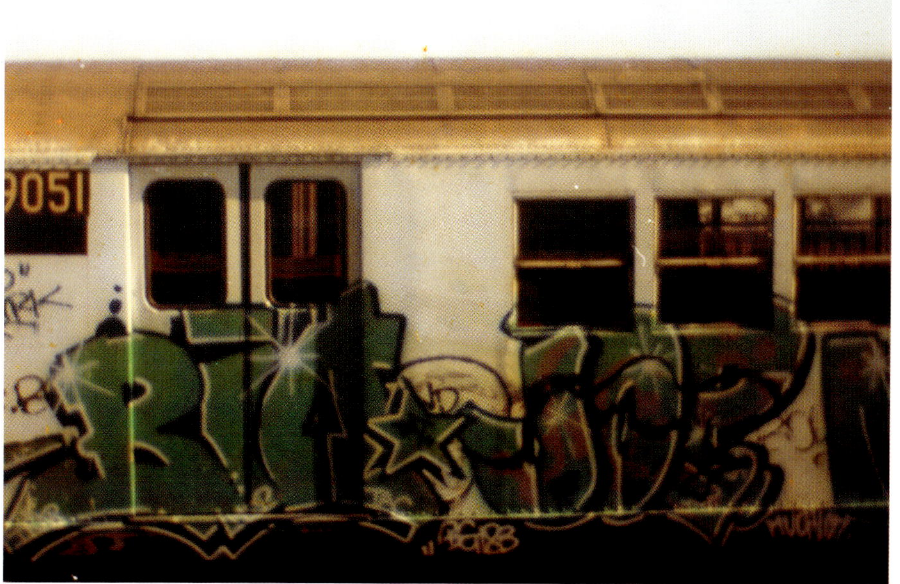

Bio (TAT) & Jop, 1984

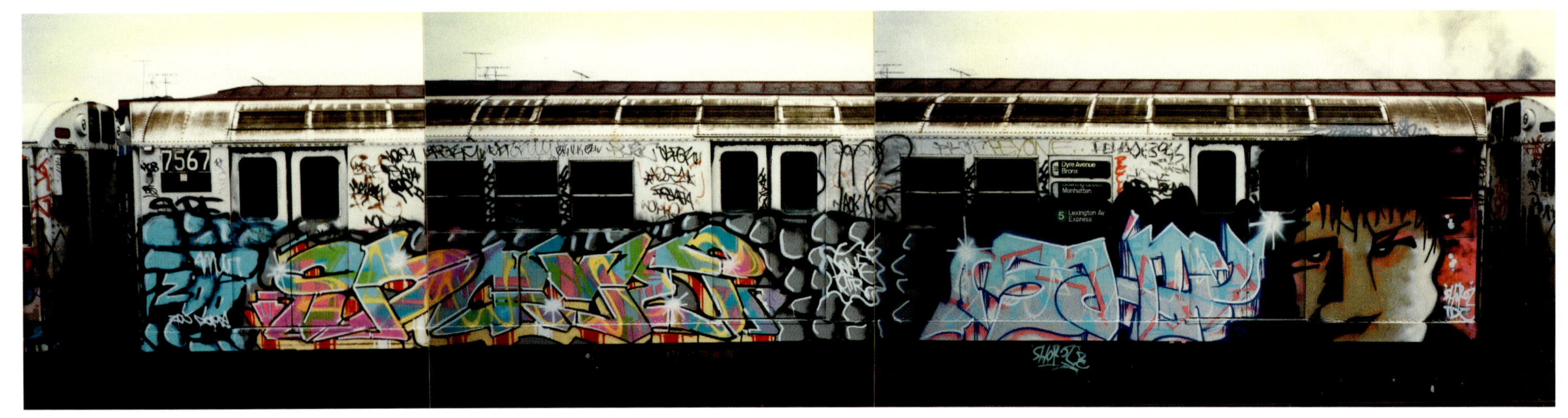

Dome & Sho (TDC), 1986

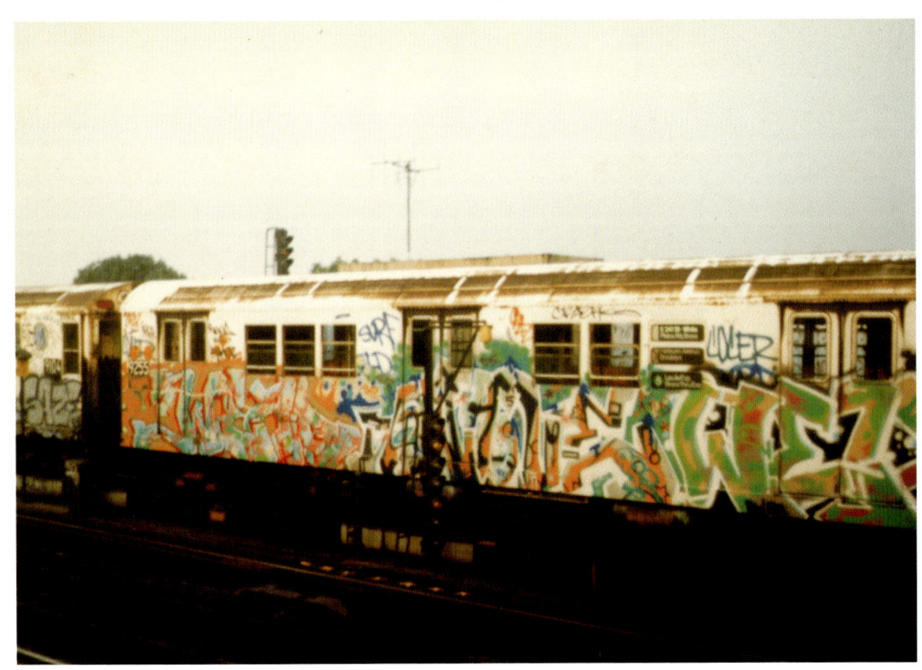

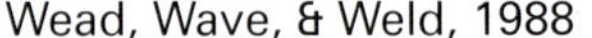

Wead, Wave, & Weld, 1988

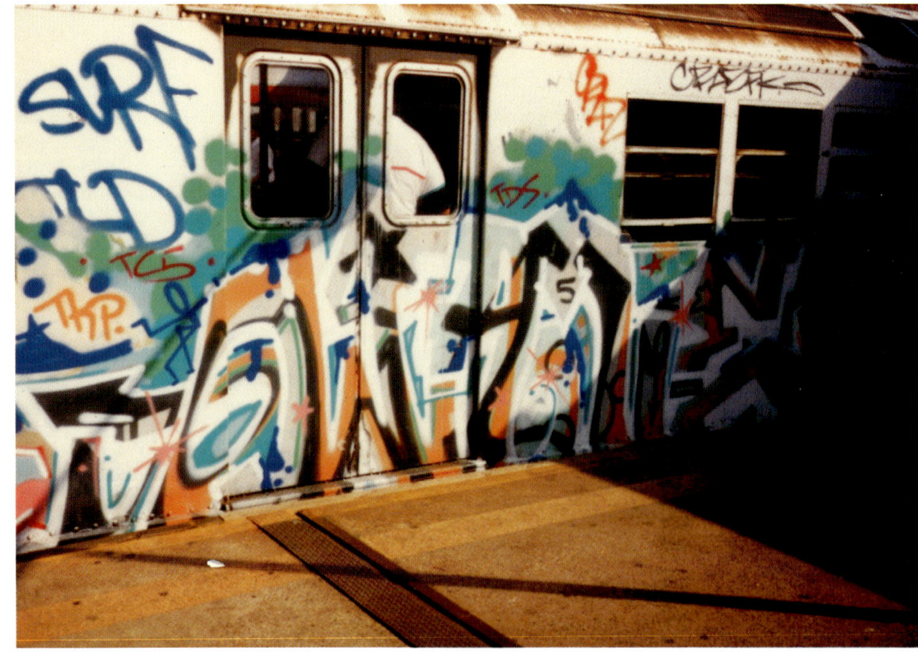

Wave, 1988

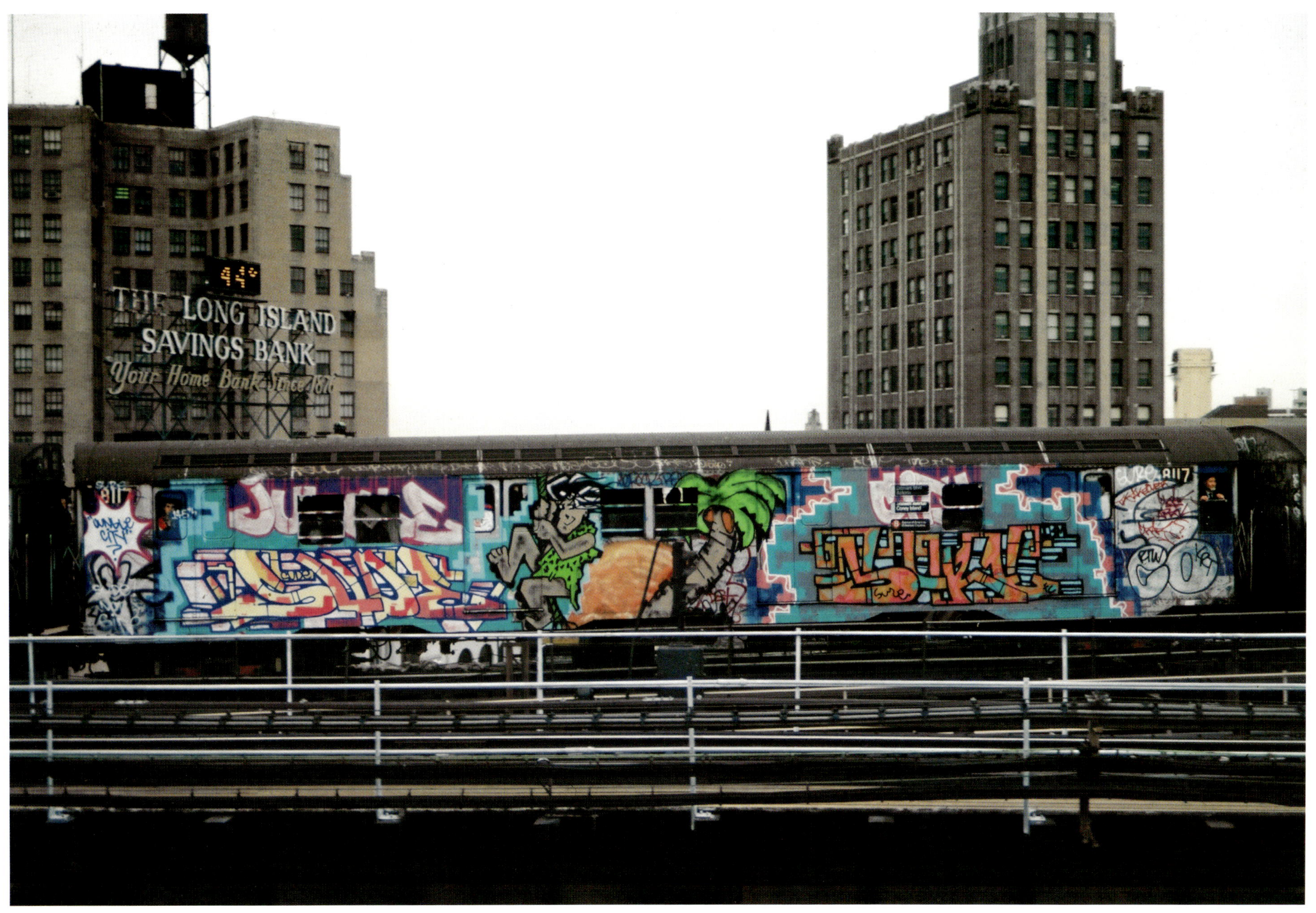

Sude & Sure, 1988

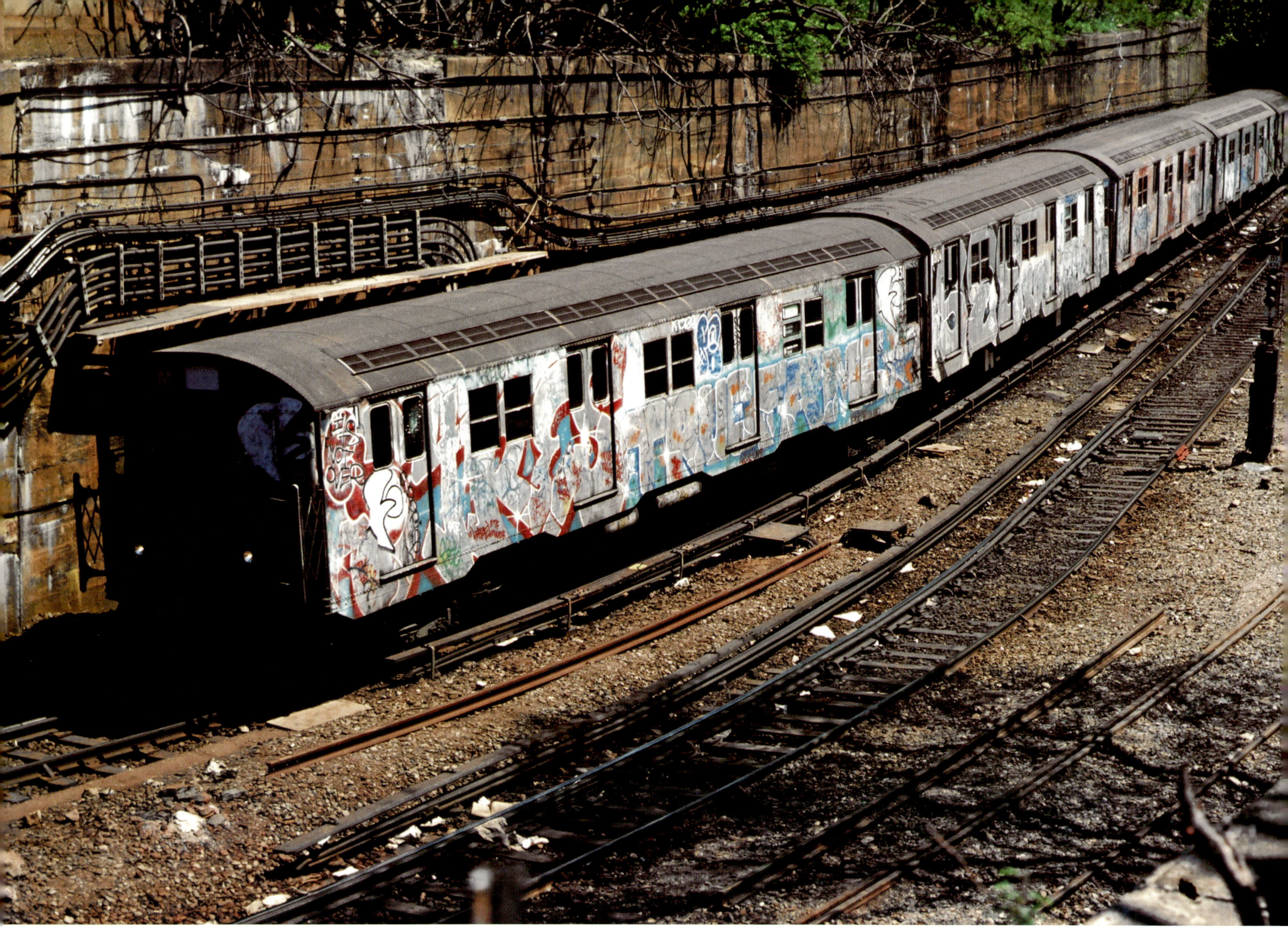

Stres (TF), 1988

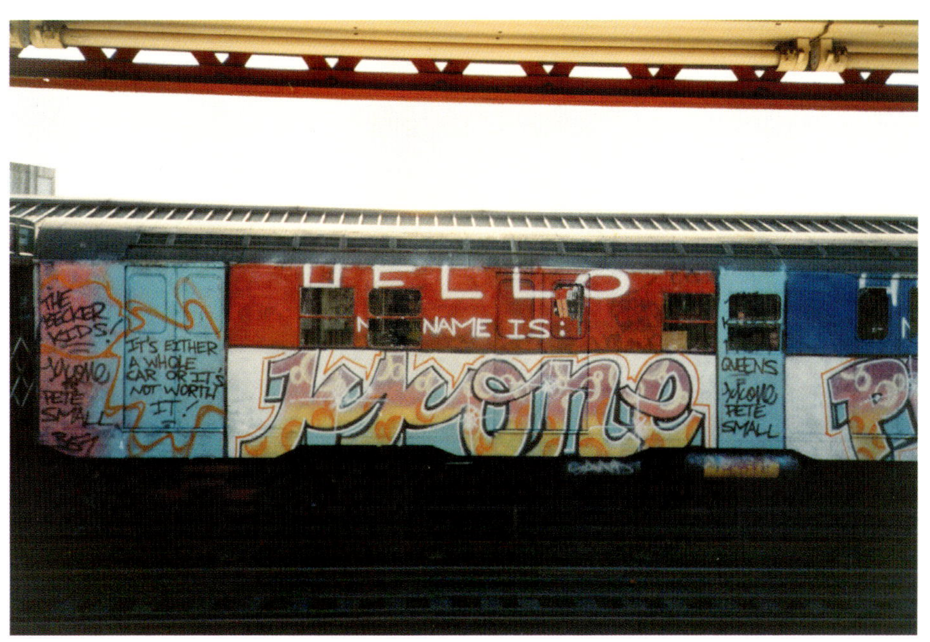

KK One, 1988

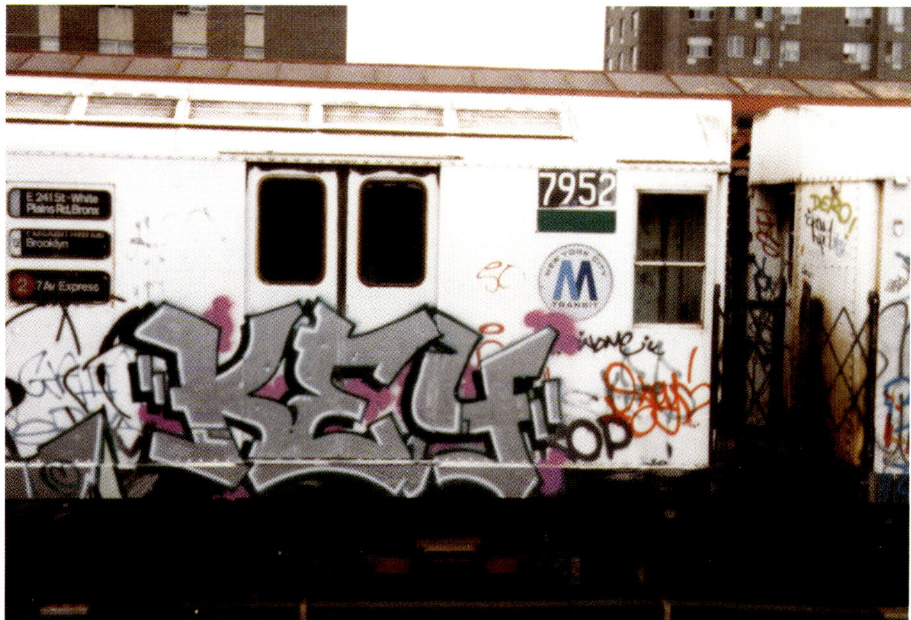

Key, 1987

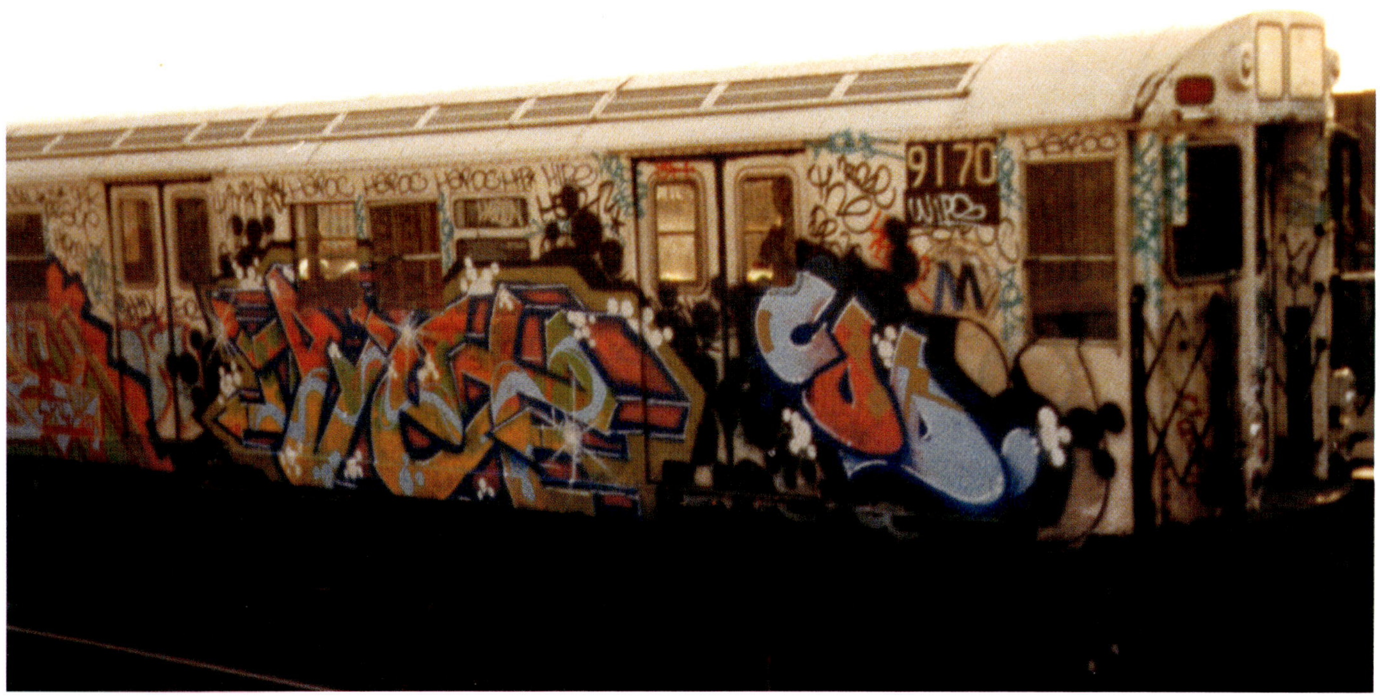

Vet (TMC), 1987

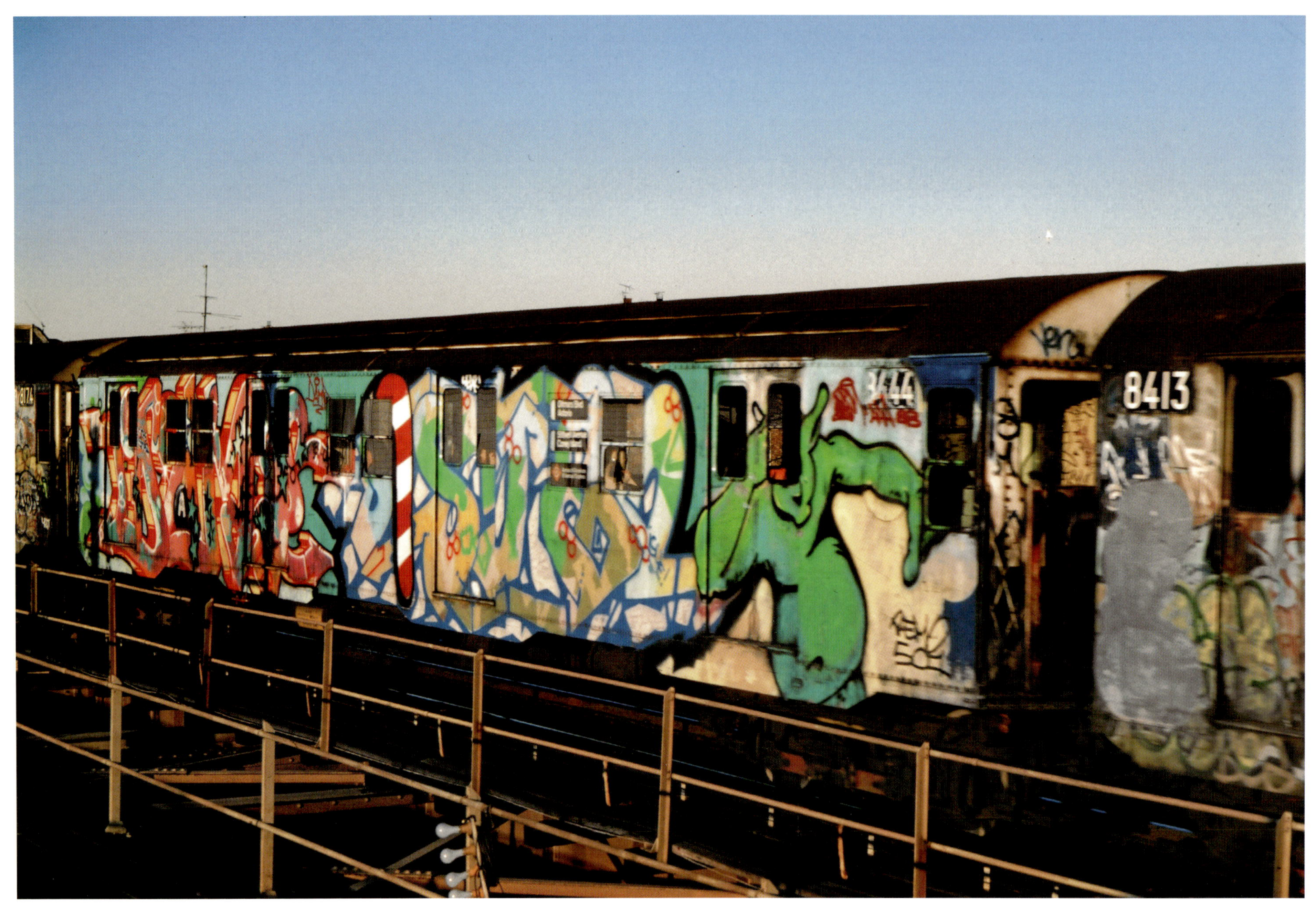

"Damp" by Sent; Isue, 1987

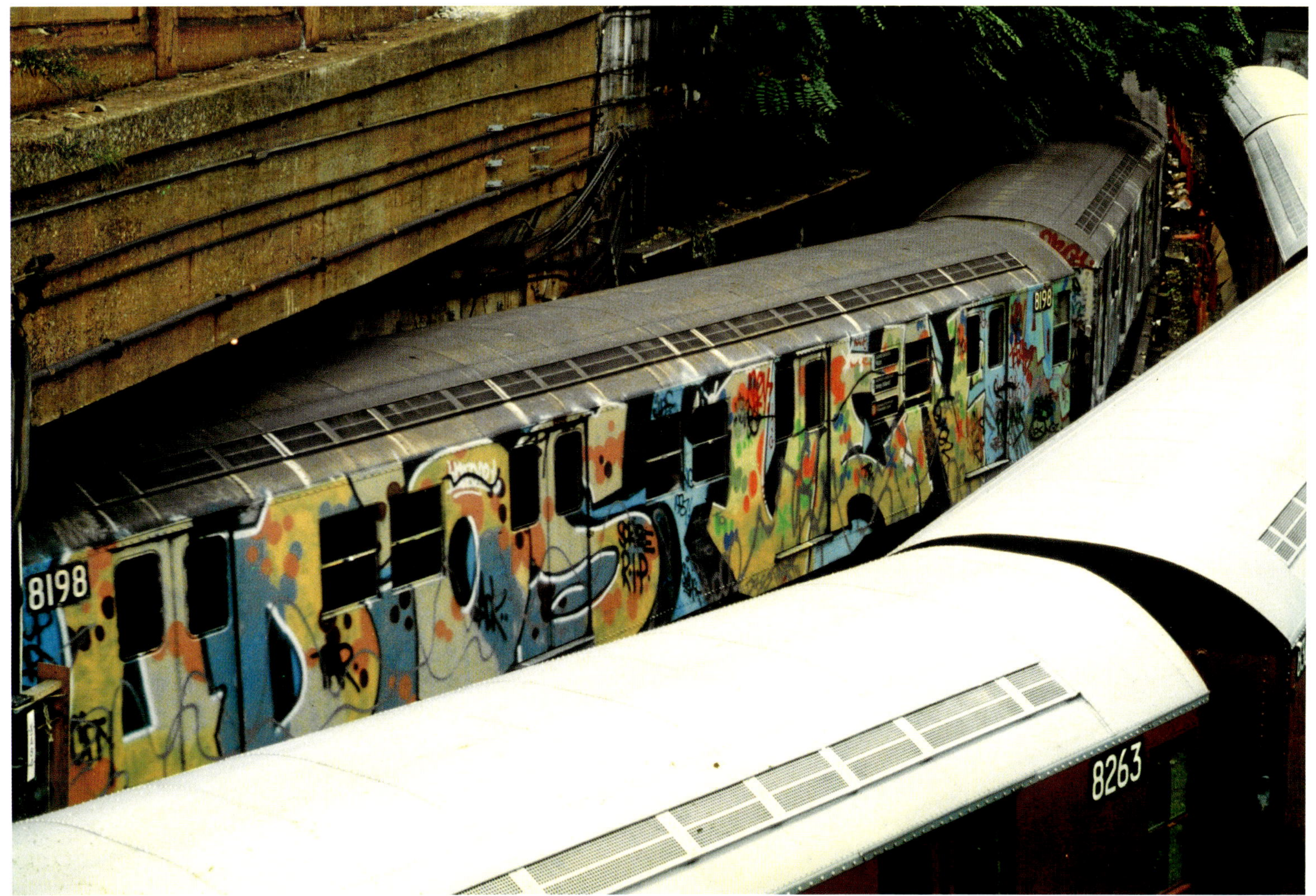

"Adios" by Wolf (AOK) & Ven (AMW), 1987

Ven and I did this on the night before Thanksgiving. It was 1987 and we did it in the 57th Street lay-up. Ghost and Tekay did a top to bottom whole car right next to this one. I adopted Adios as an alter-ego name from my old homey Dash2.

—Wolf aok

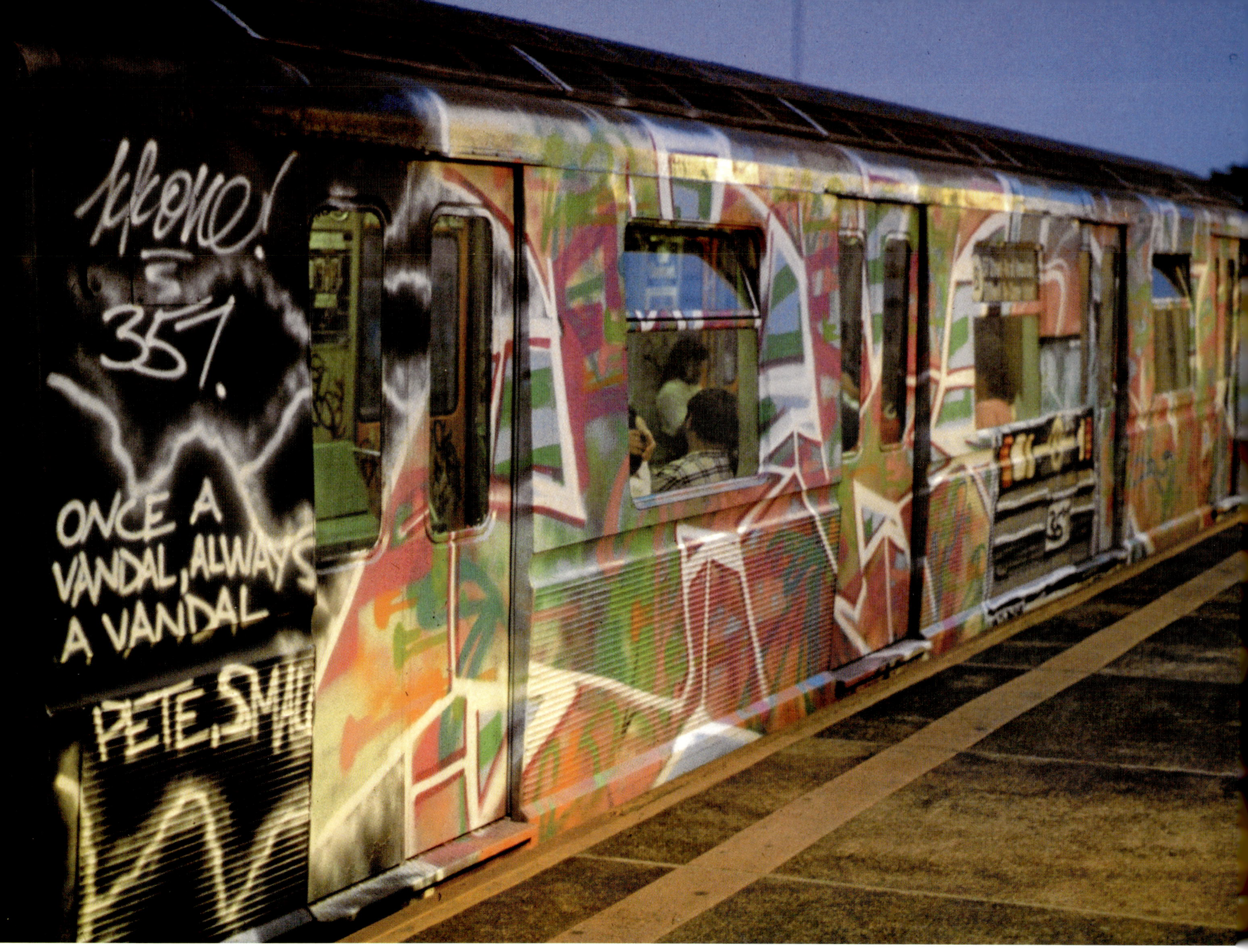

KK One, 1988

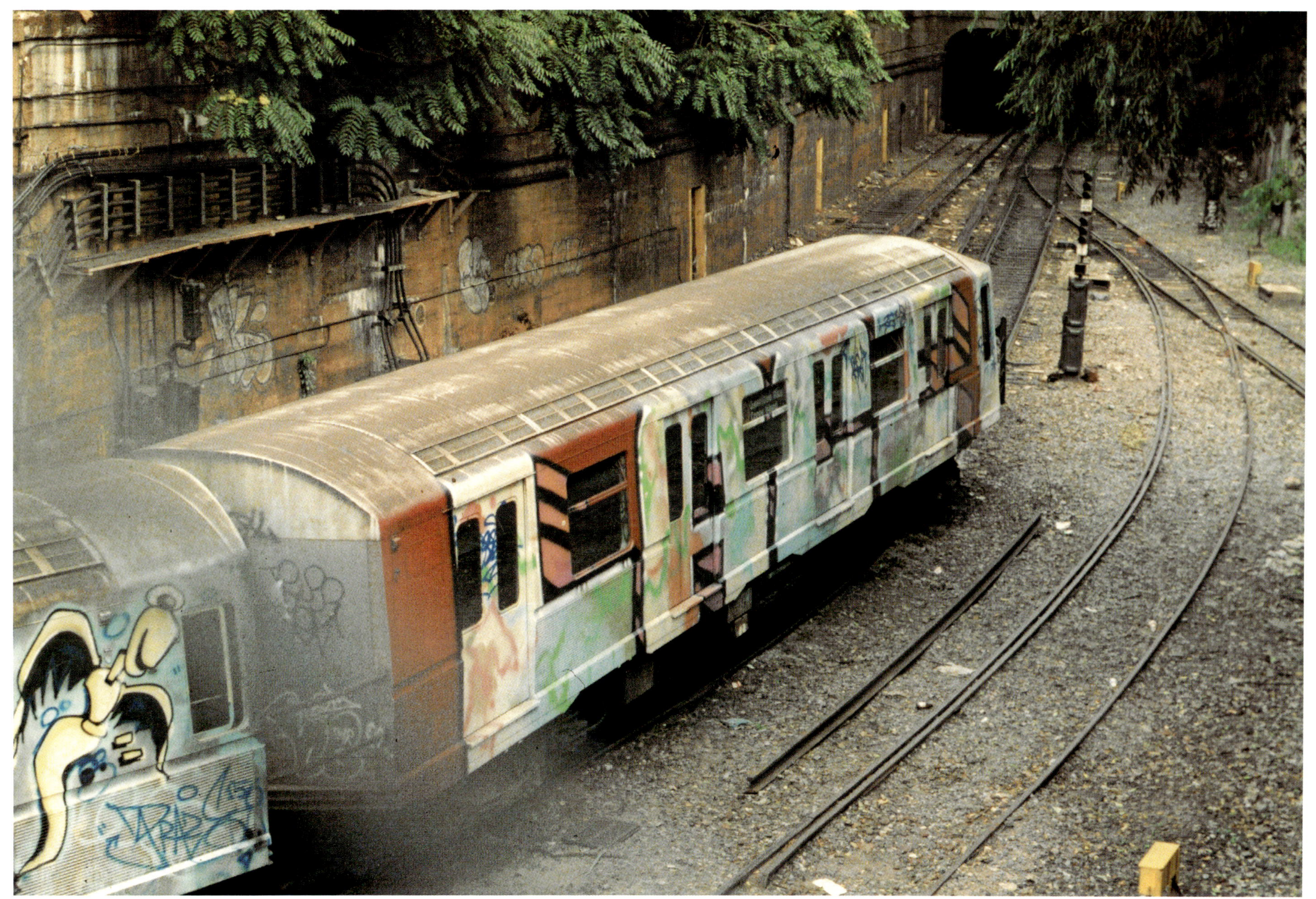

Lace, 1988

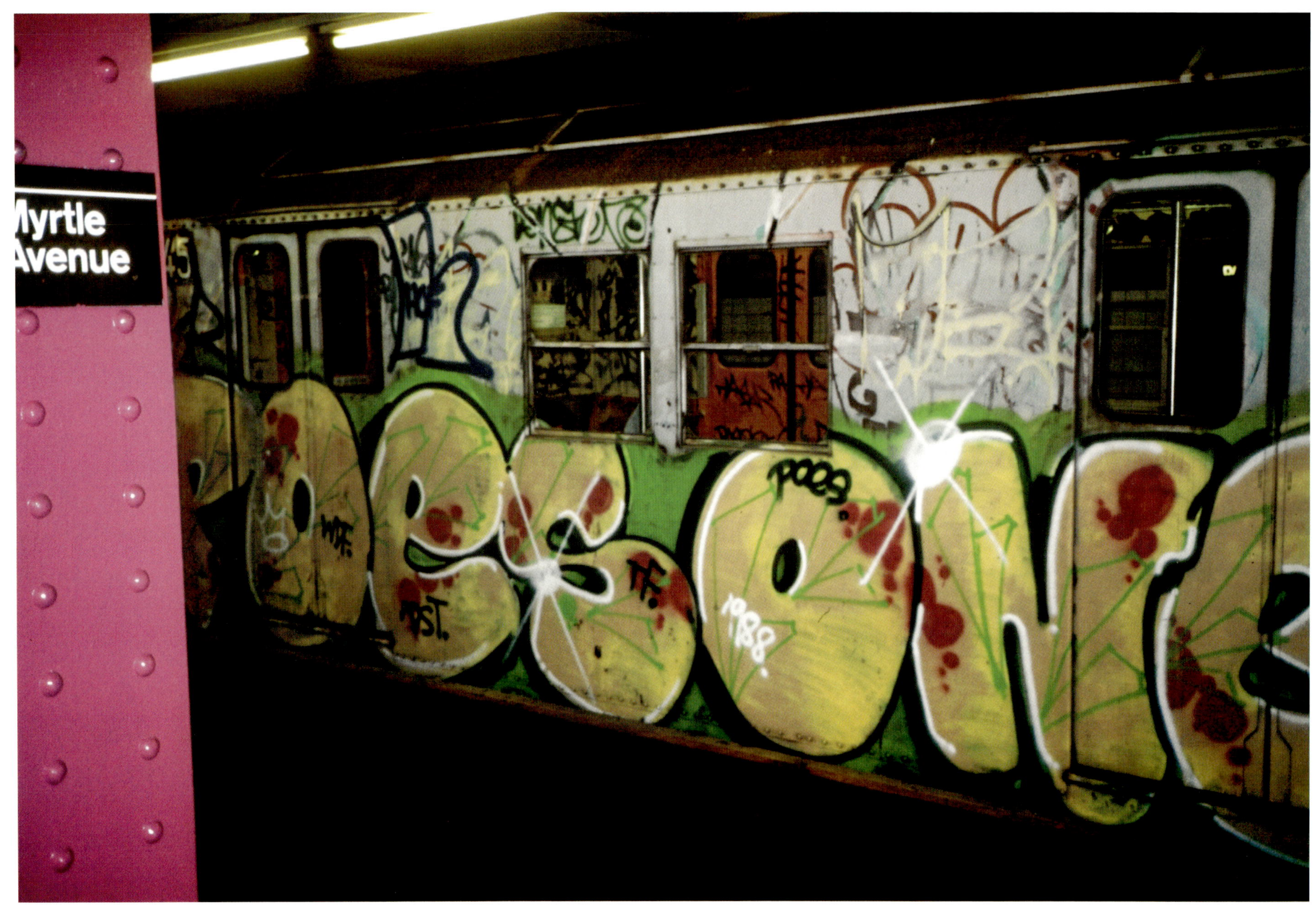

Poes (TF), 1988

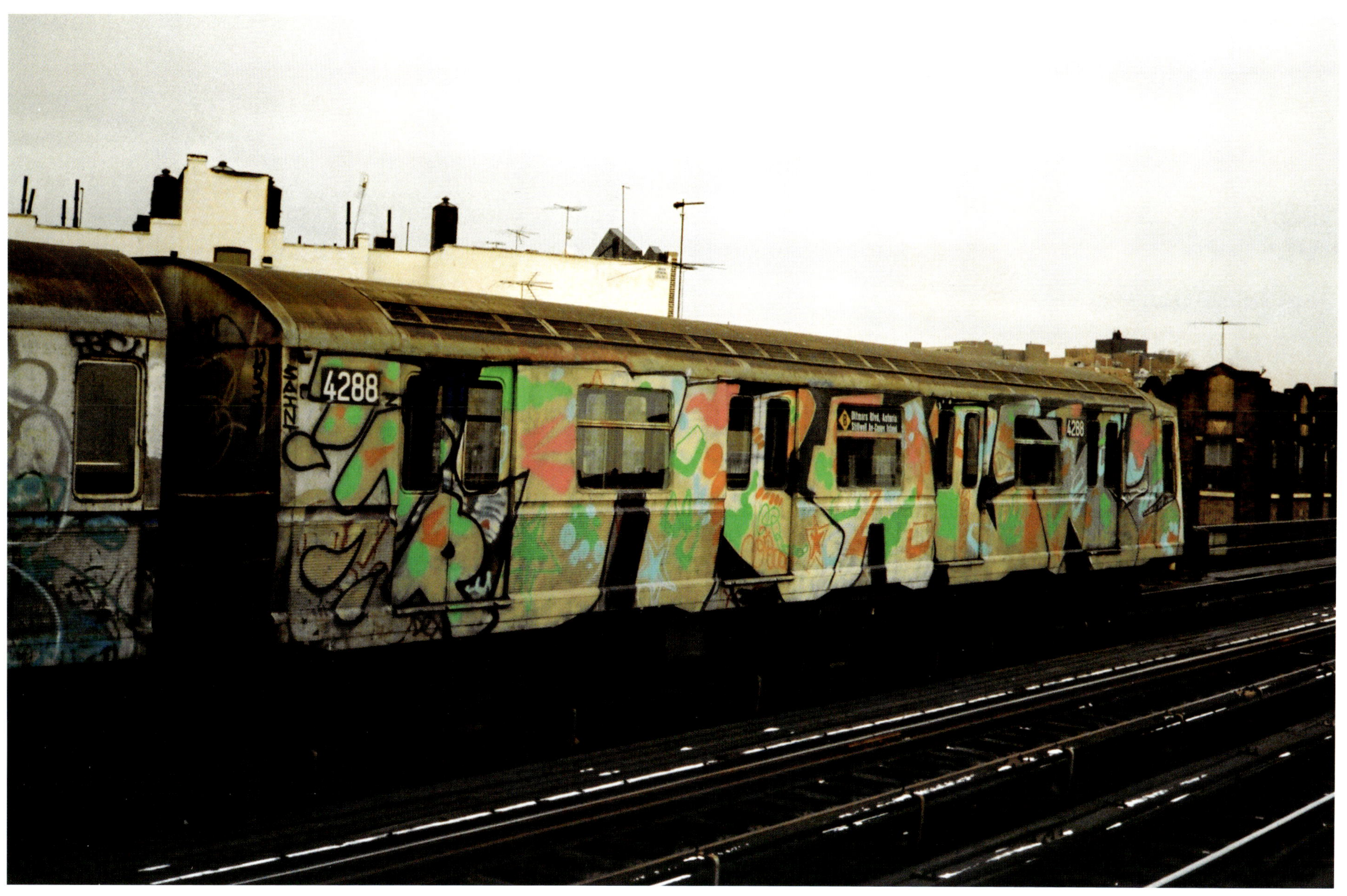

"Track2" by Tekay (TNR), 1988

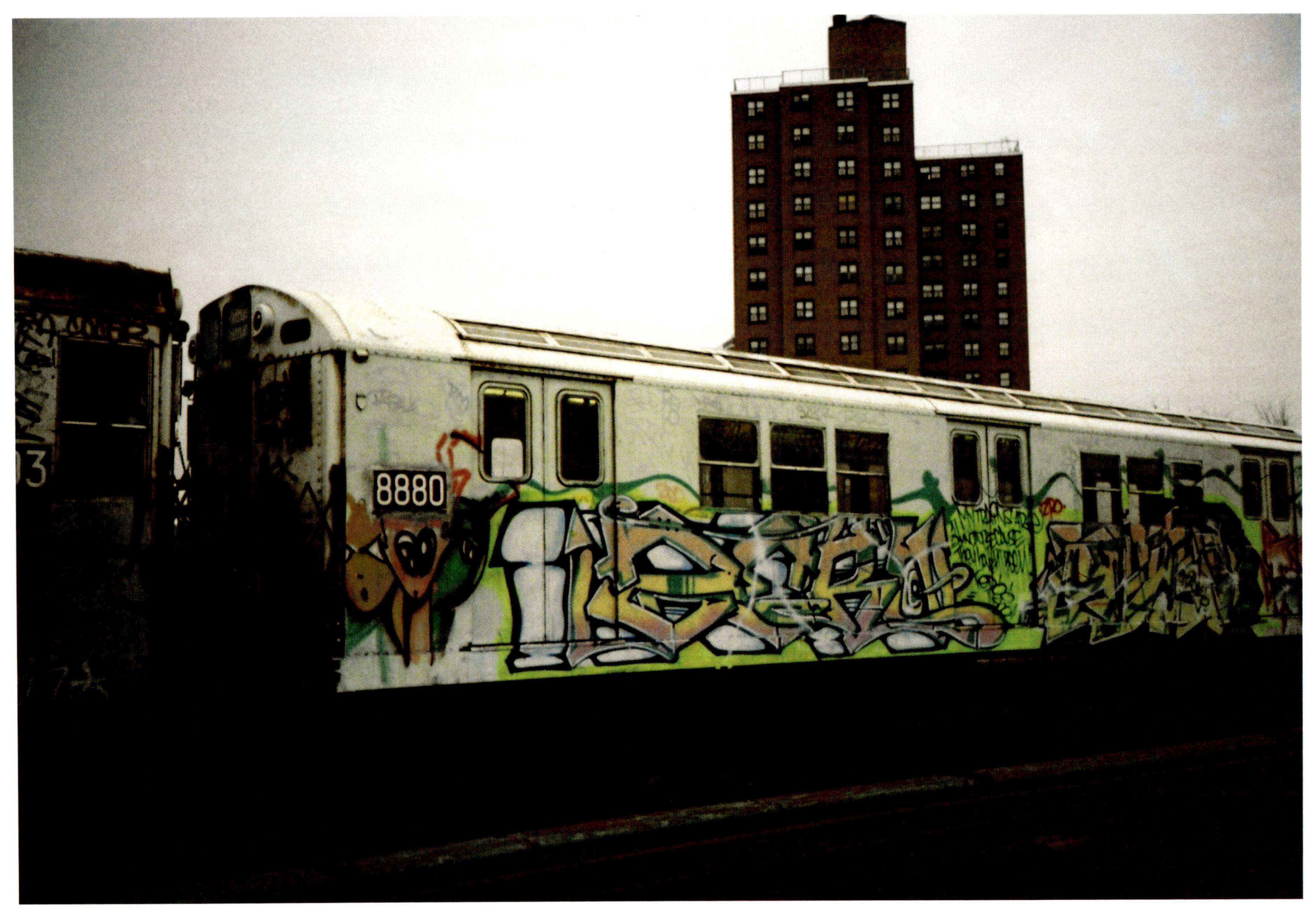

“Zero” by Dome & Sho (TDC), 1988

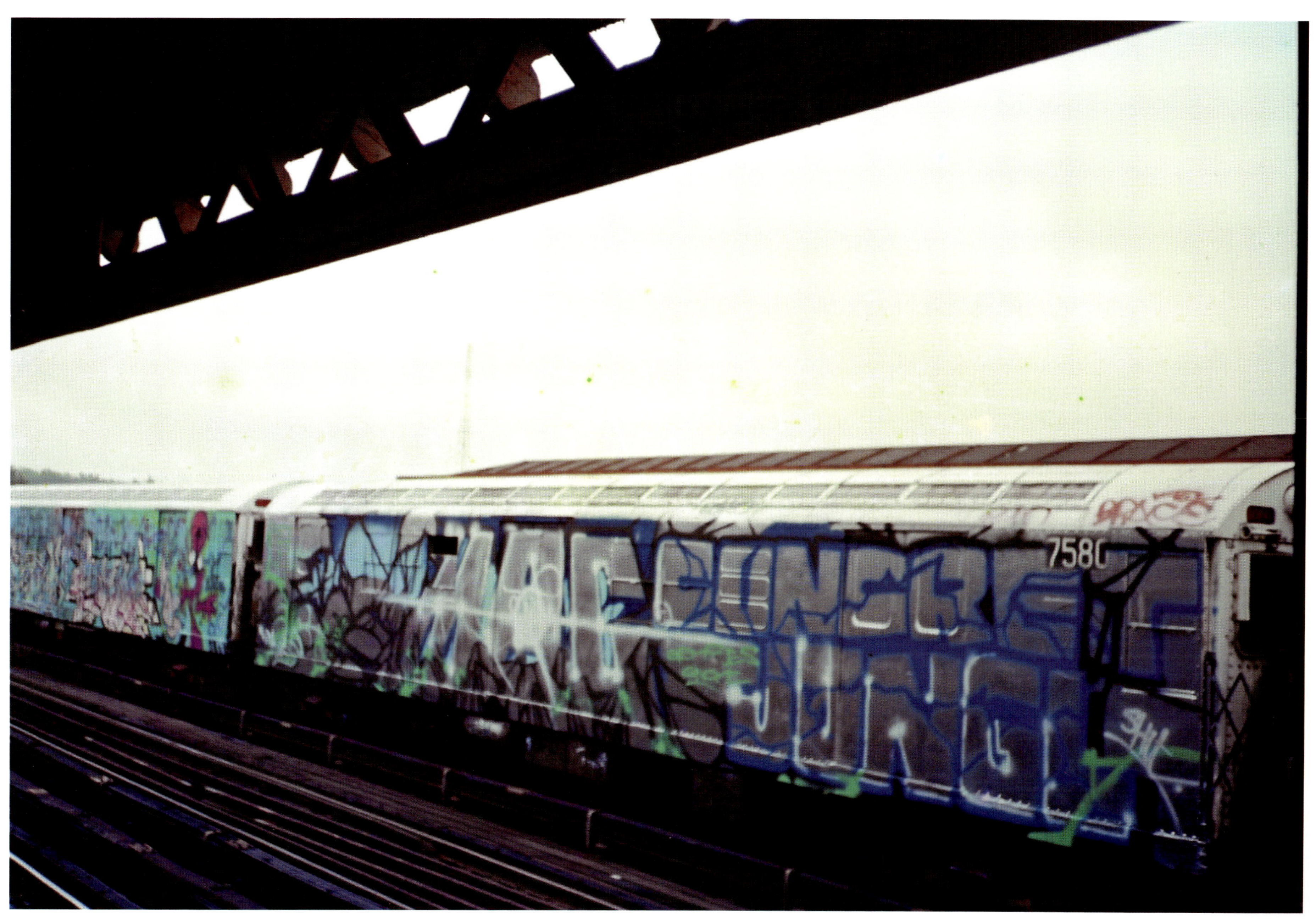

"Mac" by Mirage, Concrete Jungle, 1988

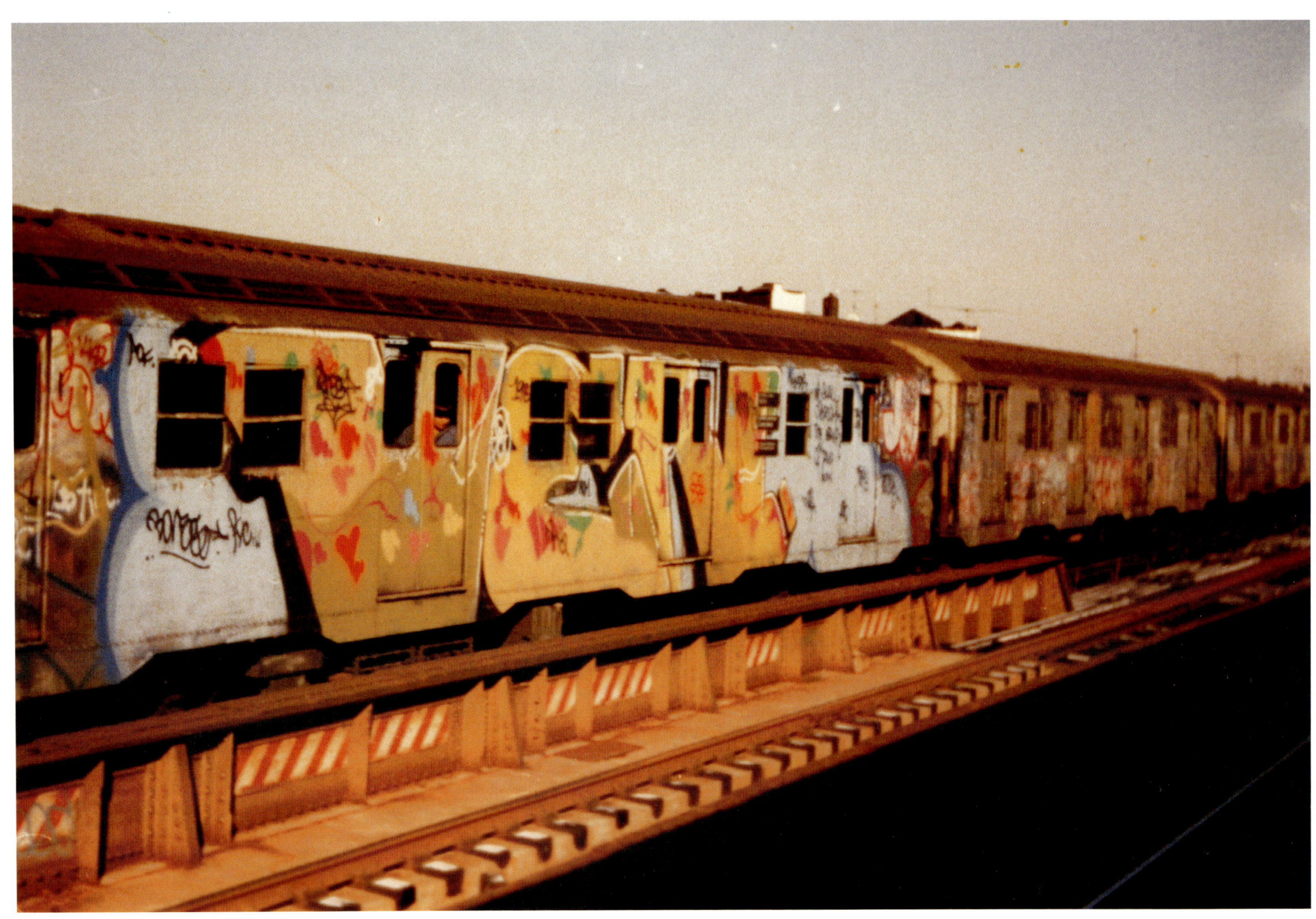

Ven (AMW), 1988

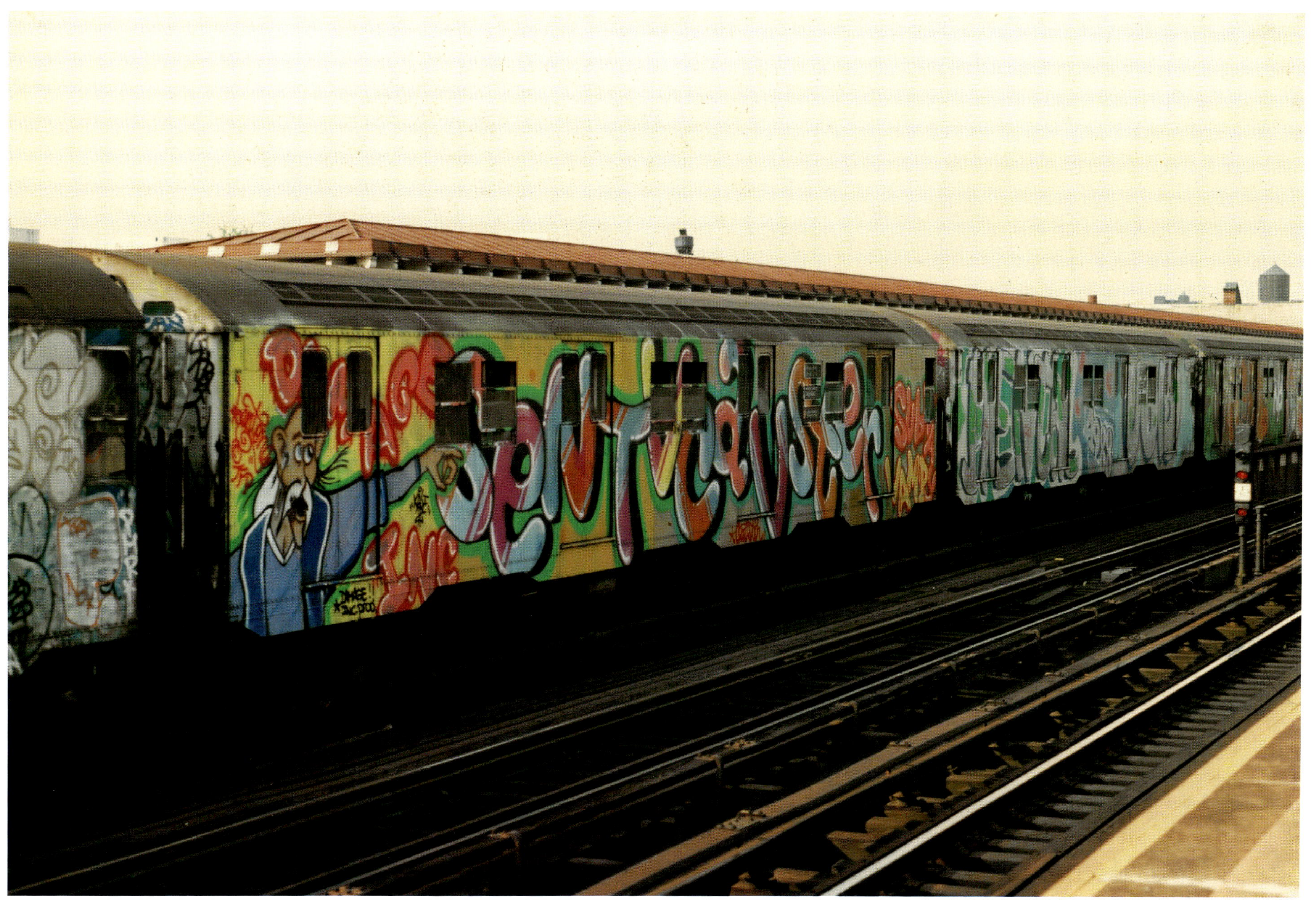

Sent & Cavster, 1988

Metropolitan Av
Queens
36 Street
Brooklyn
M Nassau Street
Local
8113
TRACK 2
DE KALB
DE KA

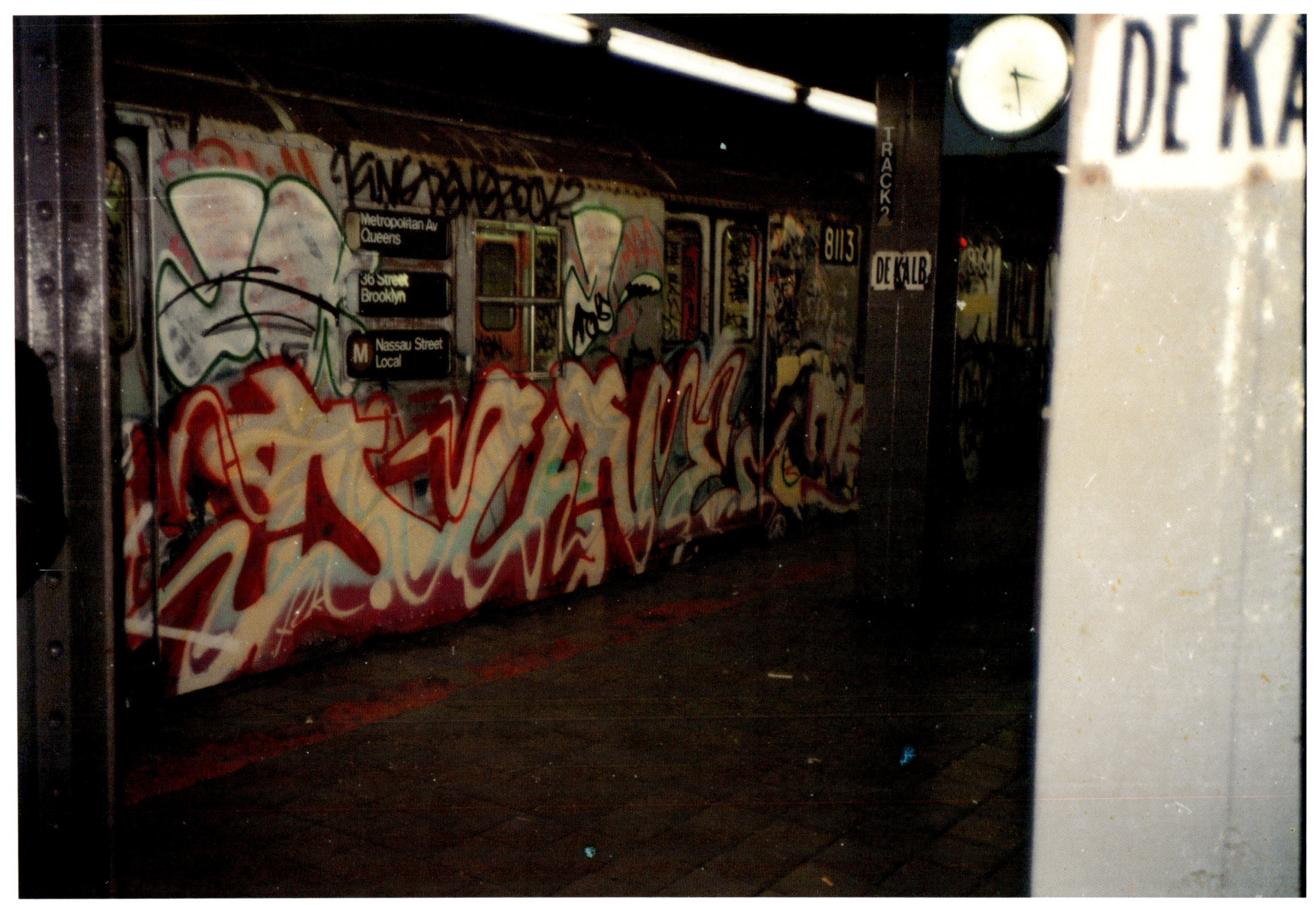

Dune, 1988

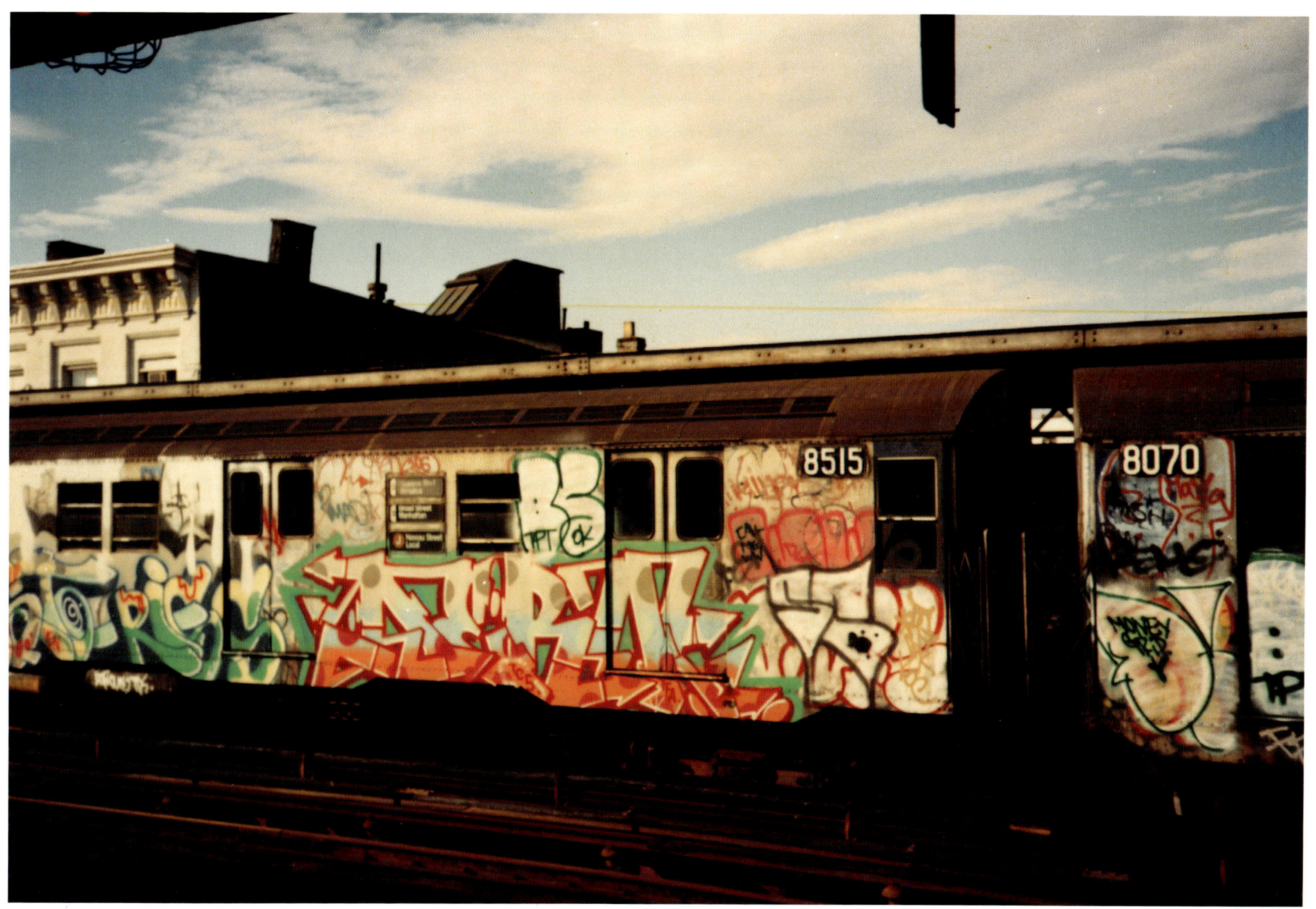

Dero (TFA), 1988

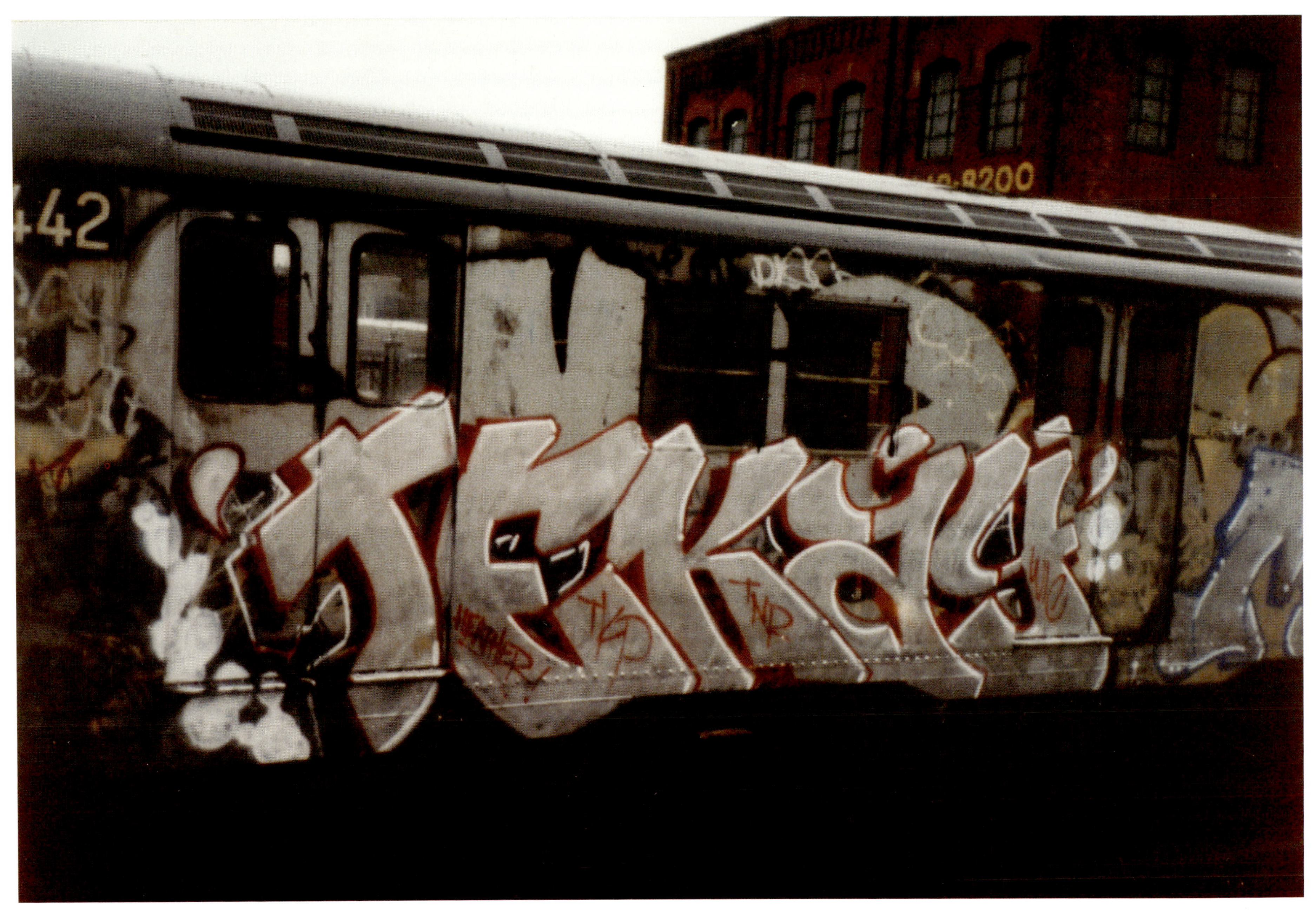

Tekay (TNR), 1987

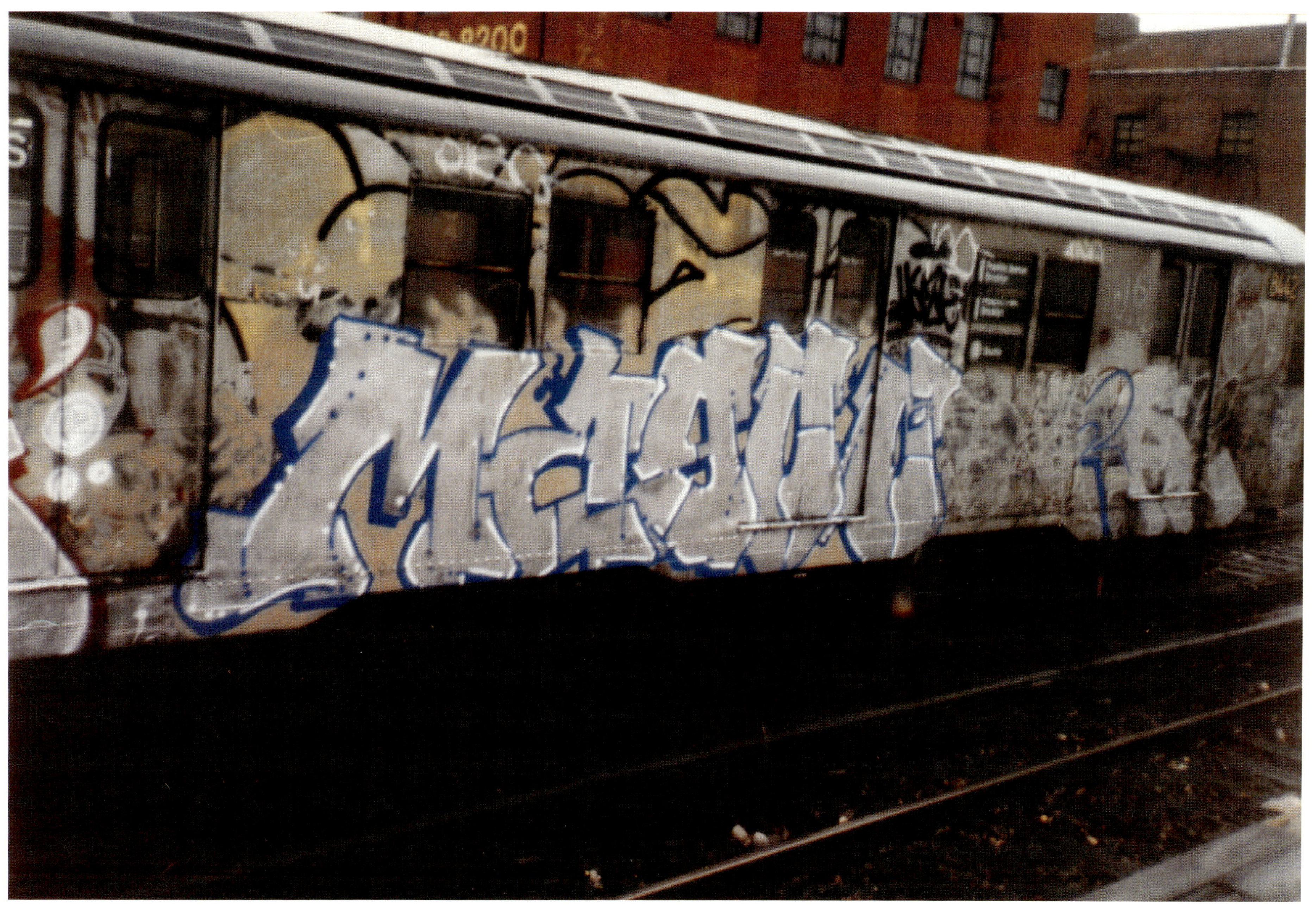

Magoo (TKP), 1987

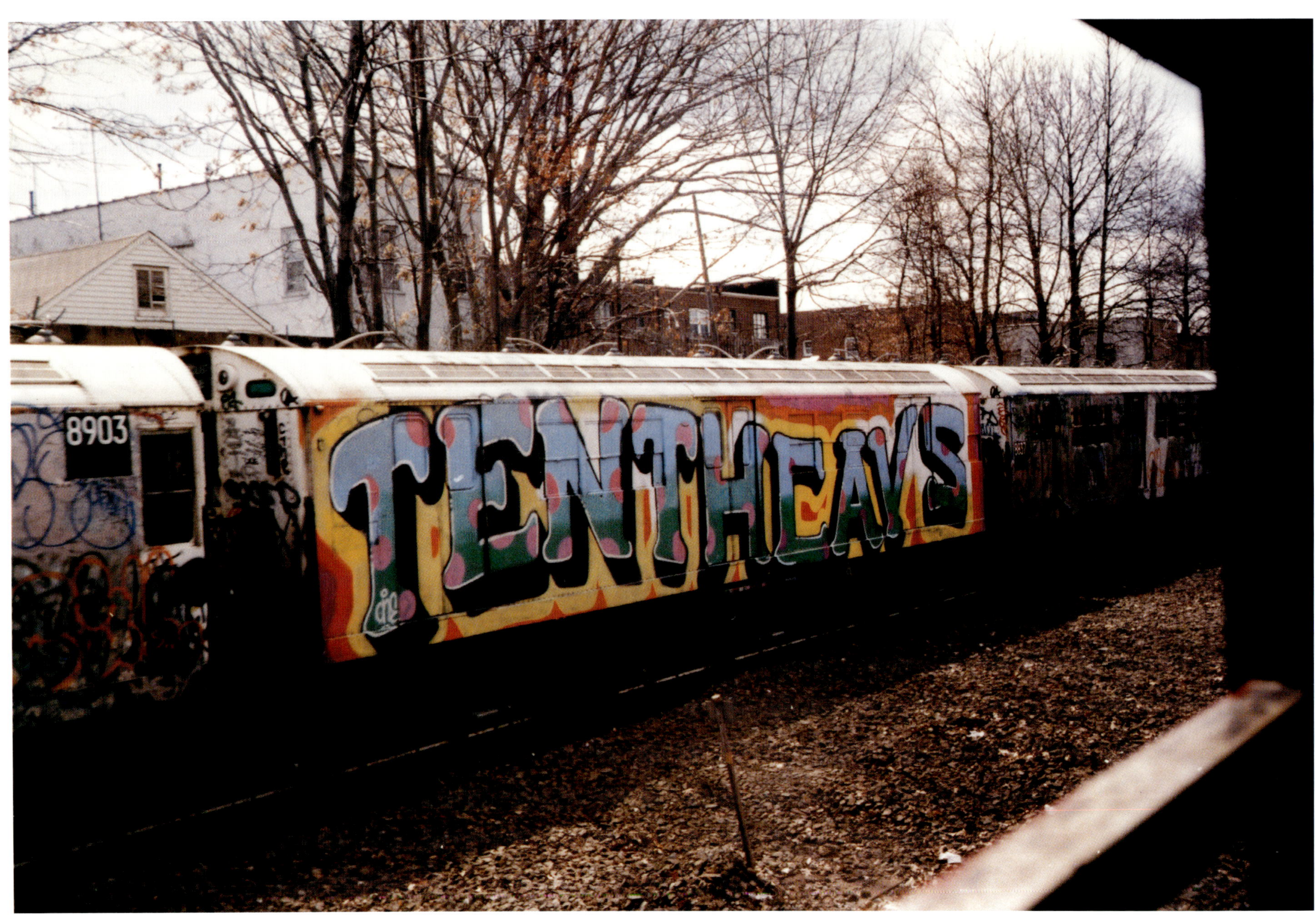

"Tenthcavs" by Sent & Cavs, 1987

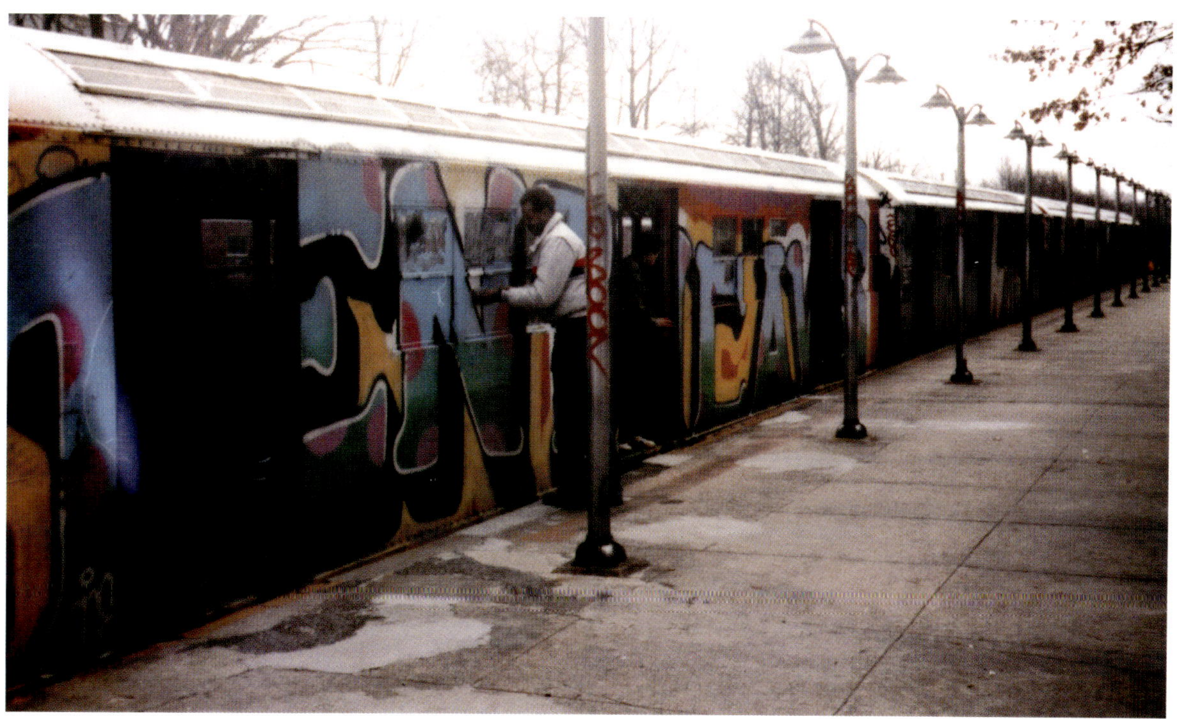

The five trains were laid-up on the 2 line from Bronx Park East to Gun Hill Road. Sent and I ventured to the Burke Avenue lay-up. Sent had the idea for this whole car "Tenth Cavs." We painted on the uptown side between Burke and Gun Hill Road. There were other writers painting and somebody yelled "5-0." The cops were in the trains and people were scattering. Some went down the el to the street. I took a chance and ran to the Burke Avenue station.

Luckily we escaped the raid, but we now we had an unfinished whole car on the line. That's considered a sin and we were on the hunt to finish that car. We spotted it one time by Pelham Parkway. It was laid up in a bad spot so we did not attempt to finish it. Another night we were in the Baychester lay-up working on another production. On our way out we spotted our unfinished whole car. Sent went back and finished it the next night. As you see in the pictures, it can be a race to catch shots of your whole car running with the windows still painted. This work bum "transit worker" would ride the train and jump out between stops and buff the windows. Luckily for us we caught it before he did.

—Cavs (SV)

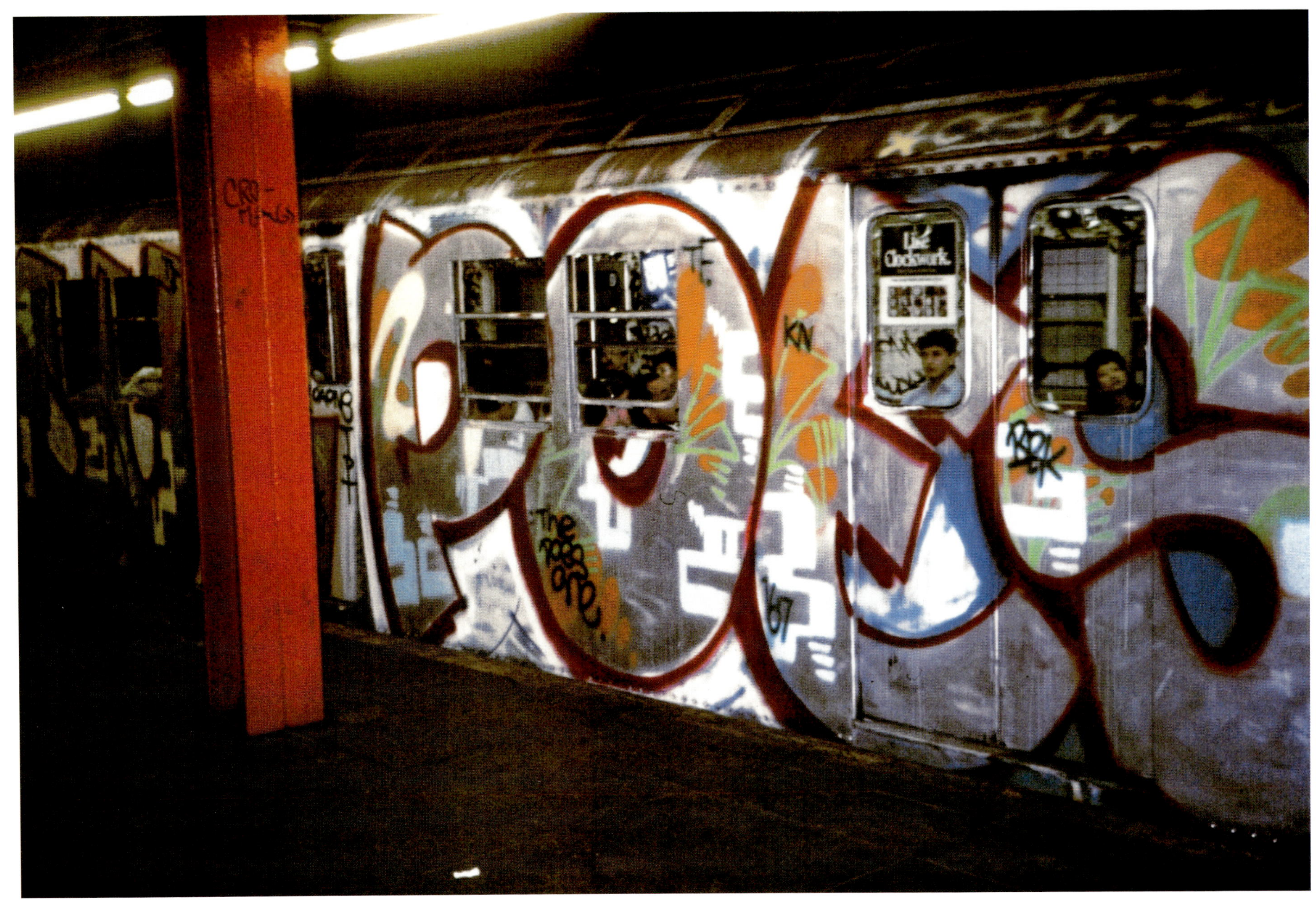

Poes (TF), 1988

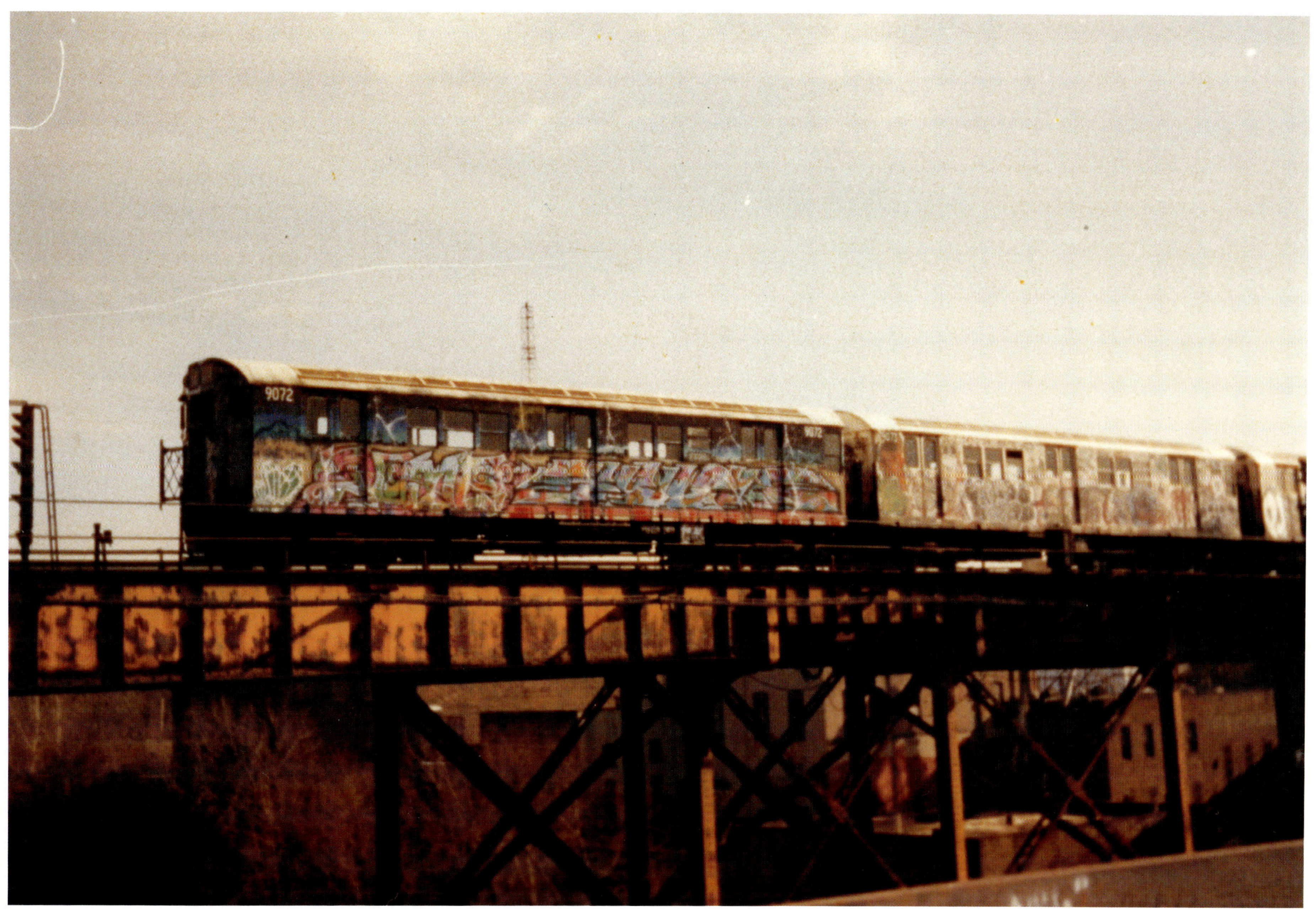

Dome & Vulcan, 1987

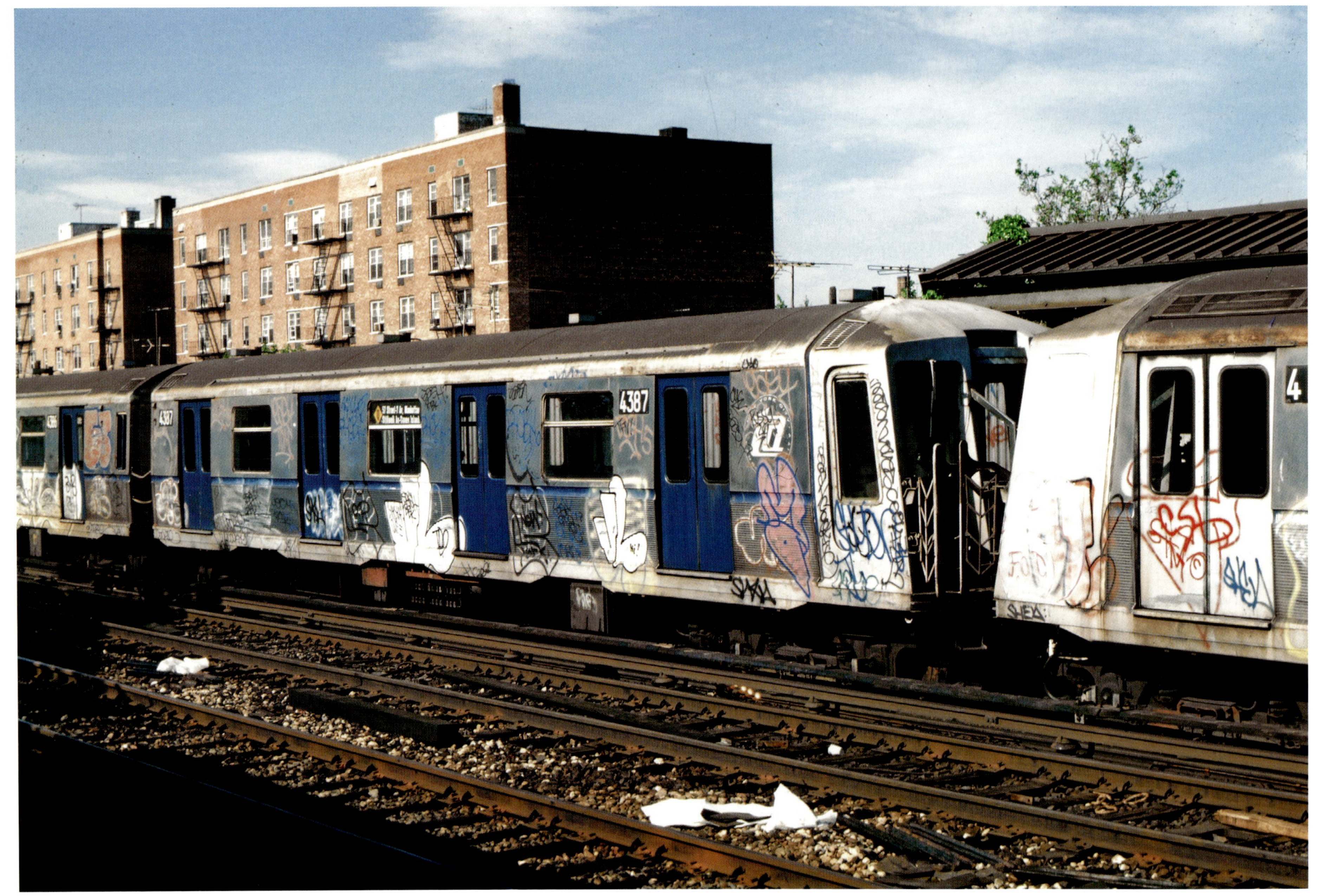

1987

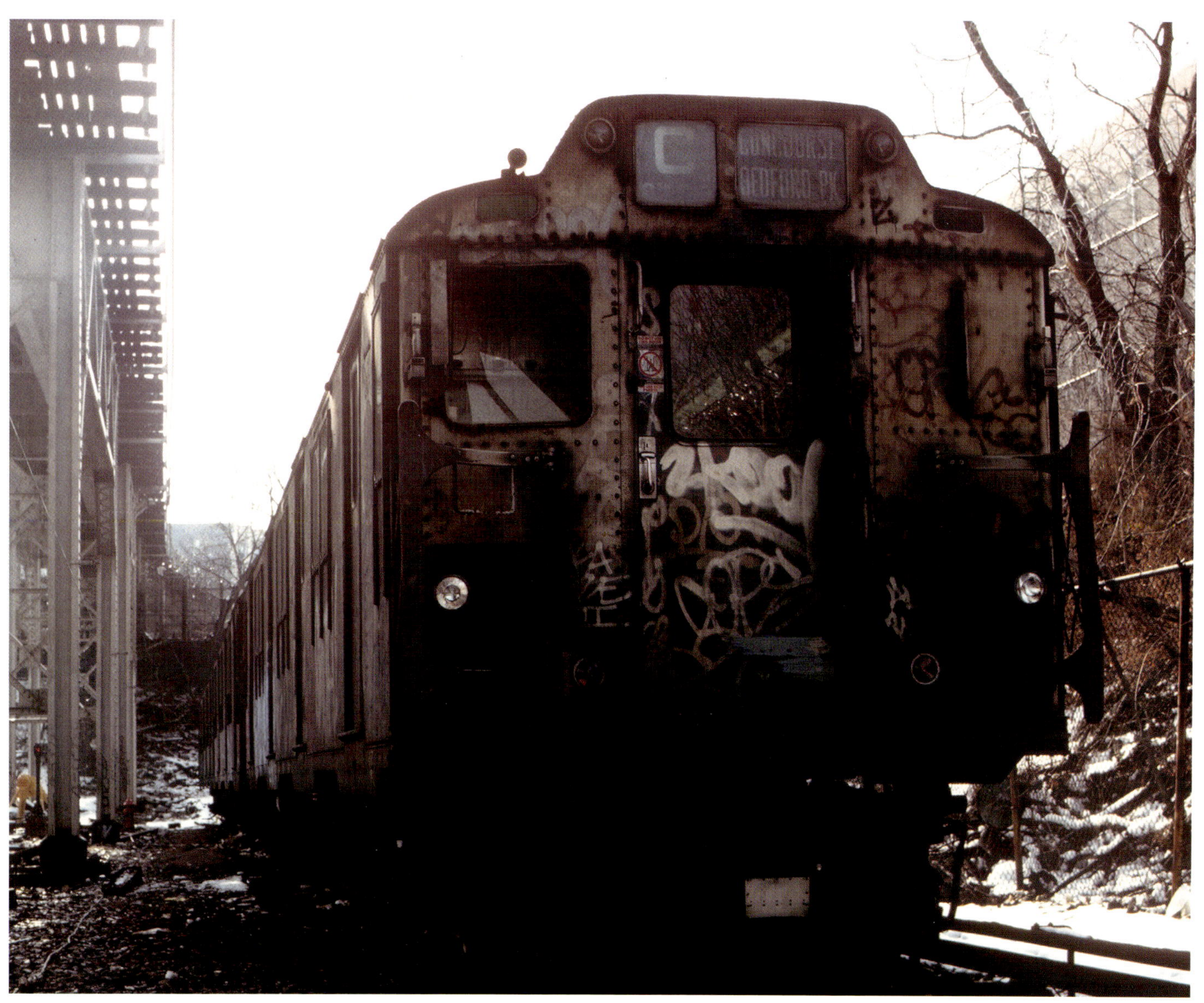

Concourse yard, 1988

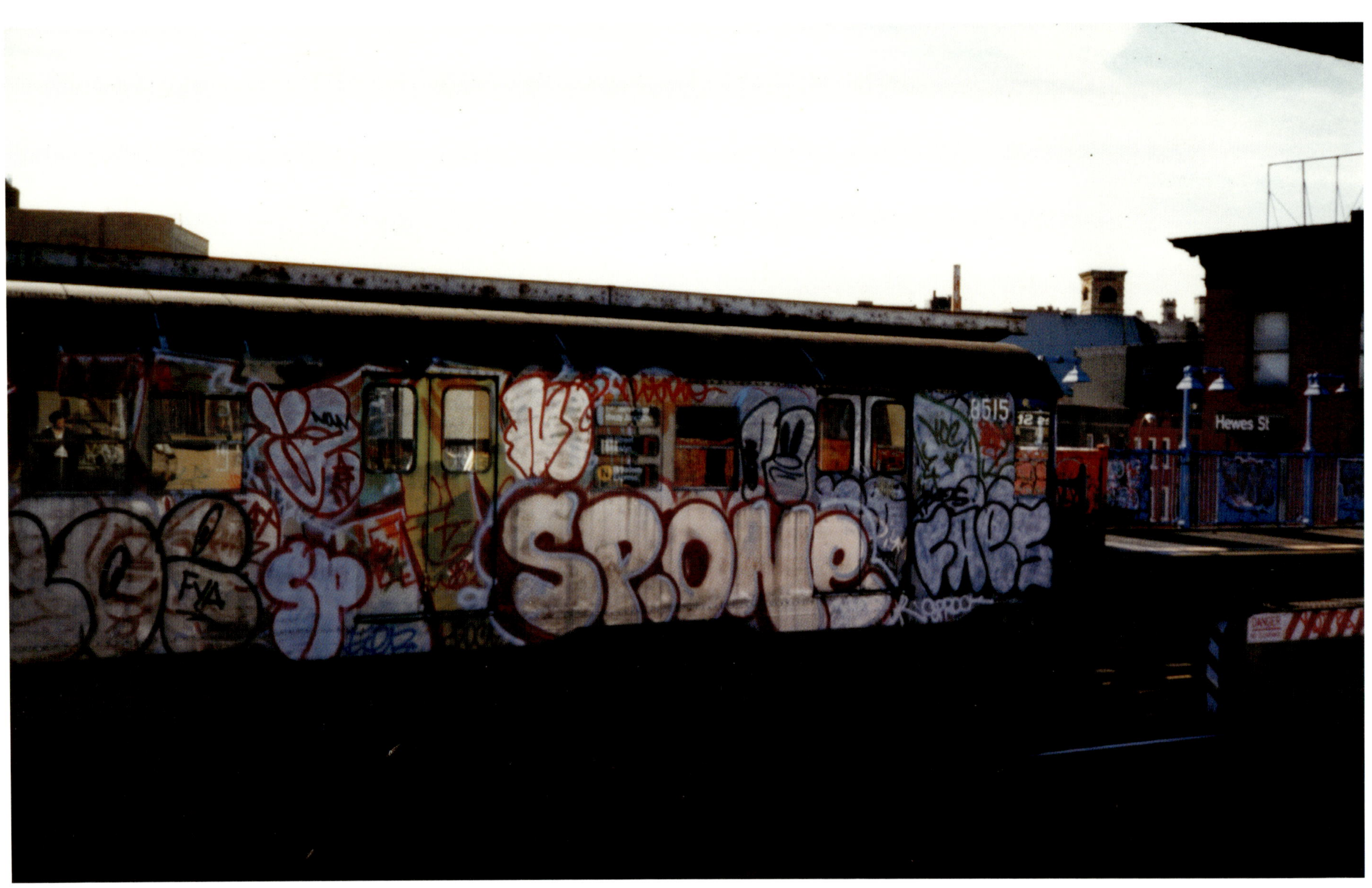
8515
Hewes St

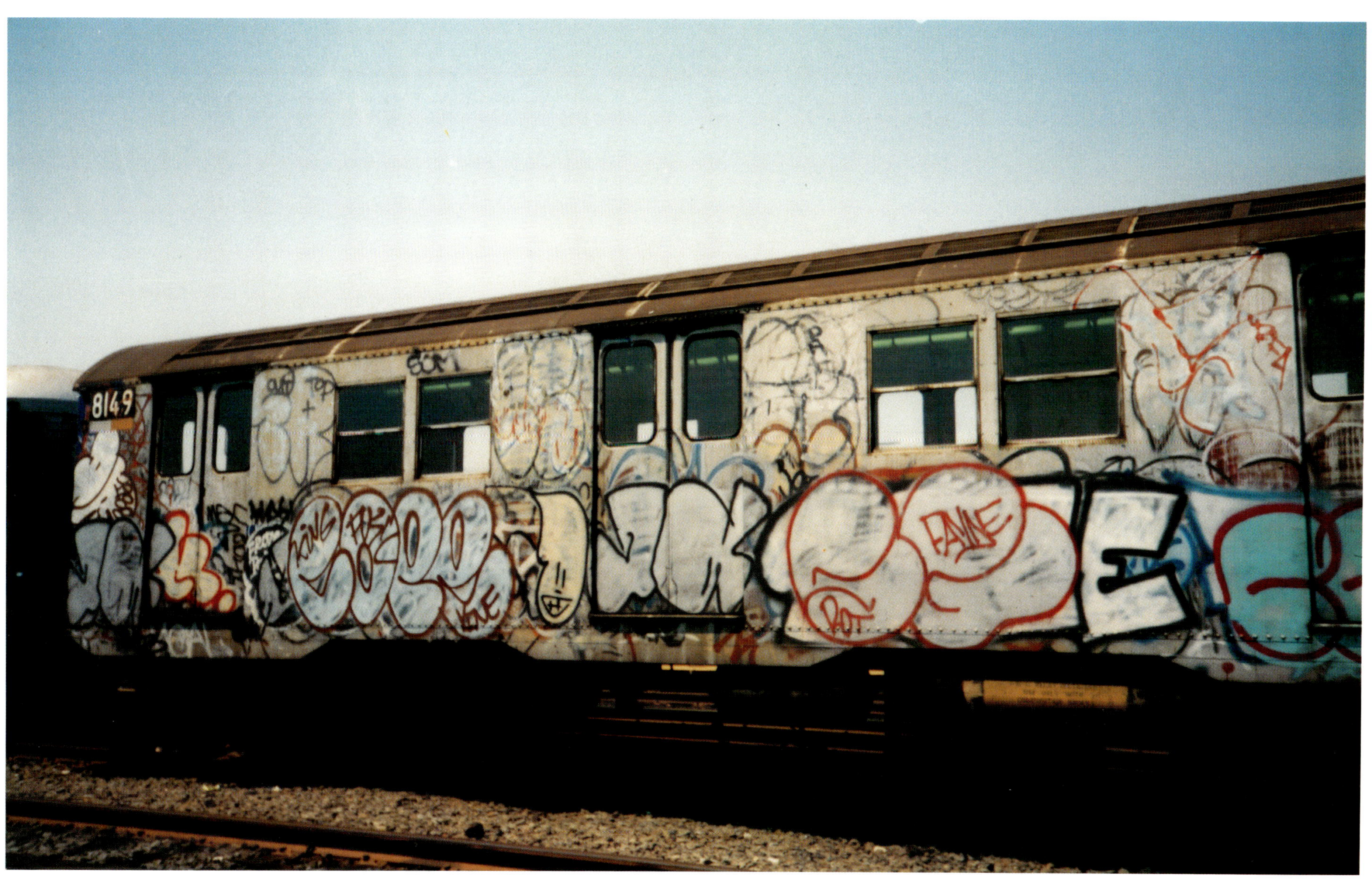

8149

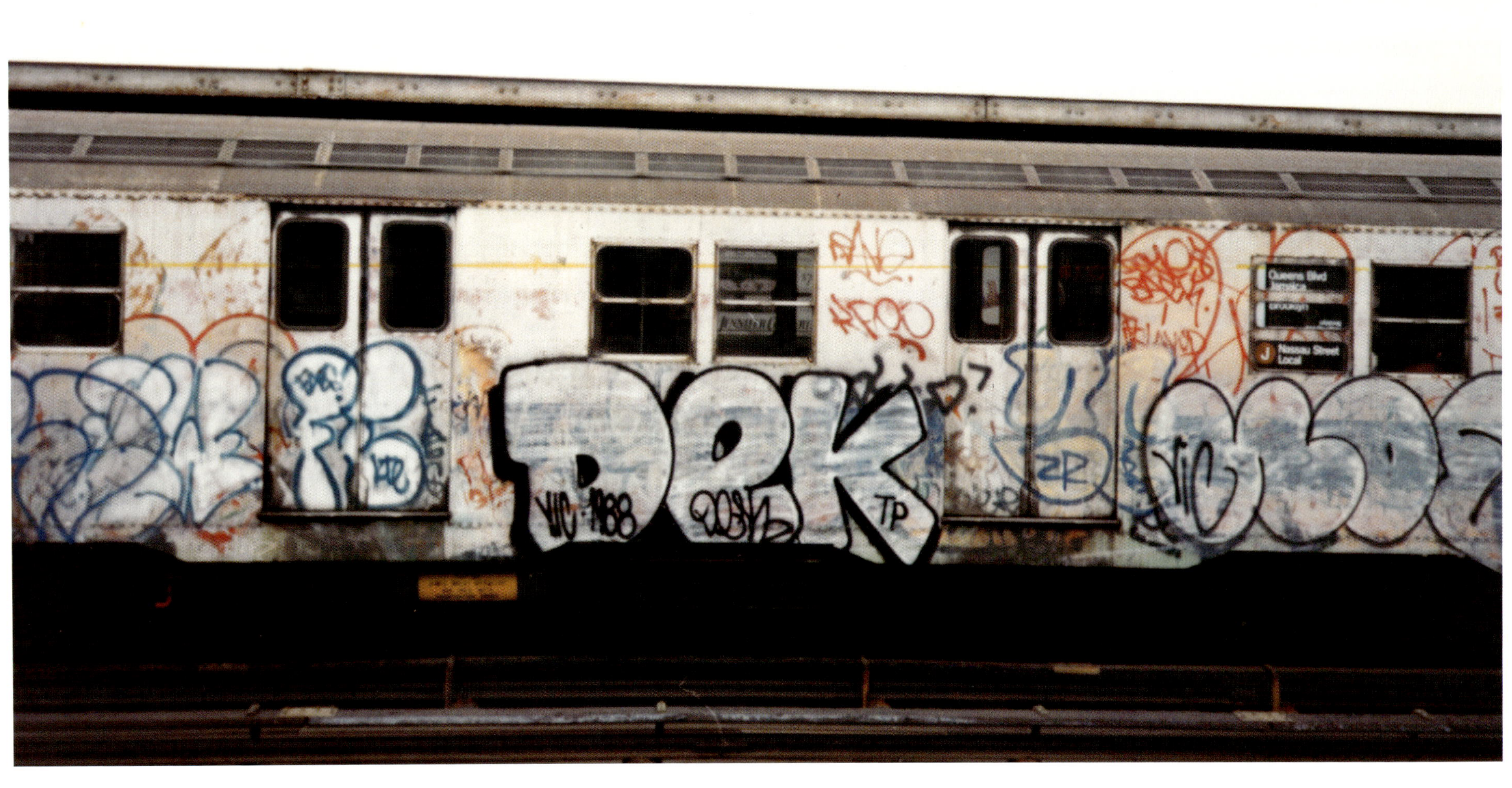

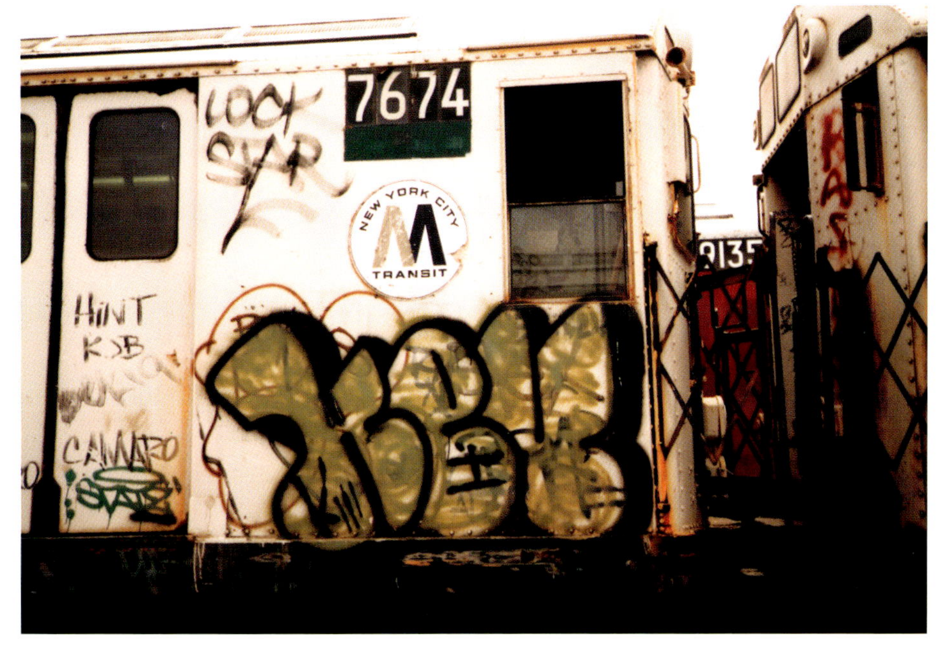
7674
NEW YORK CITY
TRANSIT

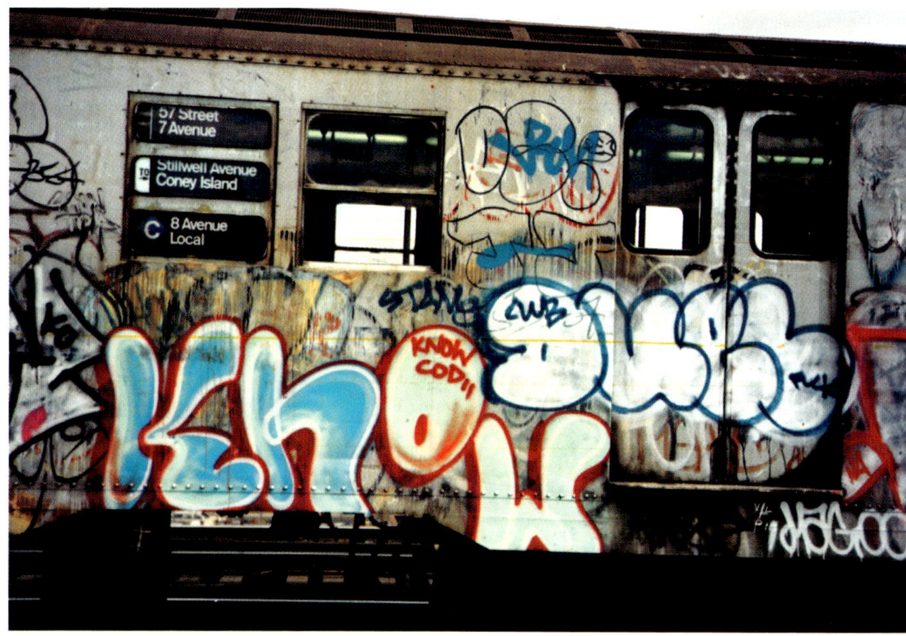
57 Street
7 Avenue
Stillwell Avenue
Coney Island
8 Avenue
Local

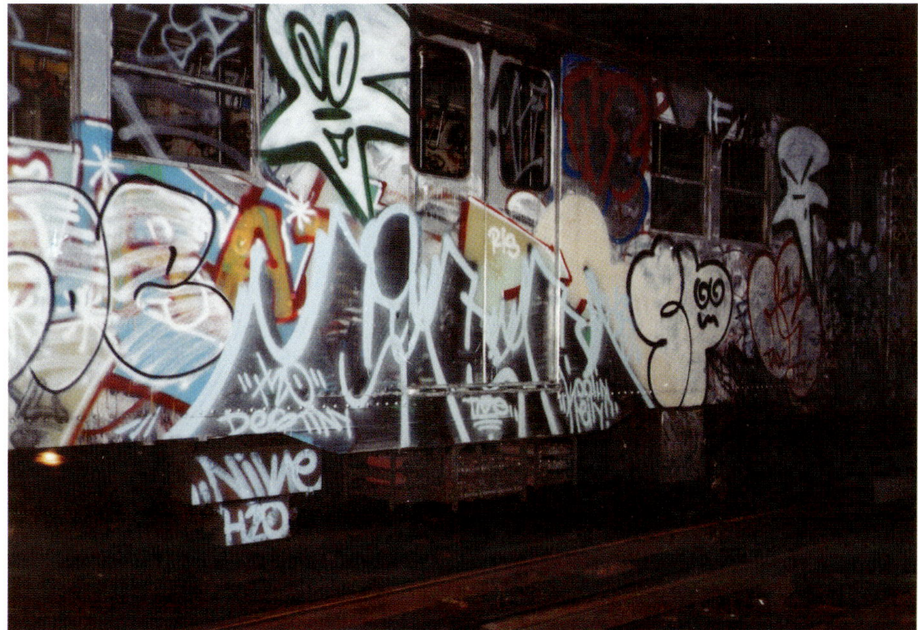

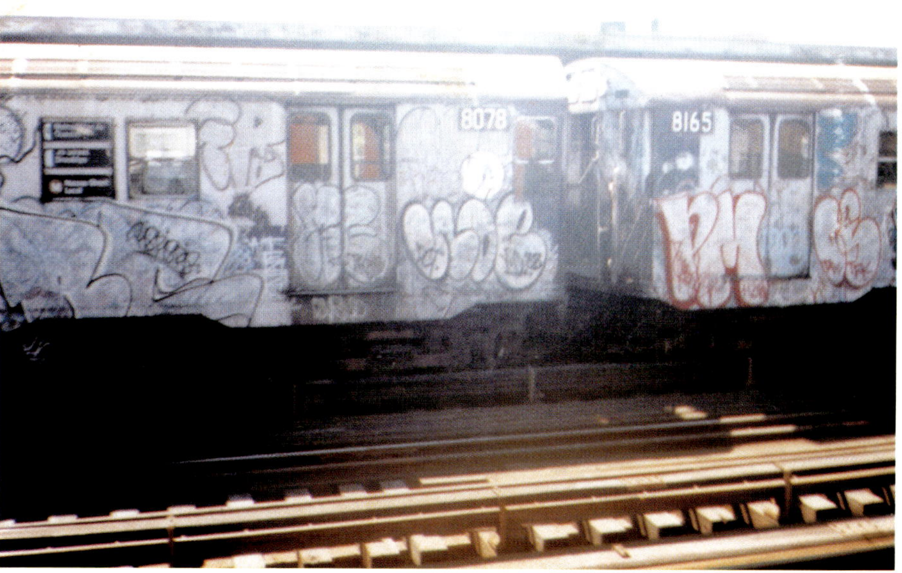
8078
8165

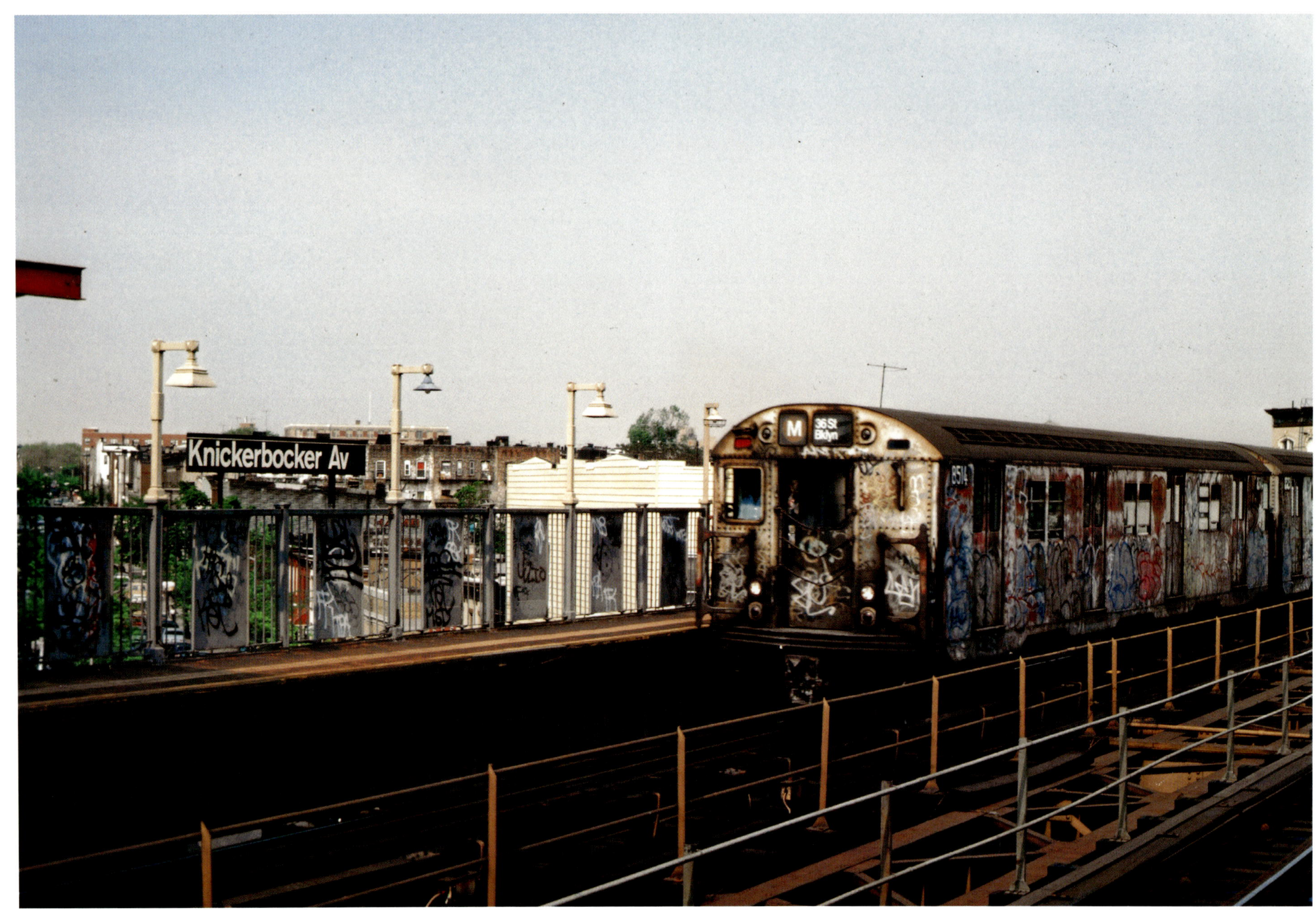

M line, 1987

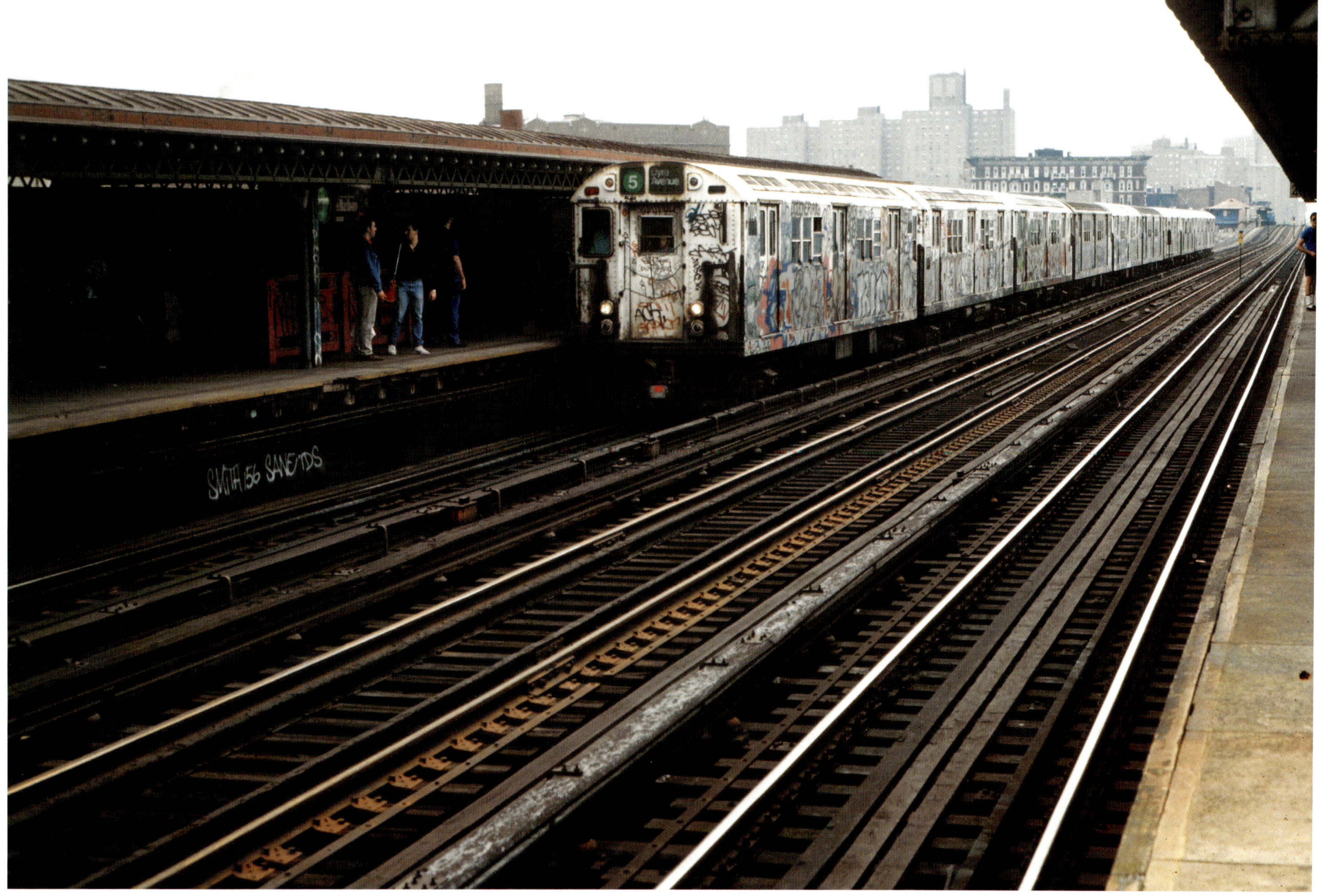

5 line, 1987

Scrap Yard

Brooklyn's dessert. No man's land. Blocks upon blocks of factories. Massive piles of abandoned brick created back in 1895 when it was a money machine for New York City. "Bush Terminal," a waterfront industrial park that met its demise in the late 1960s never recovered and only traces of the years past remain...cobble-stoned streets, trolley tracks, massive factories either closed or abandoned. There was a darkness in the air, no cars, no one around for what seemed like miles. Everything was old school, hardcore, smashed...the occasional car flipped over, sidewalks of broken glass, alleys littered with hypodermic needs and crack vials. Similar to a miniature city after a full-fledge riot, one could find an emptiness. Every building around you was either white or institutional gray. Old train rails in the street ran right into the sides of concrete walls. The entire neighborhood was a dead end, but if you were a graffiti writer back in the mid 1980s, it was a graffiti amusement park. This was Sunset Park, Brooklyn, zip code 11220. It was gritty and hardcore, ready and willing. From blue collar to welfare, sun up to sun down, this place had raw emotion. It was only fitting that the MTA placed its graveyard here on the river.

Home of graffiti's best kept secret. 44th Street and 1st Avenue. Initially referred to as a "Waste of Paint," as credible as "Ebbets Field." Somewhat legalized, always twisted, as a graffiti writer it felt like you were in the Devil's Playground. It was like something you've never seen, certainly something you will never see again, "The Scrap Yard." No fences, no guard house, no nothing. You walked in off the street. It was an MTA free for all! Endless subway cars entwined with dirty freights, a sick mixture of steel that went for blocks and blocks, lane after lane, steel on top of steel. It was beautiful!

The ill-est museum on the face of the earth. If you got there soon enough after something rolled in off the line, you were able to preserve it with a photo or just take the entire piece home with you. It wasn't uncommon to see people taking home a conductor's door, a panel, maps, anything. It was yours for the taking. All of these trains were going to be dismantled, and you best believe graffiti writers did most of the it first.

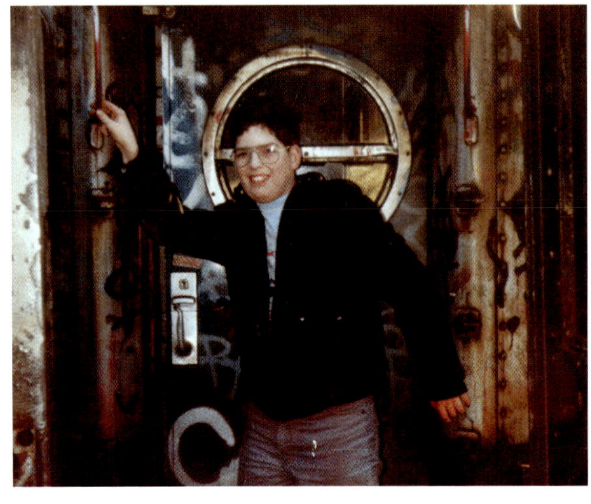

1984

It was a crazy place during a crazy time. Graffiti started making its own comeback and it had a lot to do with this place. Wholecars, panels, bombin', whole trains, insides. Writer after writer coming out of retirement just to rock some shit. Taking their time, mad writers always showing up. Beef, crews, cats gettin' vicked. Old school heavyweights sitting in beach chairs drinking beer out of the cooler while doing a whole car on a Sunday morning. Writer's don't care, the workers didn't care, for a time the cops didn't care.

Sane, Smith, Wolf, Zephyr, Bind, Lace, KK, PK, Case 2, Mirage, Cav, Vev, Revs, DB, Dune, Trike, Ant...the list could go on forever. Too bad the graffiti writers couldn't let the scrap yard go on forever. It's in a graffiti writer's blood to destroy, and that's exactly what they did. It didn't take long for the MTA to slow it all down. Within their yard, upon the ground they covered in stones and oil-stained wooden boards you could see glass everywhere. Spray paint cans by the hundreds. Trains would come in and every window would get smashed within a few days, doors open, seats flipped, everything bombed. Any time of day you could see little kids climbing on the steel. Even the freights were getting it. It was no surprise to see a new Bind whole car next to a freight that was cracked open and spilling thousands of boxes of "Special K" cereal onto the tracks.

There was a time when all you had to worry about whether the neighborhood kids were coming through like packs of wild dogs, but now the MTA had had enough. Cops started showing up, vandal squad would set up camp. Security cars would be rolling. Before you knew it, a fence was up and the trains were gone. It turns out that they moved them to what they thought was a more secure facility a few blocks away on 36th Street. Of course the writers got that one too and it all started over. Eventually the MTA ran out of trains to scrap, and once again Bush Terminal killed something that was once so alive.

—Joey PM

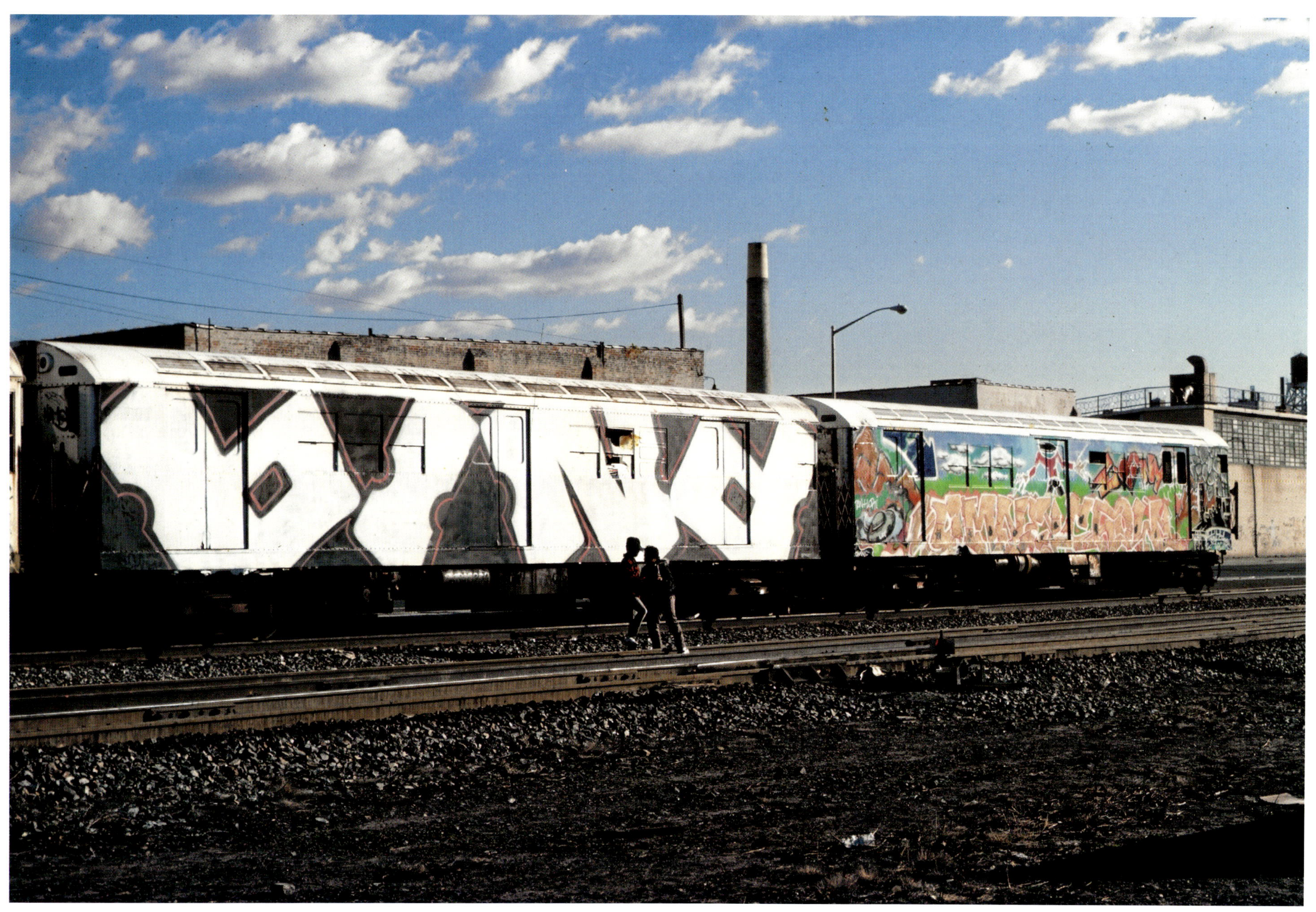

Bind, top to bottom; Omne Chow, whole car, 1987

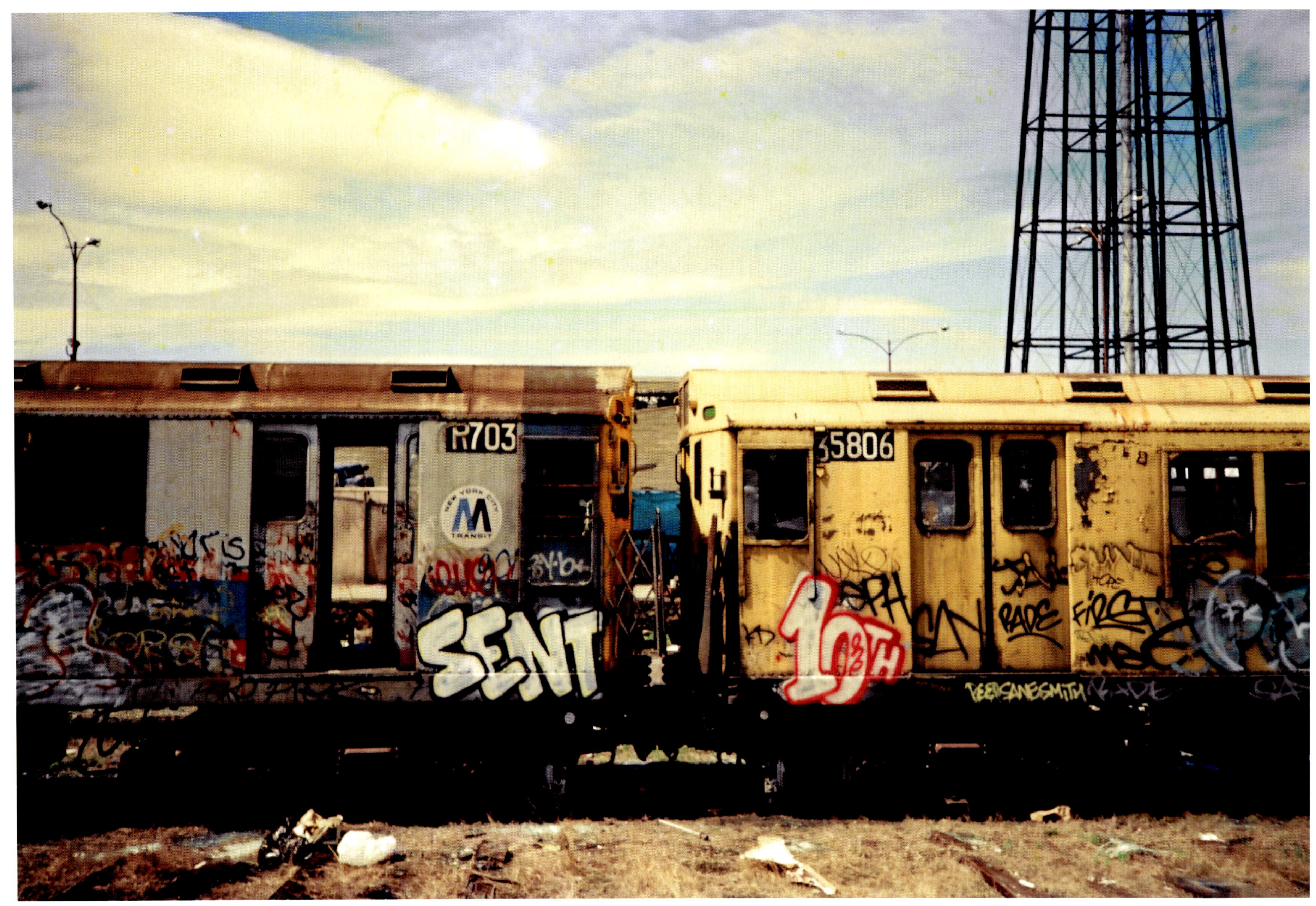

Sent (TFP), 1988

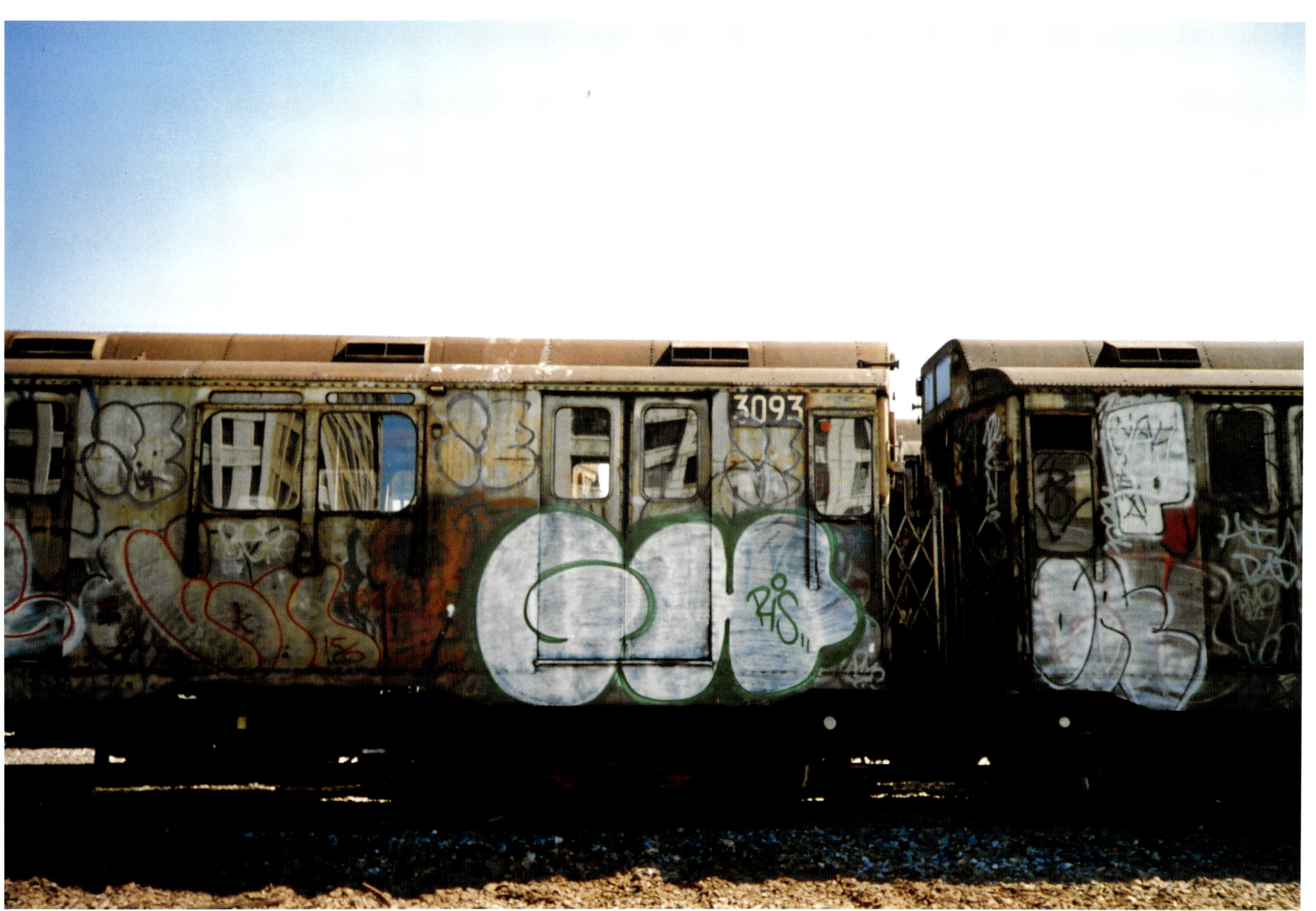

"GH" by Ghost (RIS), 1988

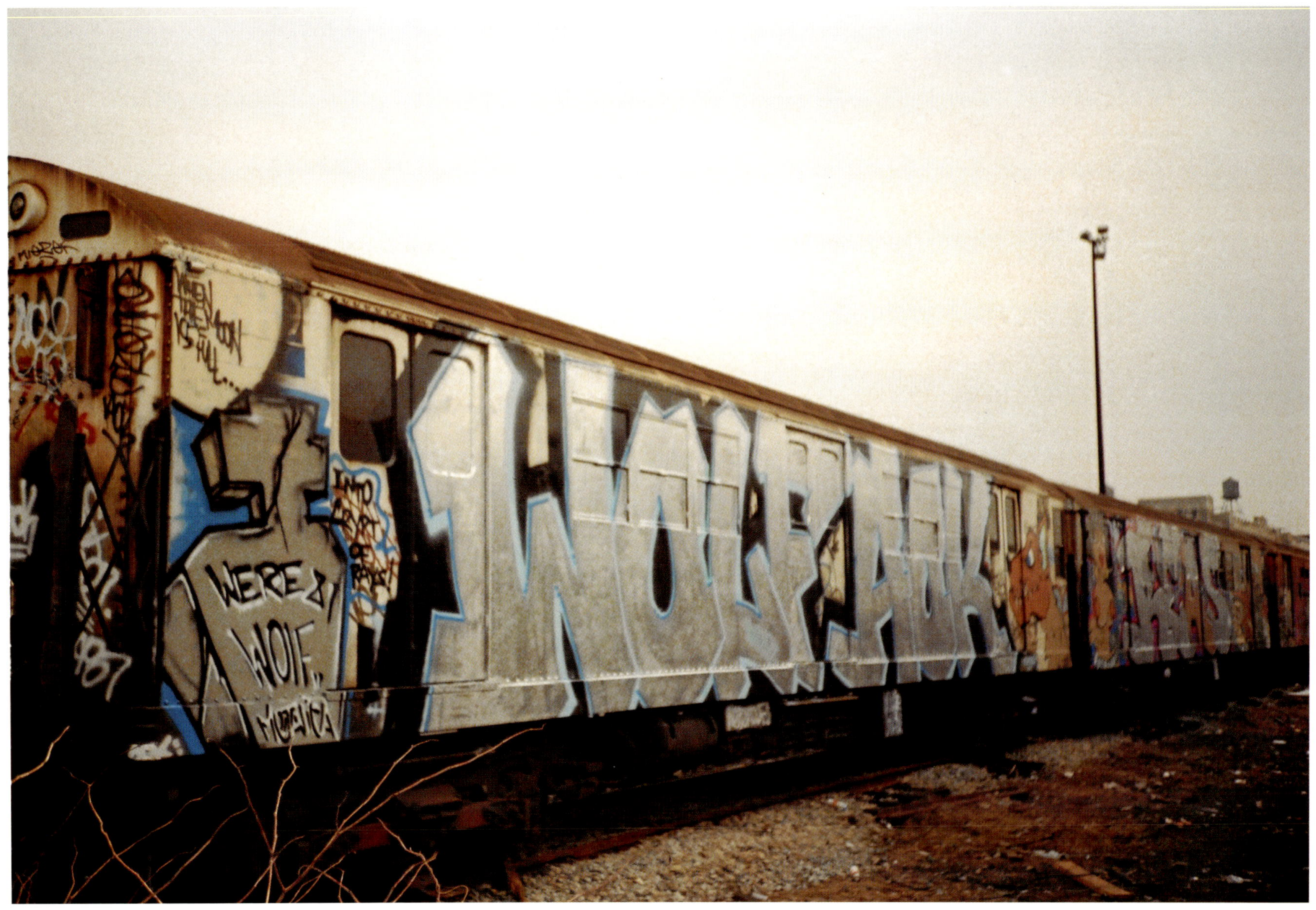

Wolf (AOK), 1987

We did these in the 2nd Avenue scrap yard. It was summer time, 1987. We used Martin paint silvers and Rustoleum. Reas did both characters that day off the top of this head. That was not at all unusual for him to do.

—Wolf (AOK)

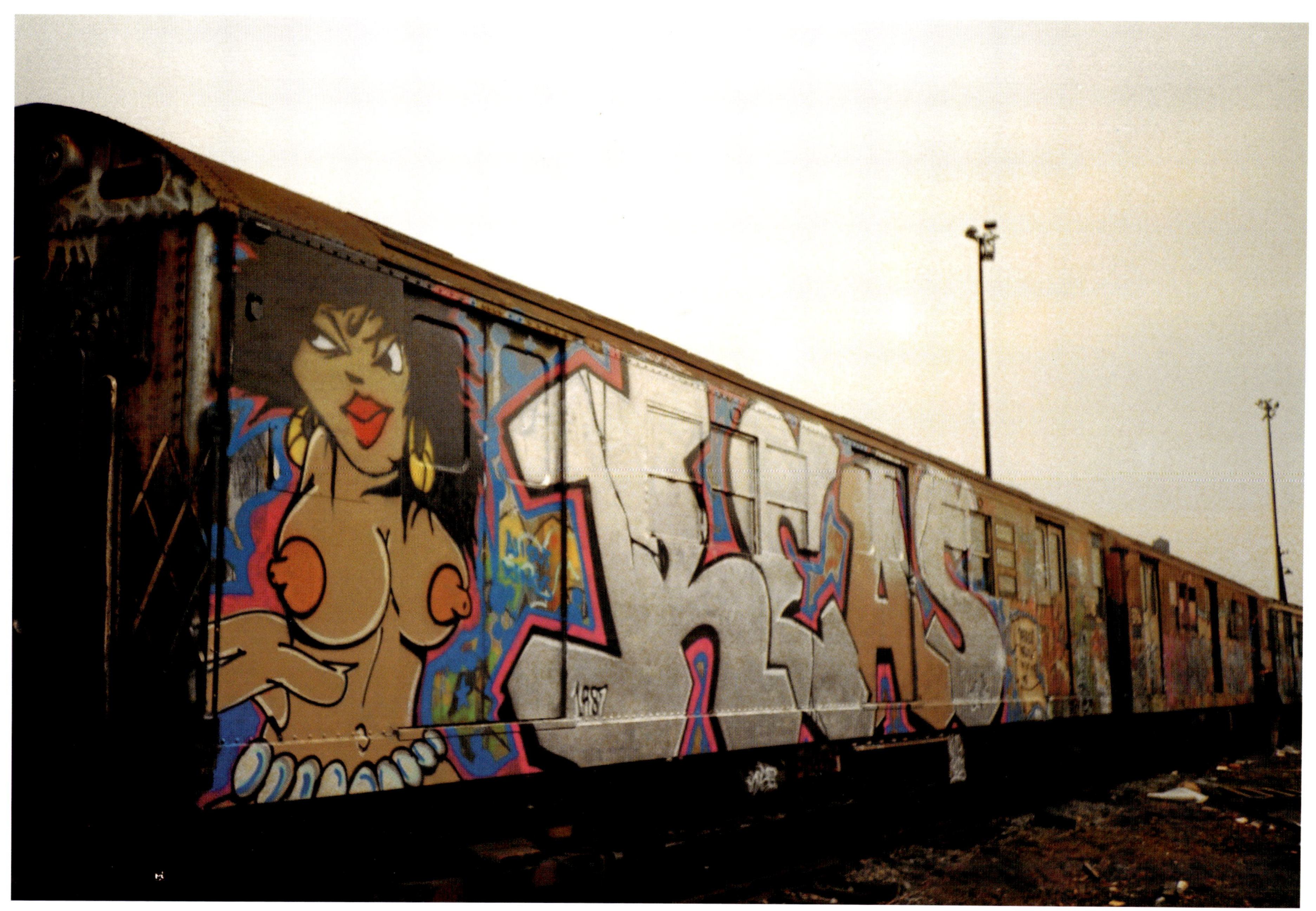

Reas (AOK), 1987

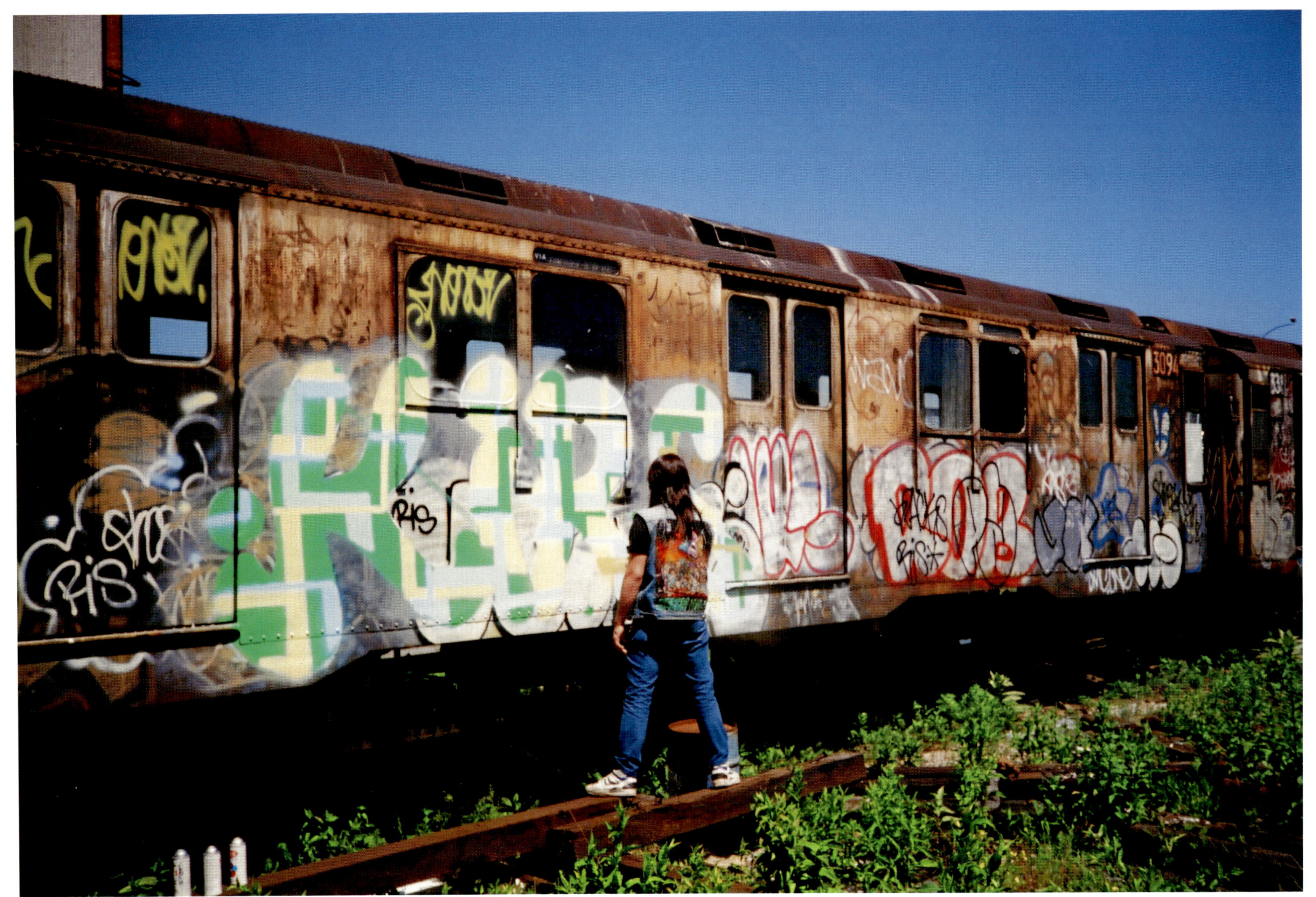

Kirs (MPC), 1988

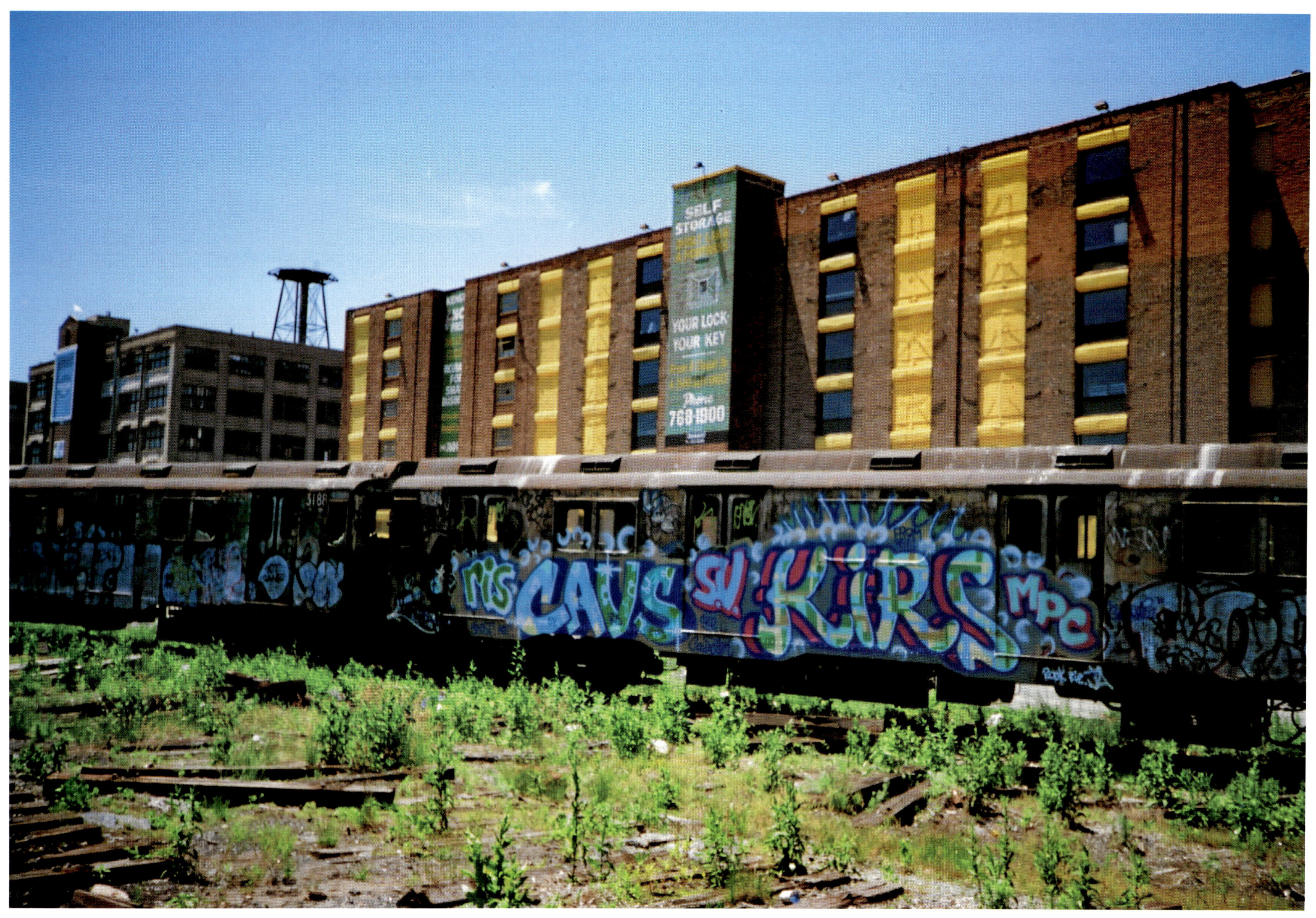

Cavs & Kirs (SV), 1988

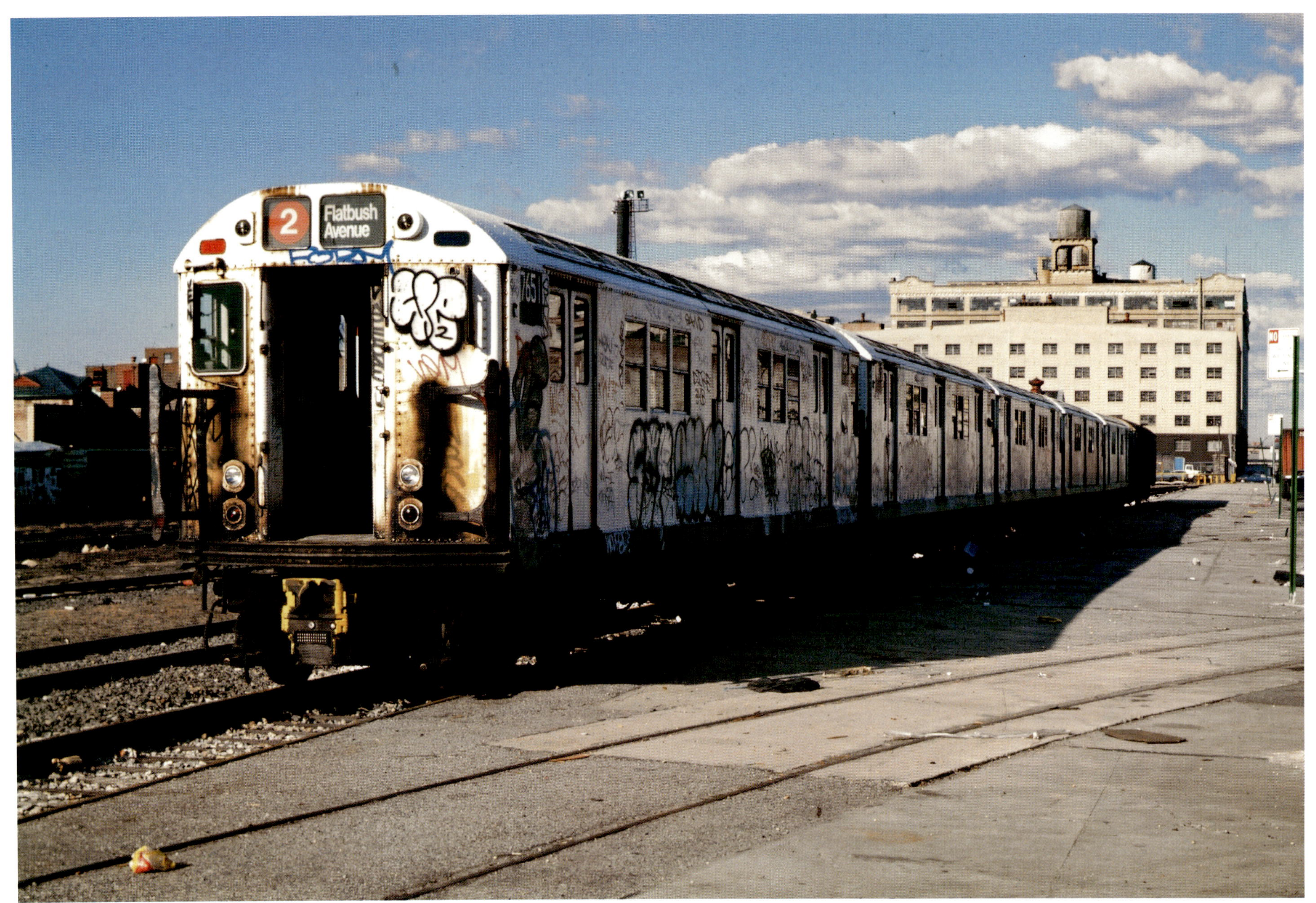

2nd Avenue, 1987

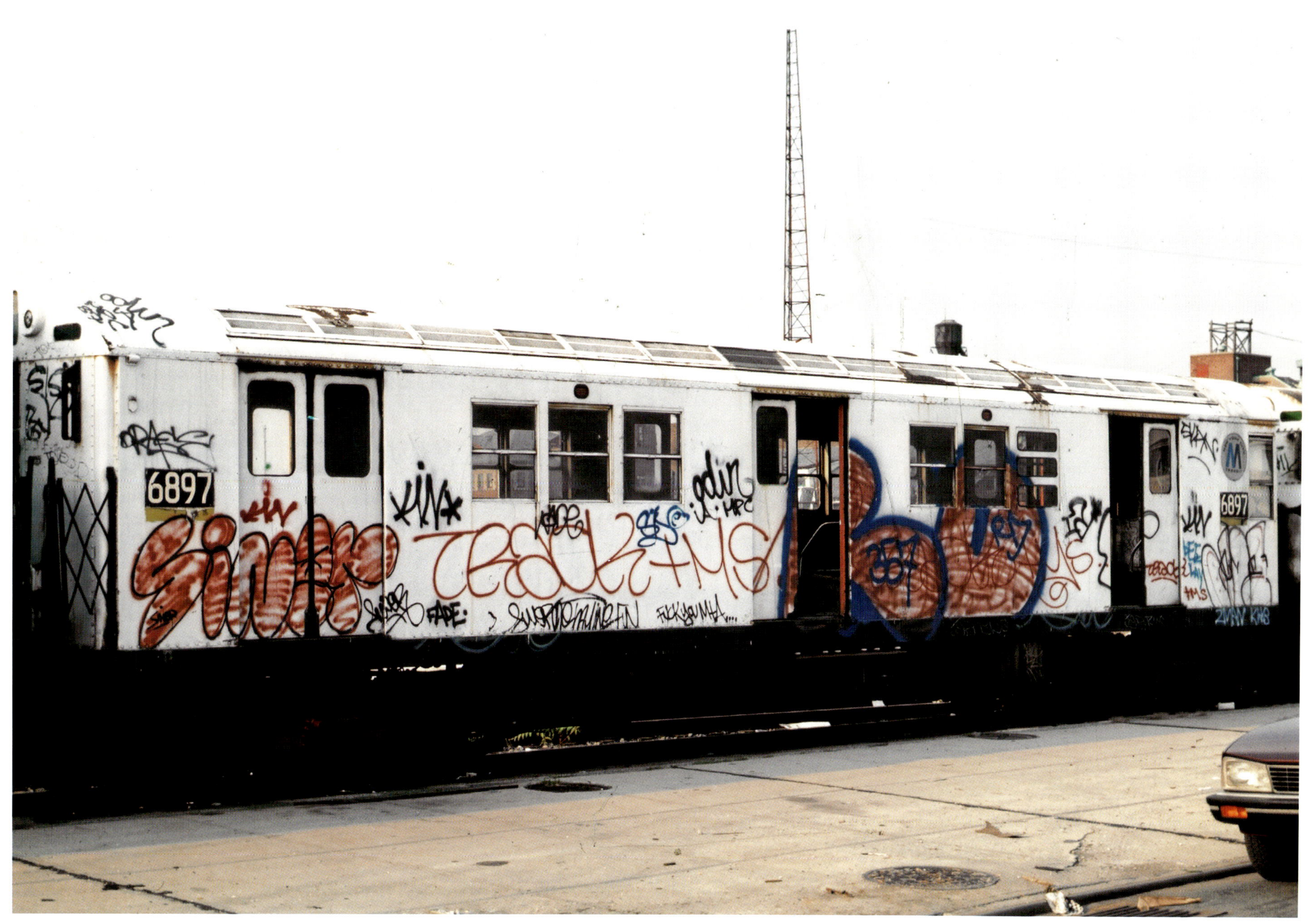

2nd Avenue, 1987

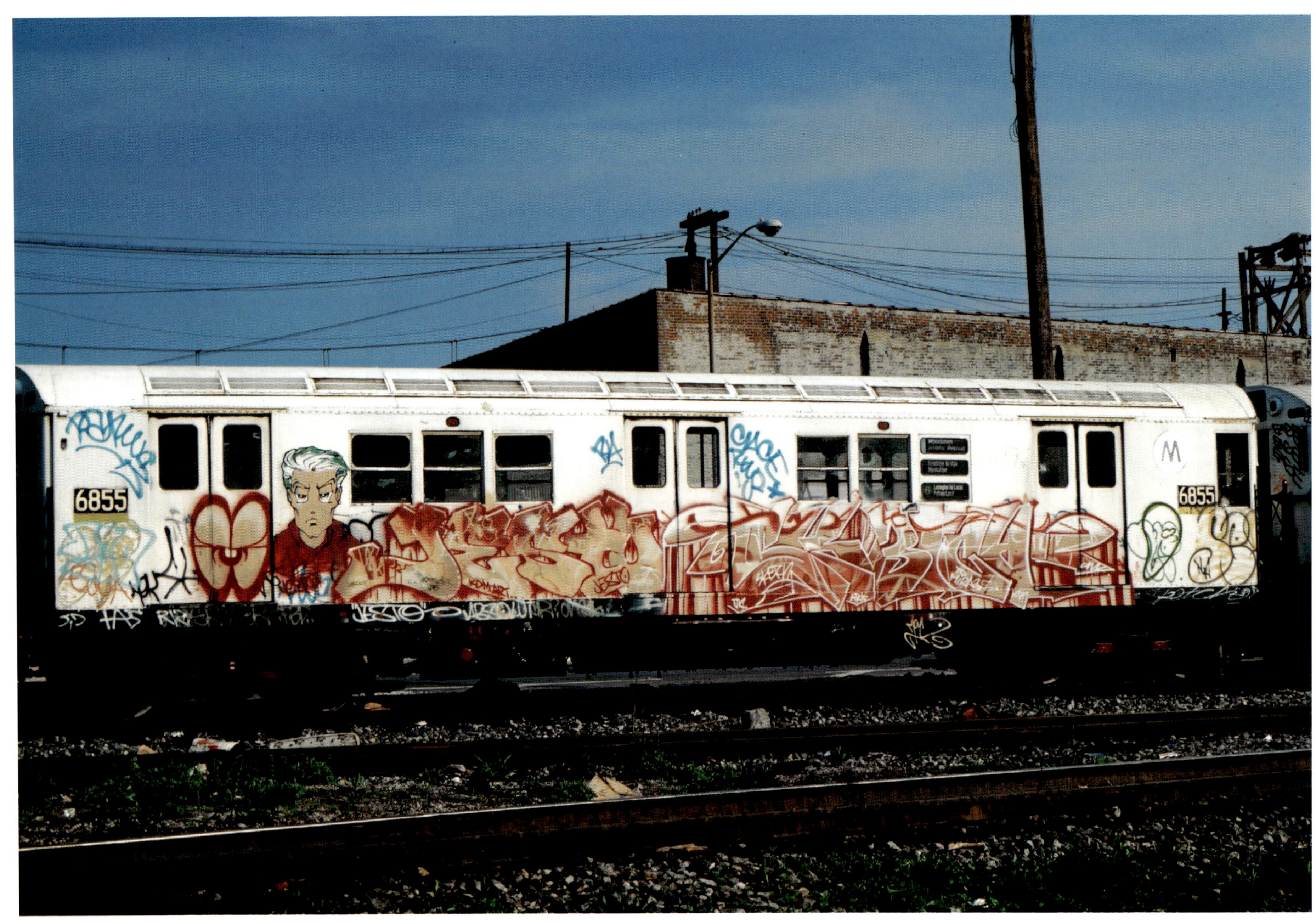

Jesto & Sketch (CWK), 1987

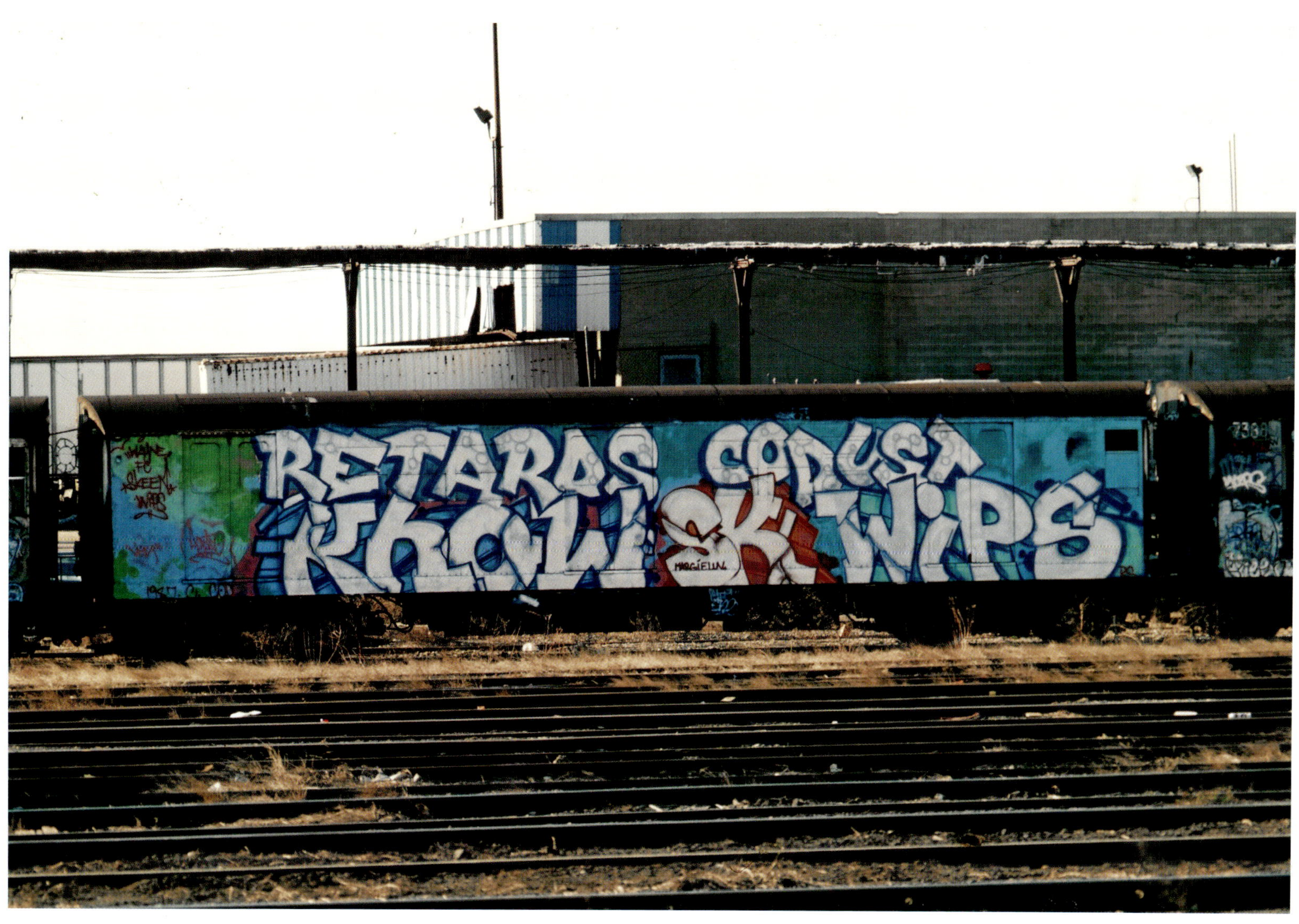

Know, SK, & Wips (COD), 1987

It was interesting to take photos of the subway in the '70s and '80s. You had a large variety of cars and different paint jobs. Today, the cars are more modern and cleaner but not as interesting. I don't take that many pictures today. The system itself, however, remains fascinating to anyone that observes it up close!

—Bill Myers, photographer and "train buff"

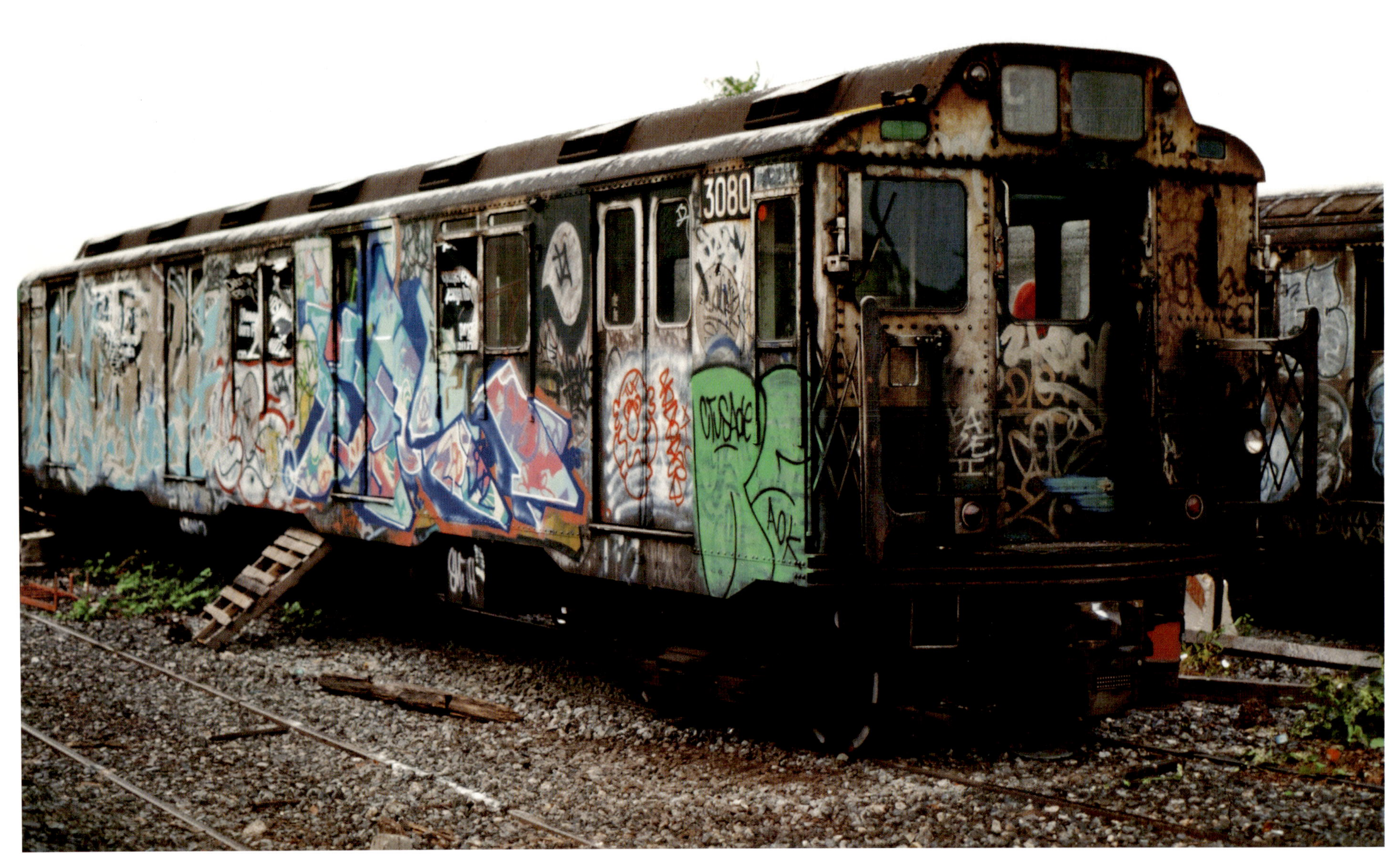

1988

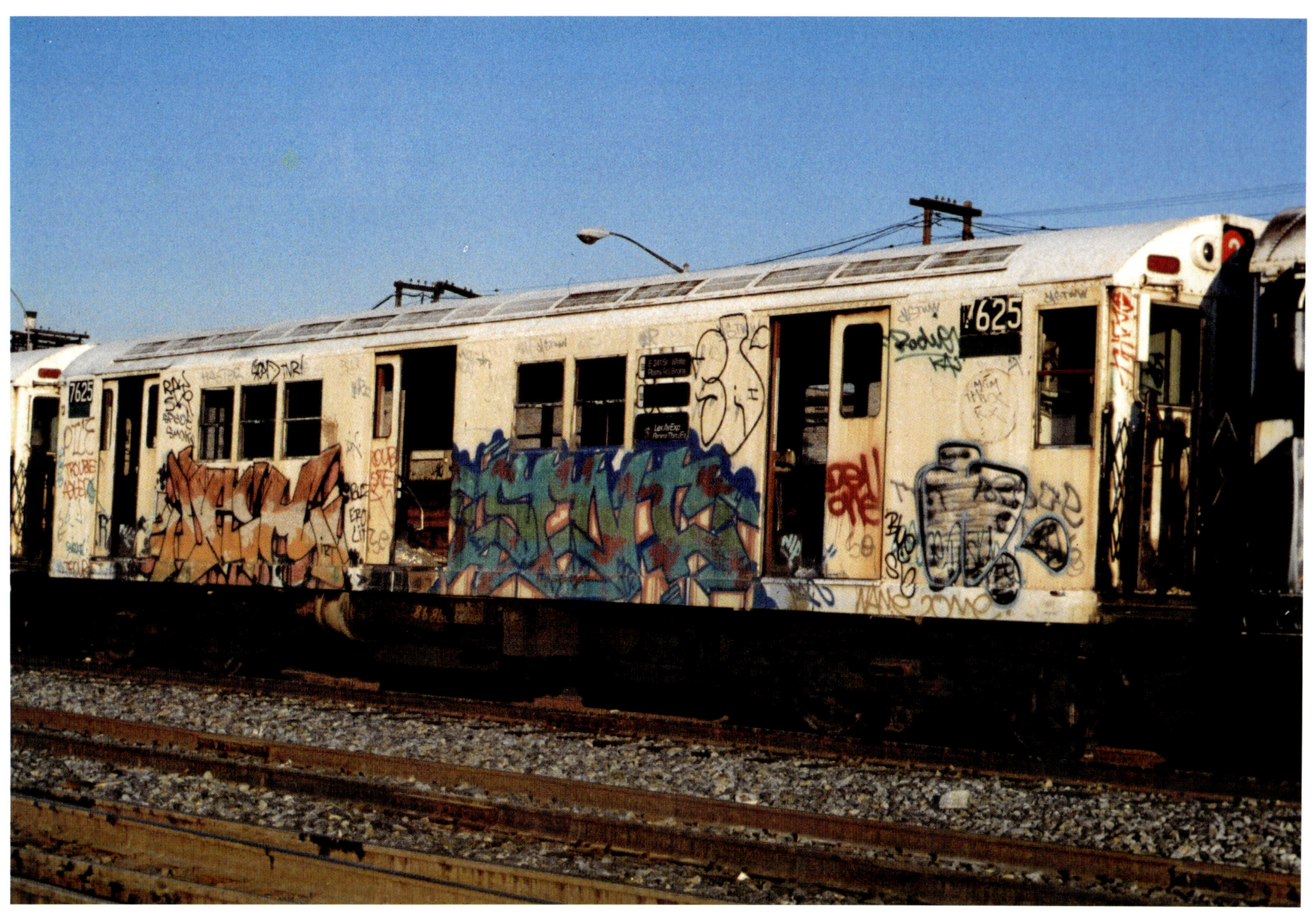

Deem & Sent (TFP), painted in 1985, photographed in 1987

KENSTON
NOW PRESENTS
THE EXTRA CLOSET
SELF STORAGE
YOUR LOCK

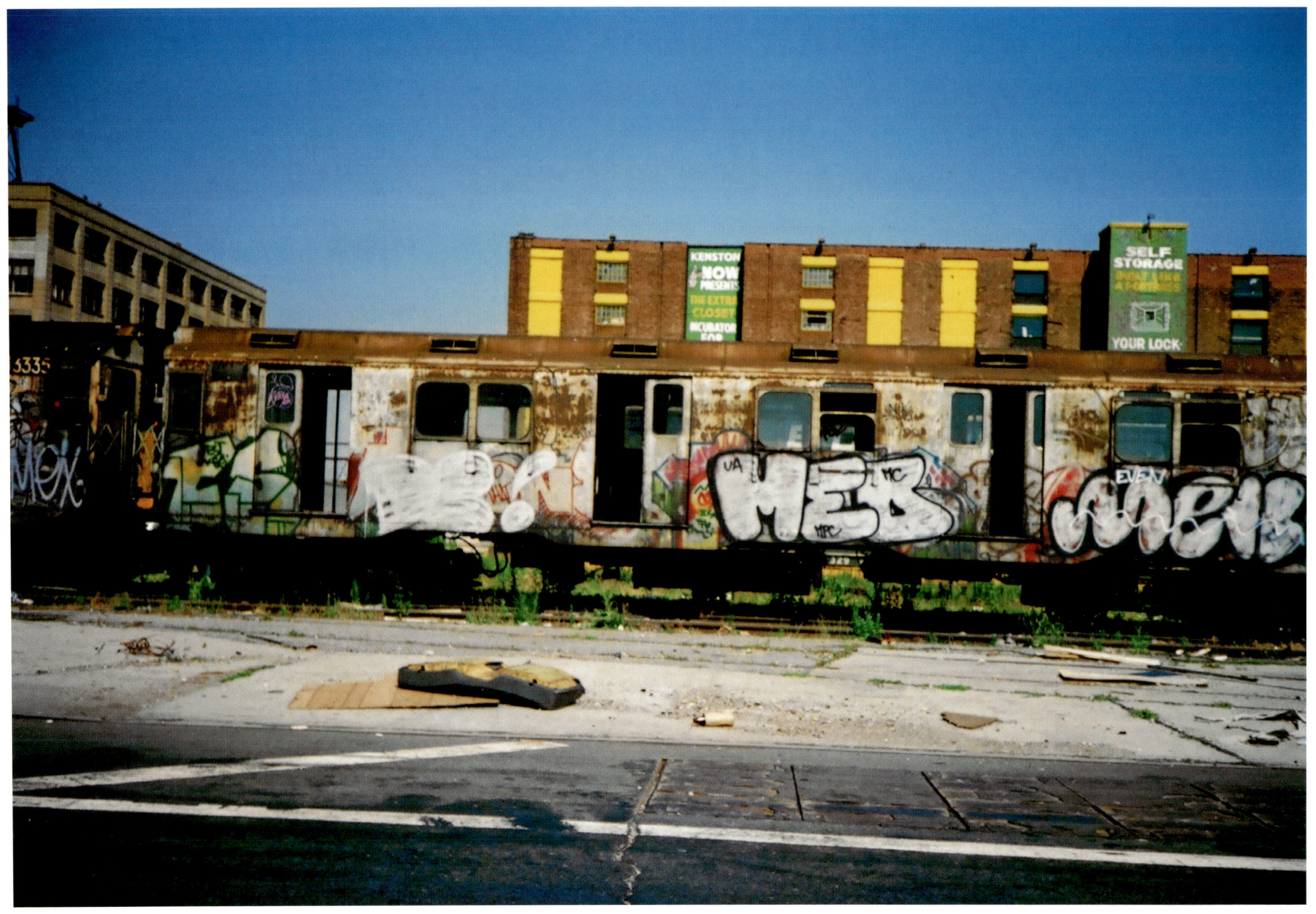

Med, 1988

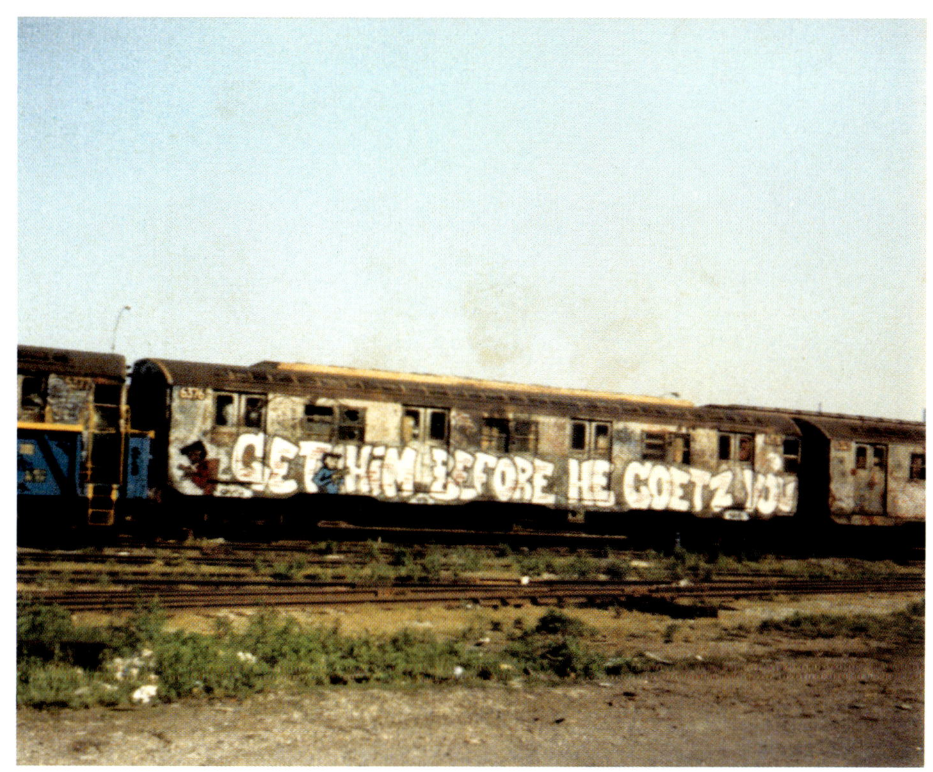

"Get him before he Goetz you." Smith, 1987, in reference to Bernard Goetz

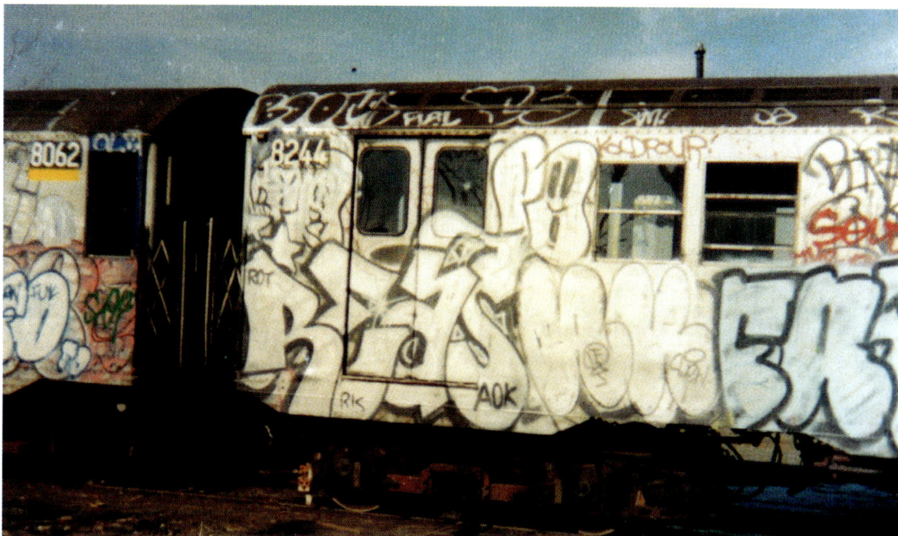

Reas (AOK), 1987

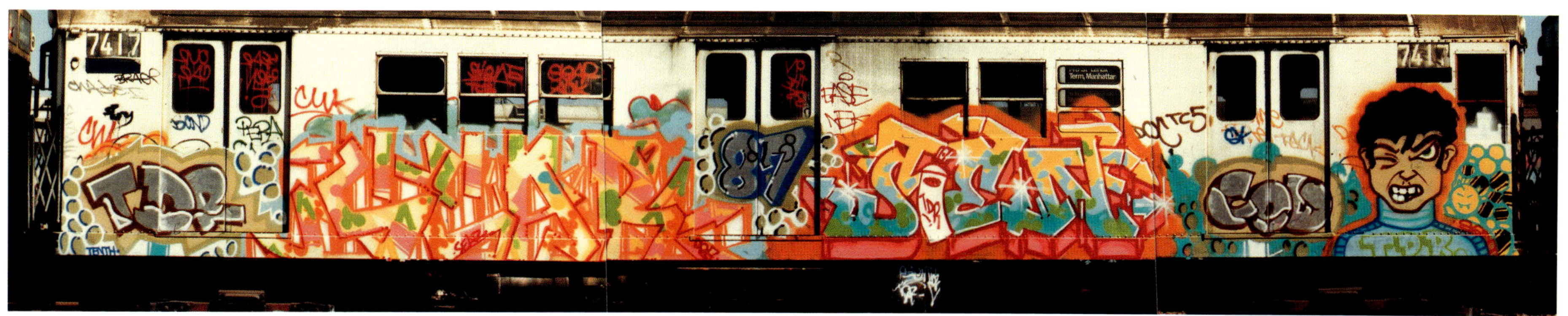

Sear & Sien 5, 1987

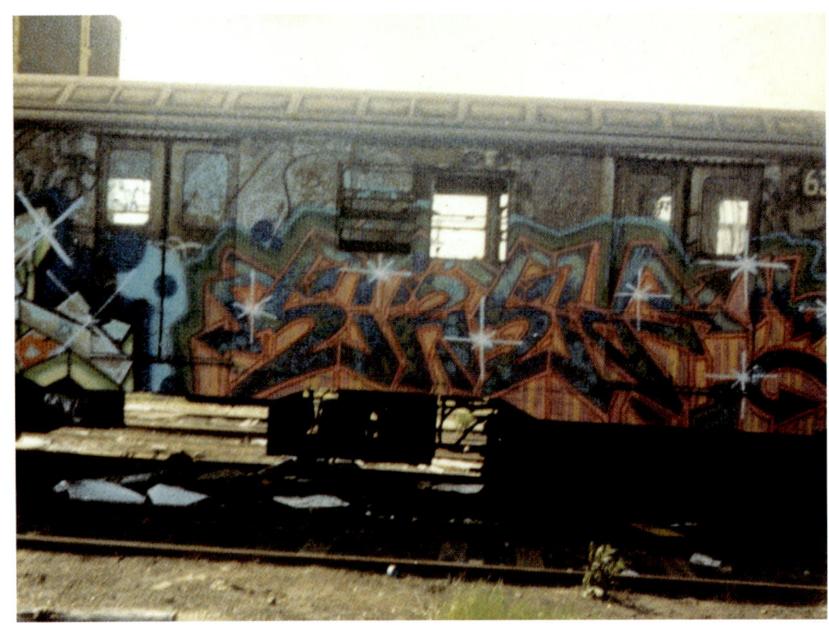

Stash, 1987

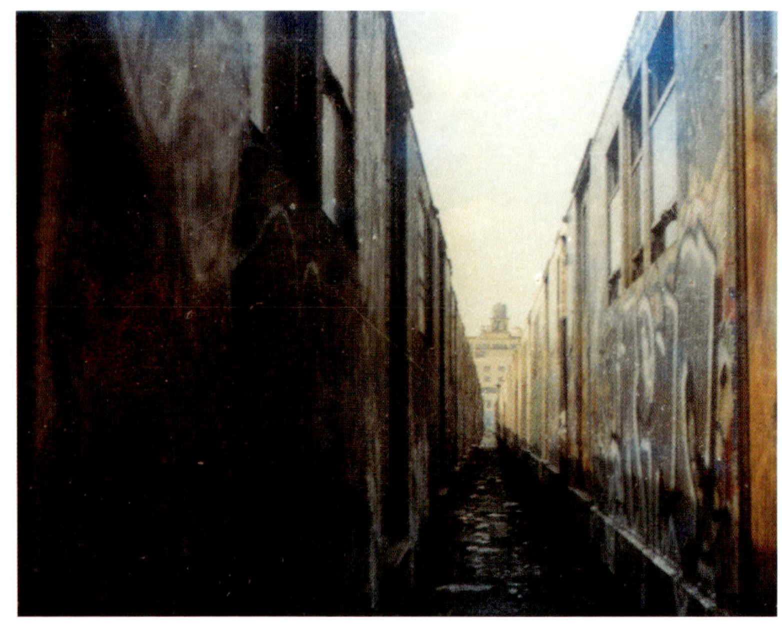

1987

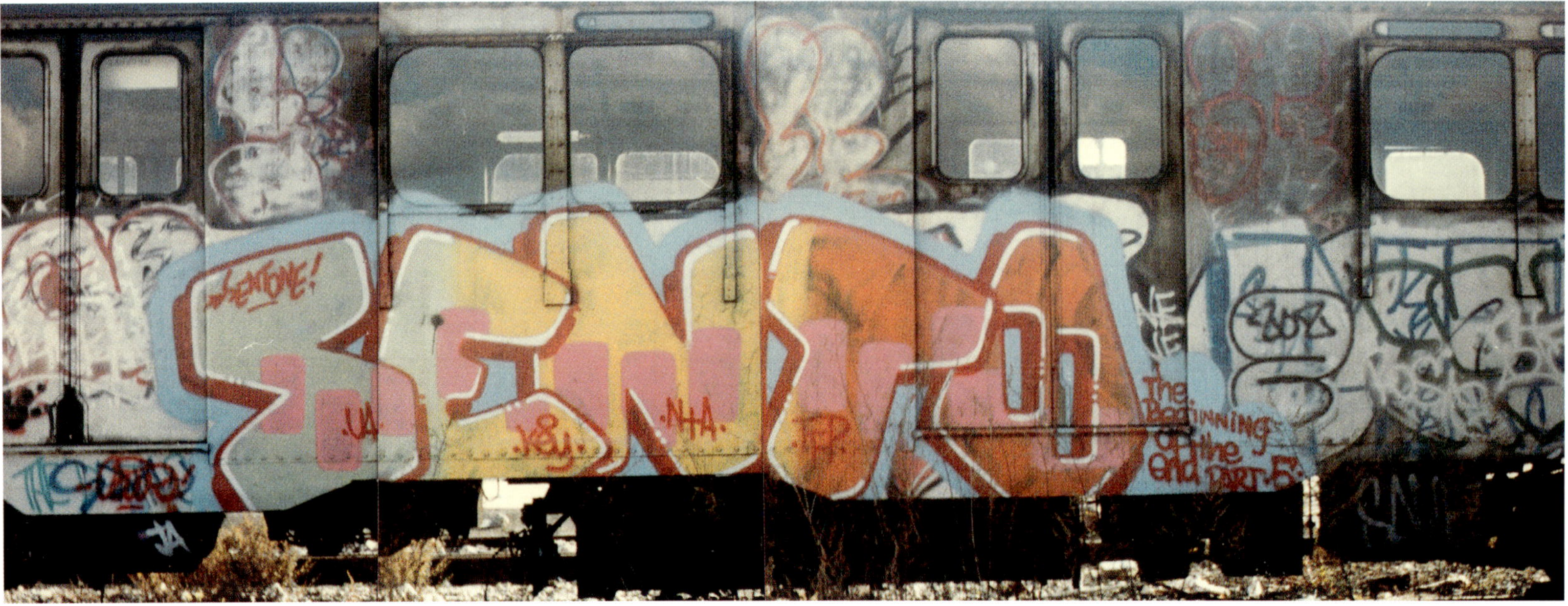

Sento (TFP)

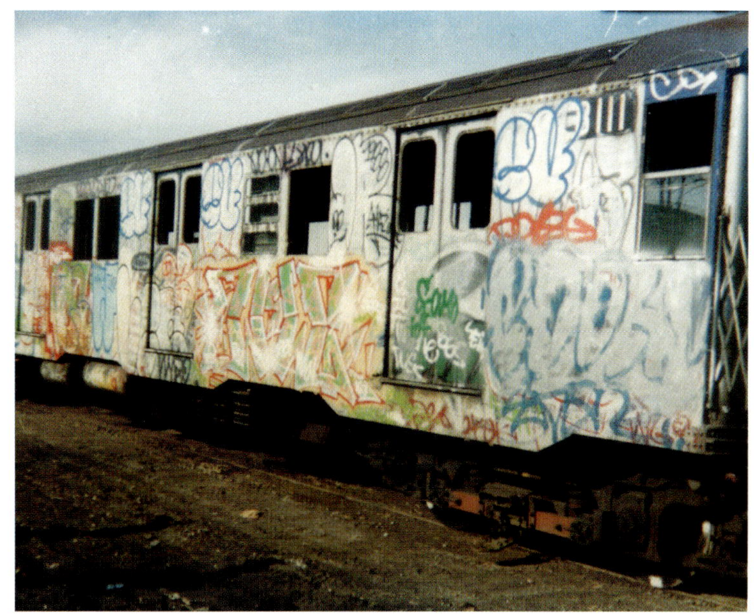

"WW" by Pema

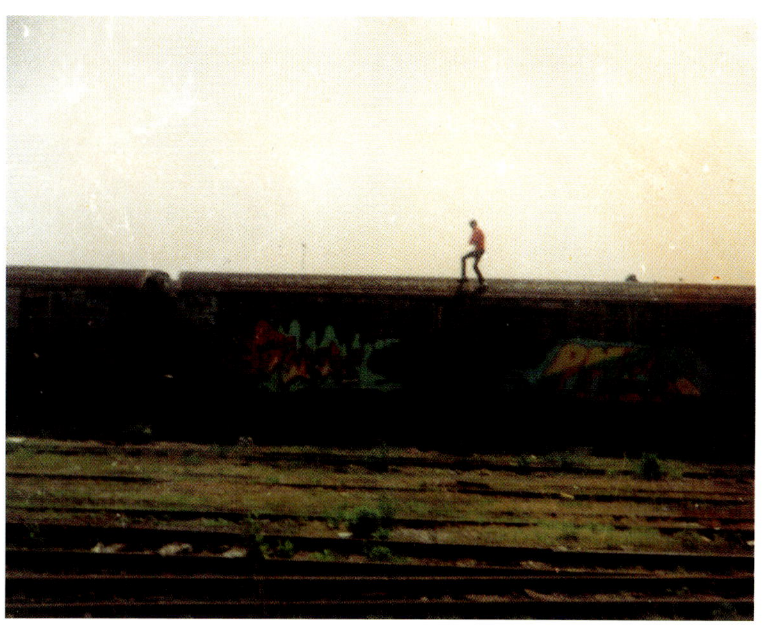

Dbone & Pmer, 1987

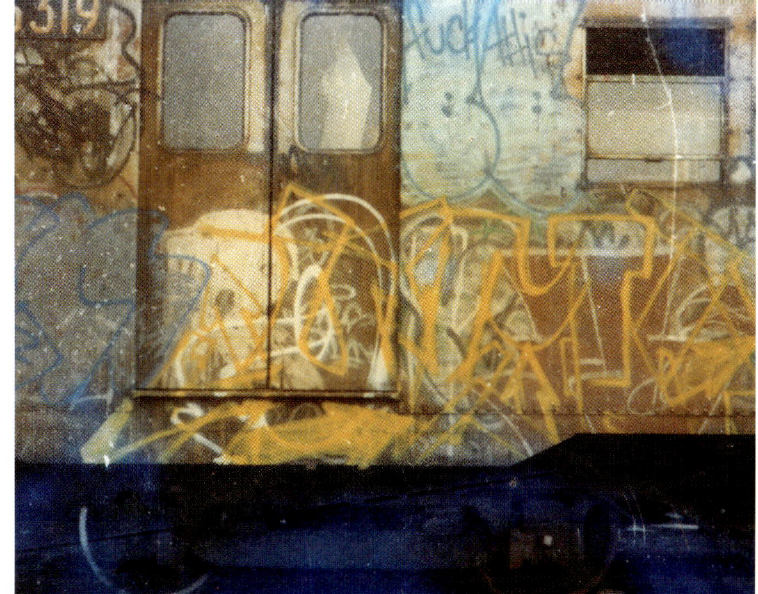

Omni outline

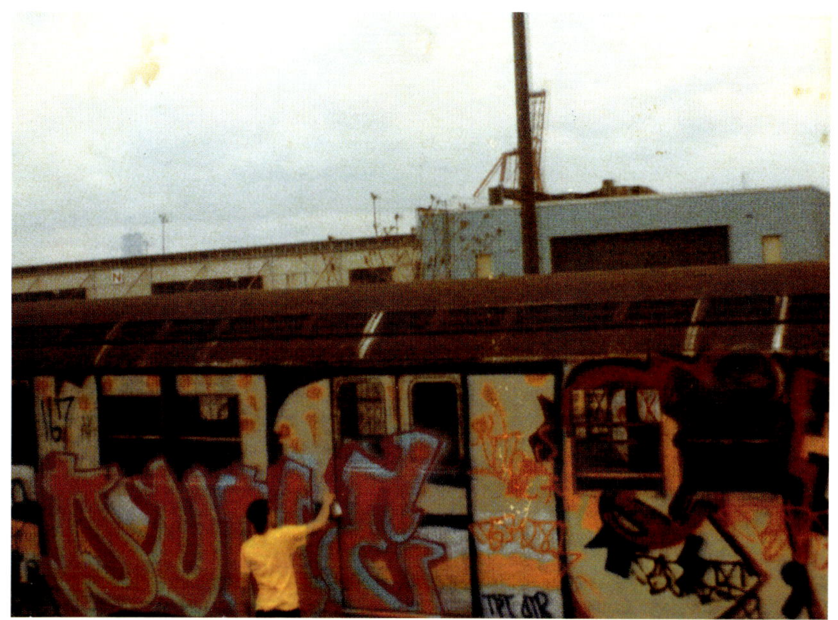

Dune, 1987

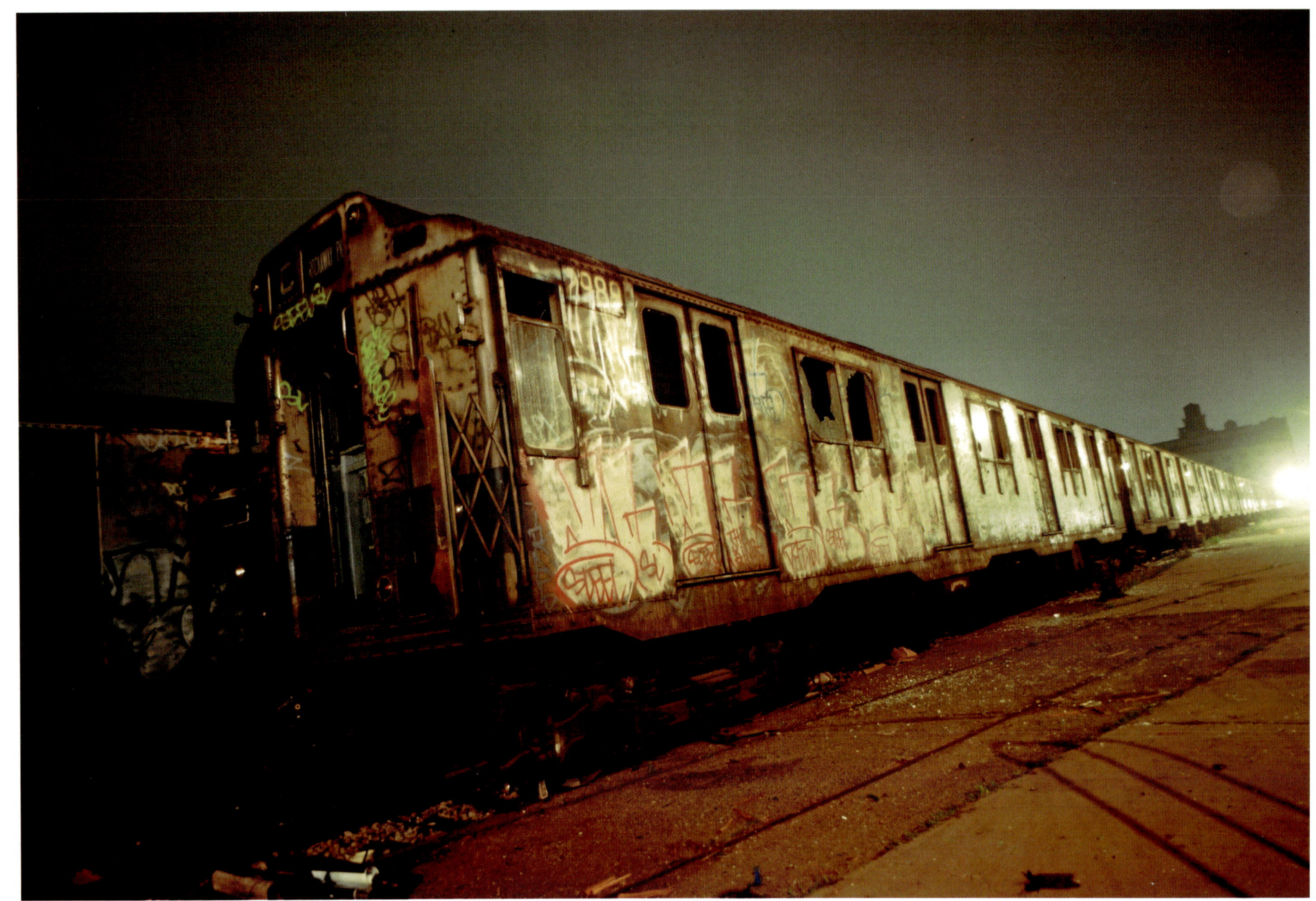

Steel

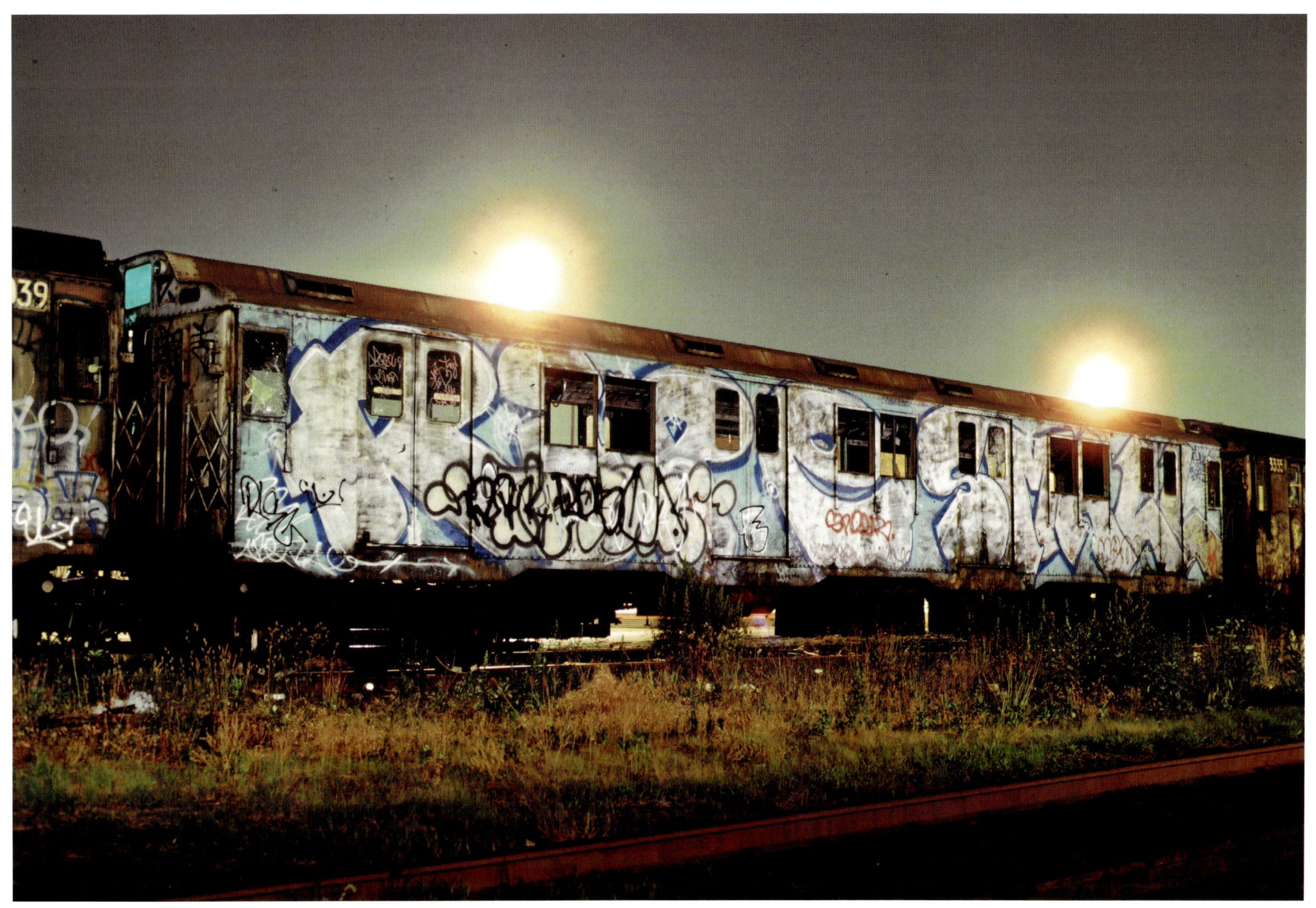

Ripe & Small, 1988

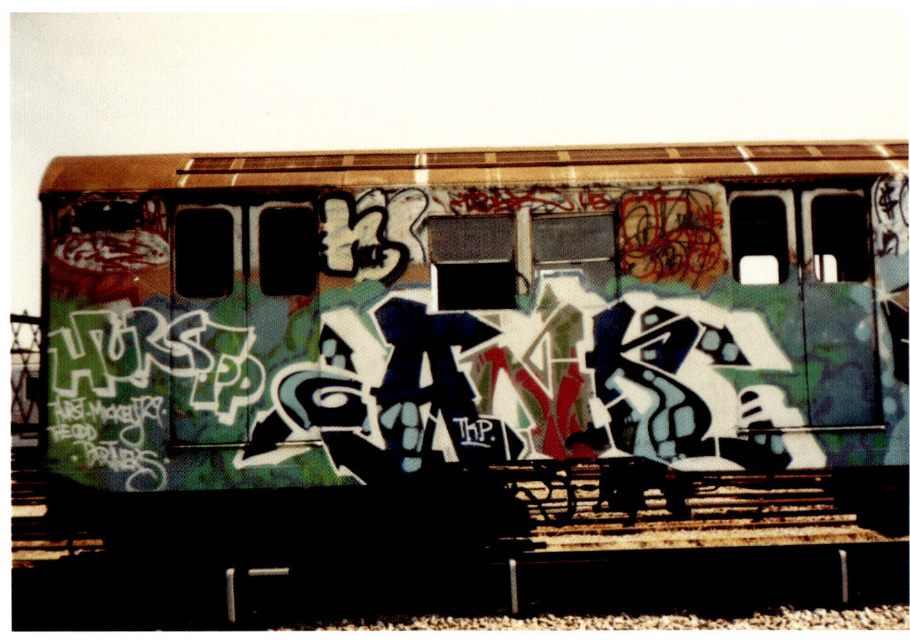

"And" by Magoo (TKP), 1989

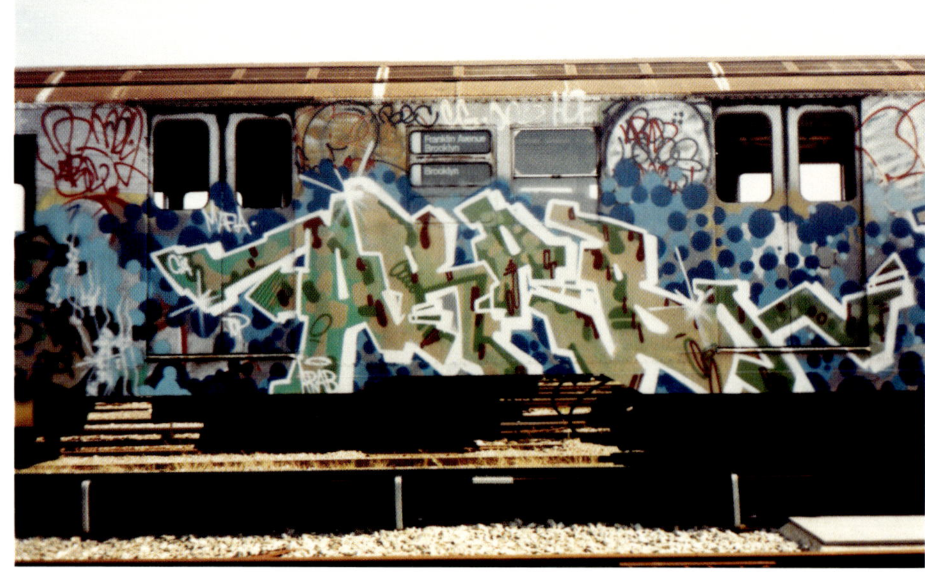

"Arab" by Doc (TC5)

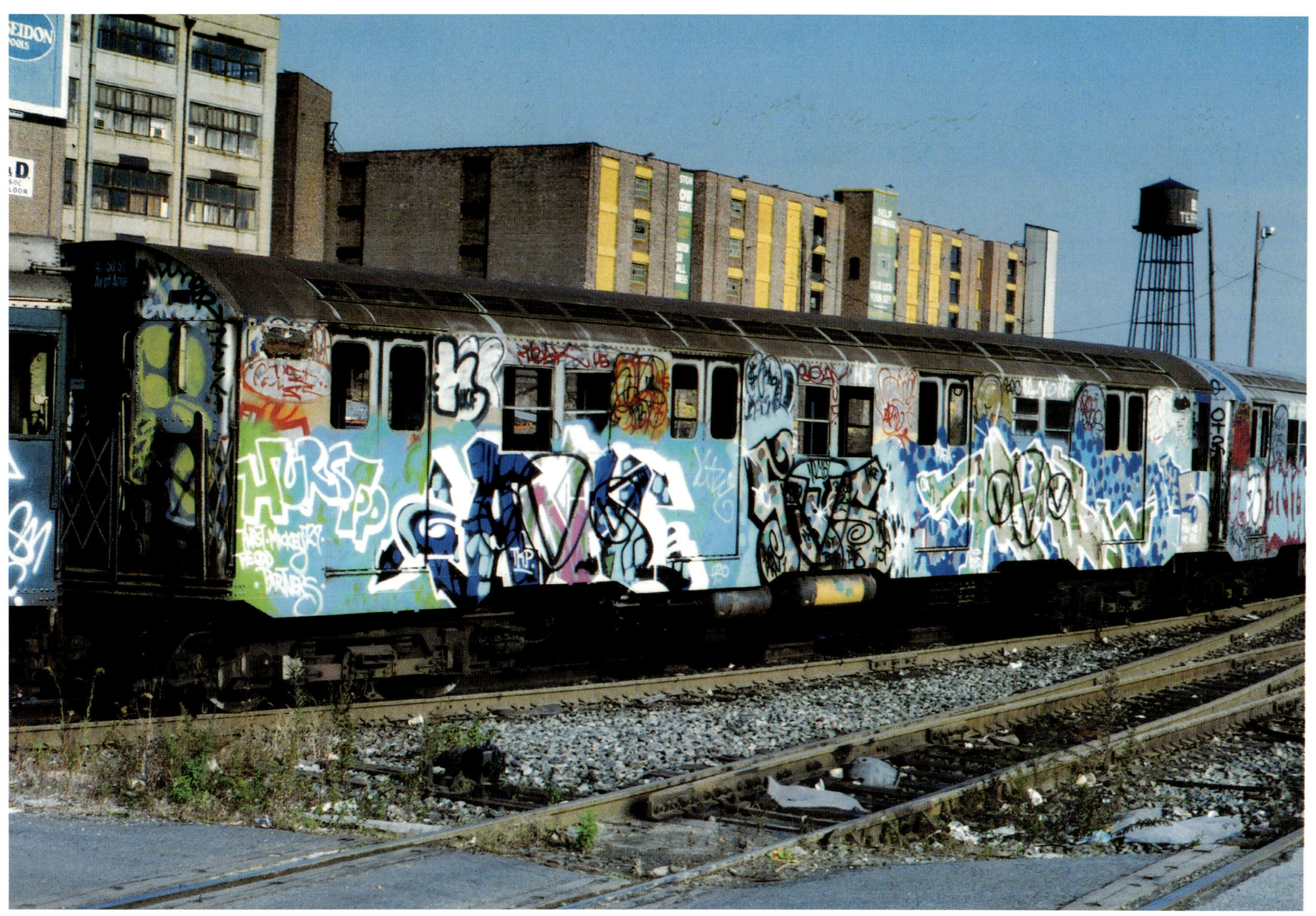

The vandal squad making their presence known. The marking of the V over the piece was their handiwork.

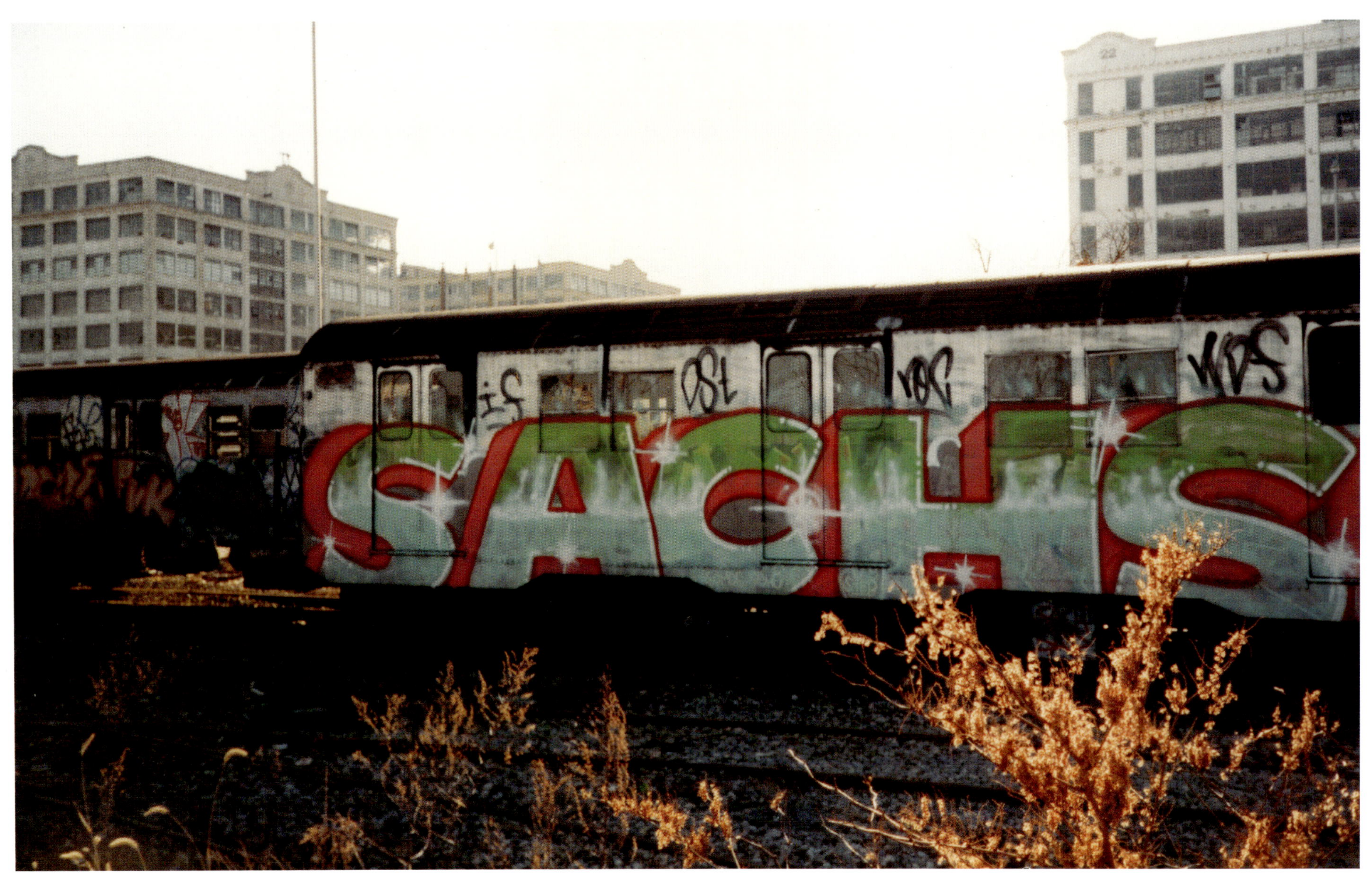

"Sachsoon," by Sach (TMB), 1989

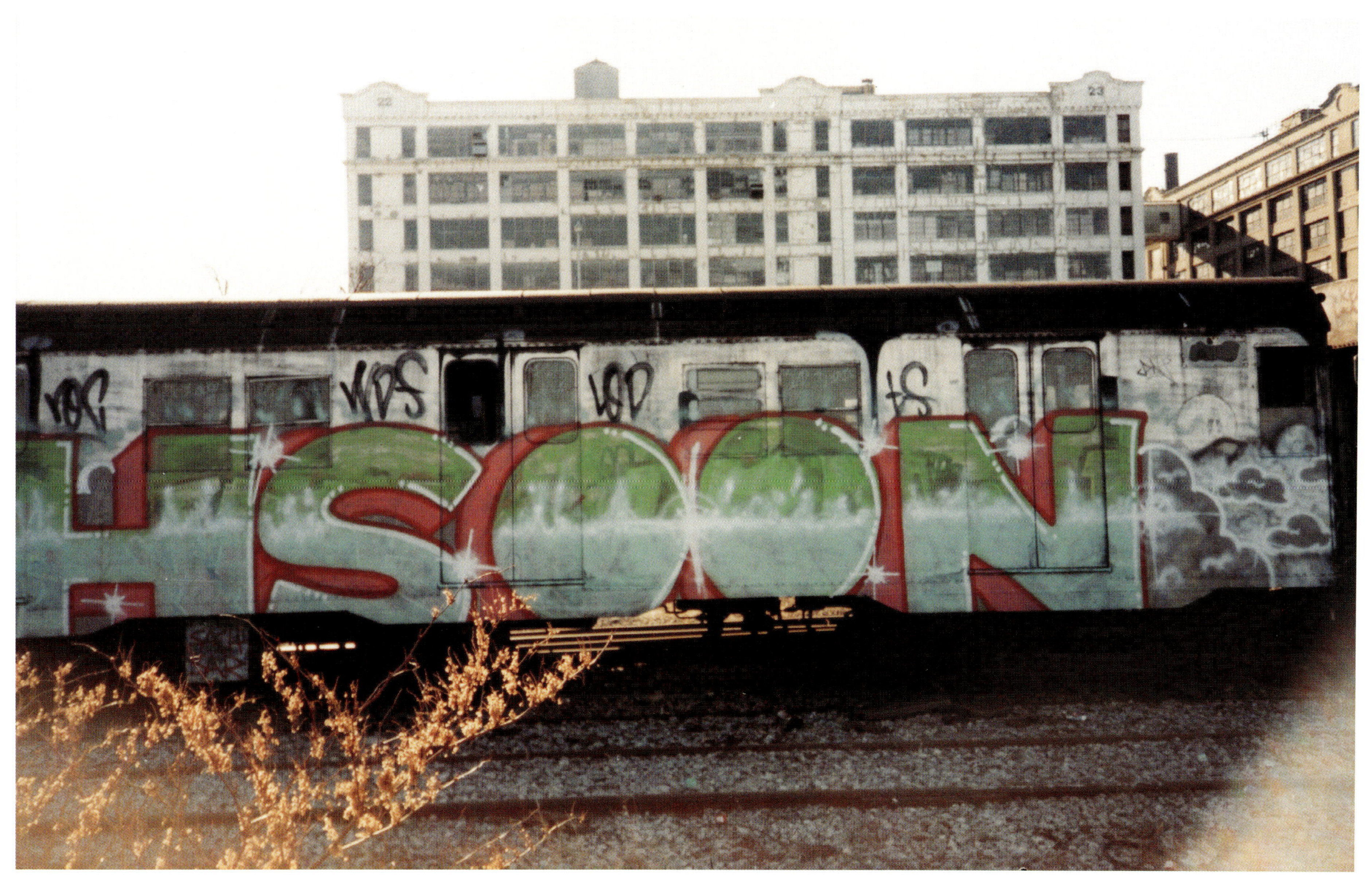

“Sachsoon,” by Sach (TMB), 1989

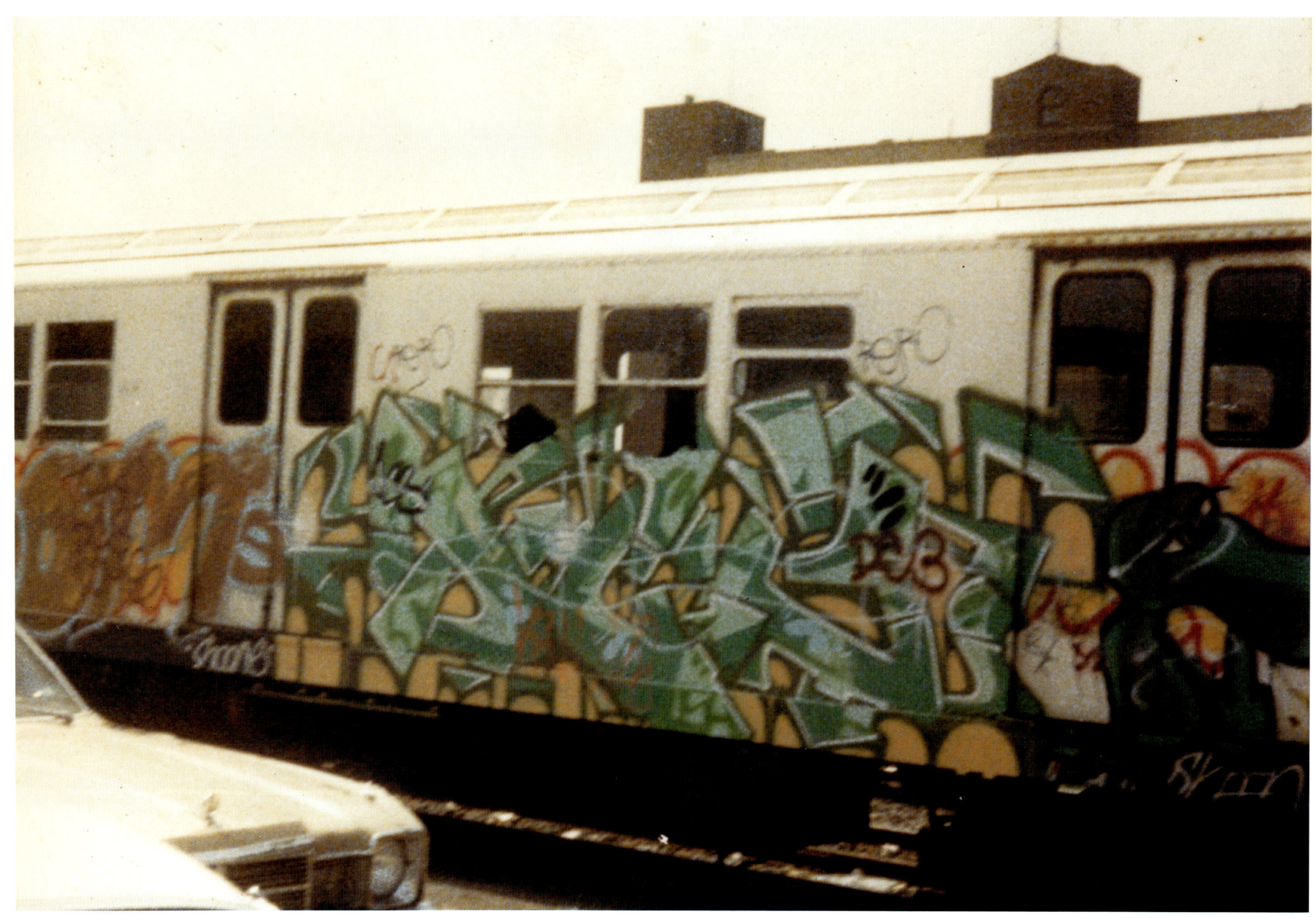

DC3, 1987

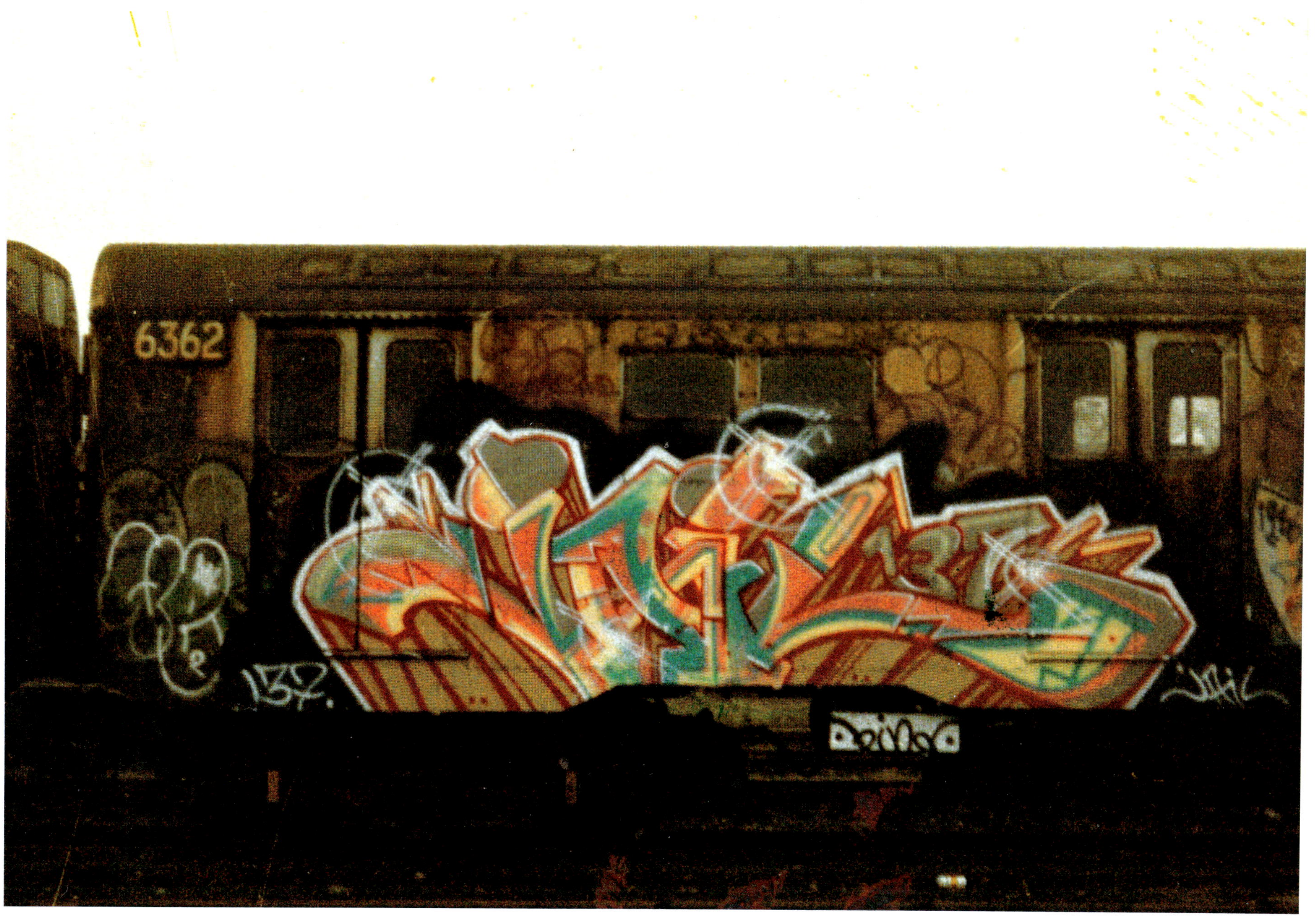

"Jail 137" by Bind, 1986

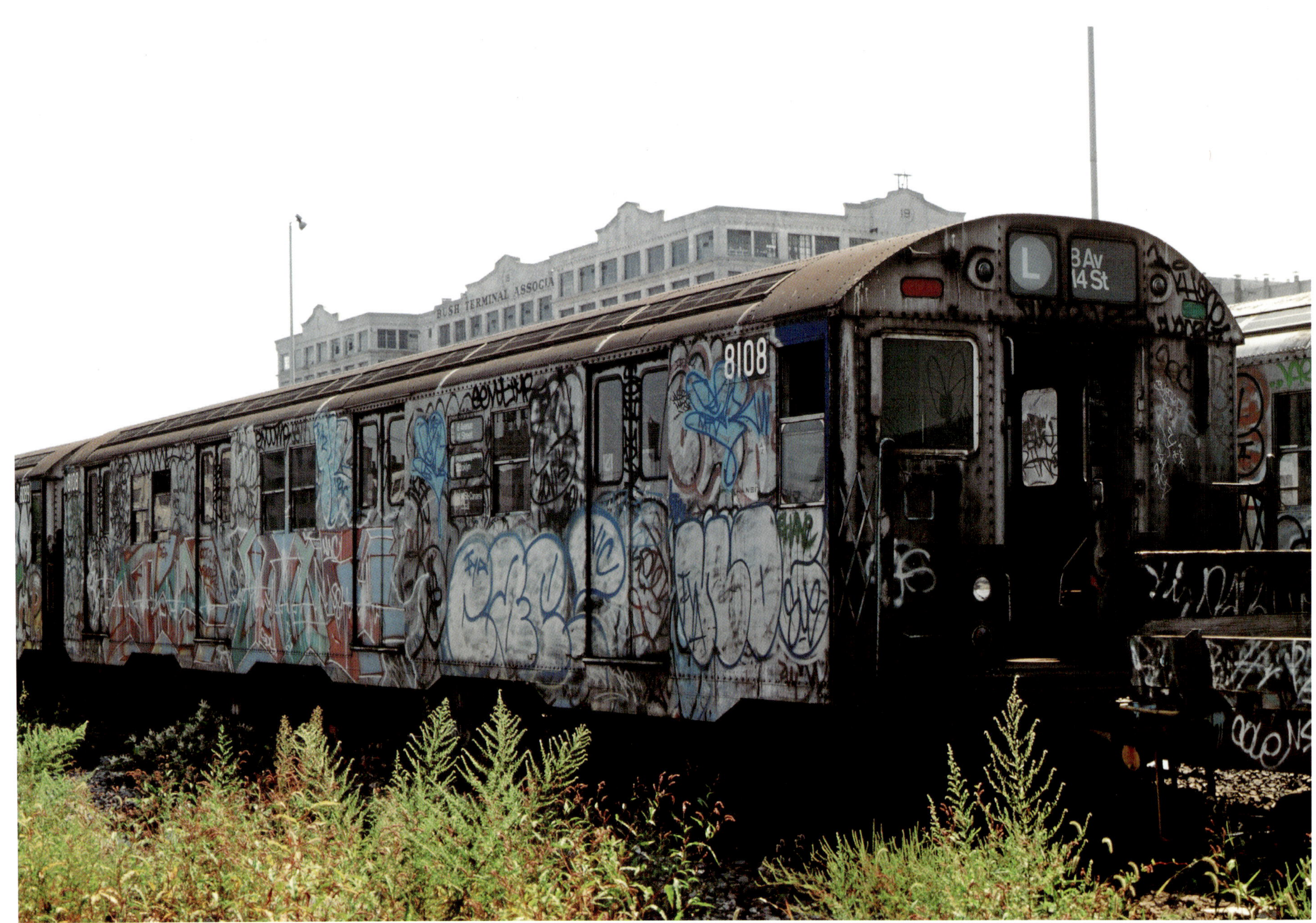

DG (NWC) & Deam (SDS), 1988

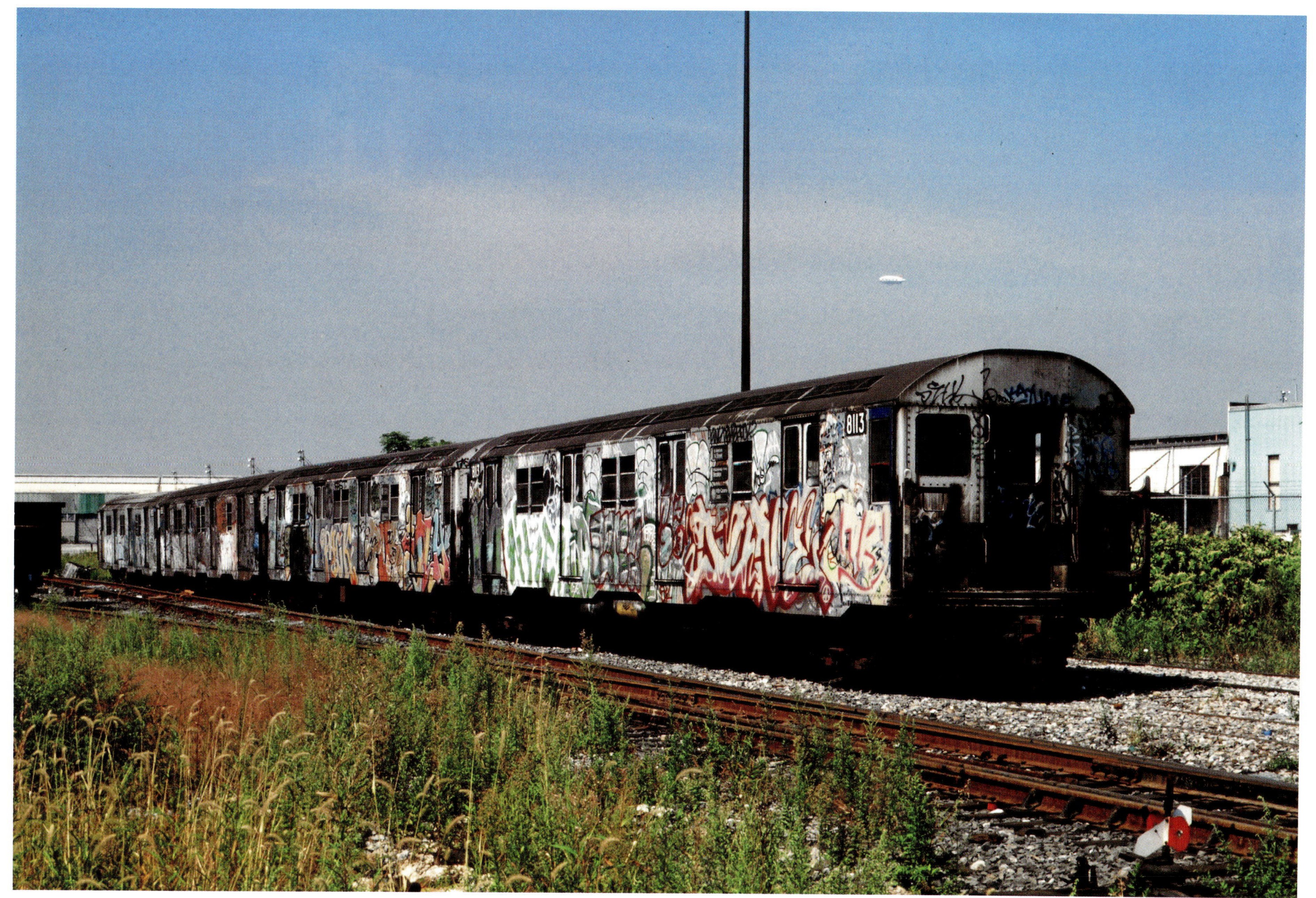

1989

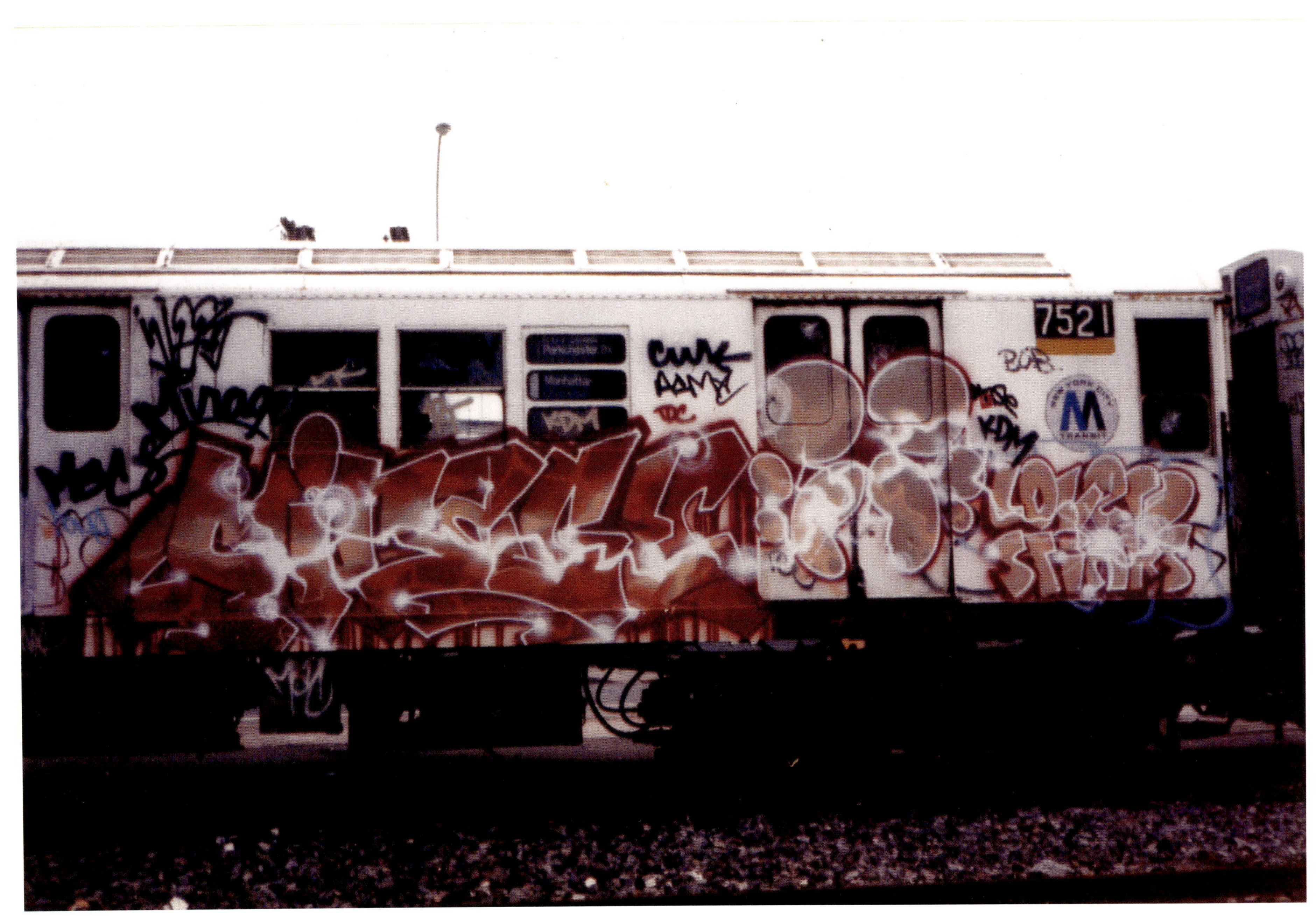

Mirage, "Rest in Peace," 1987

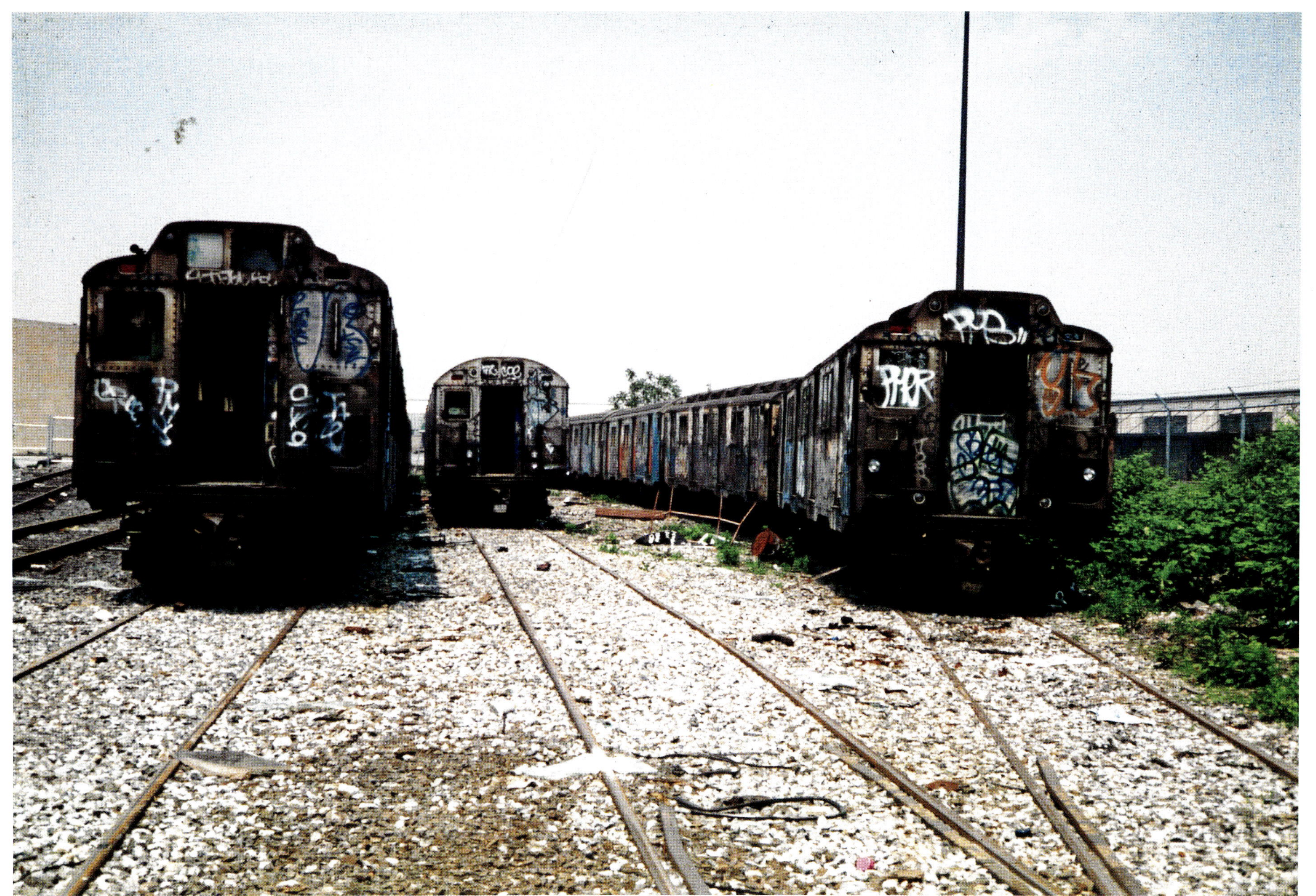

1989

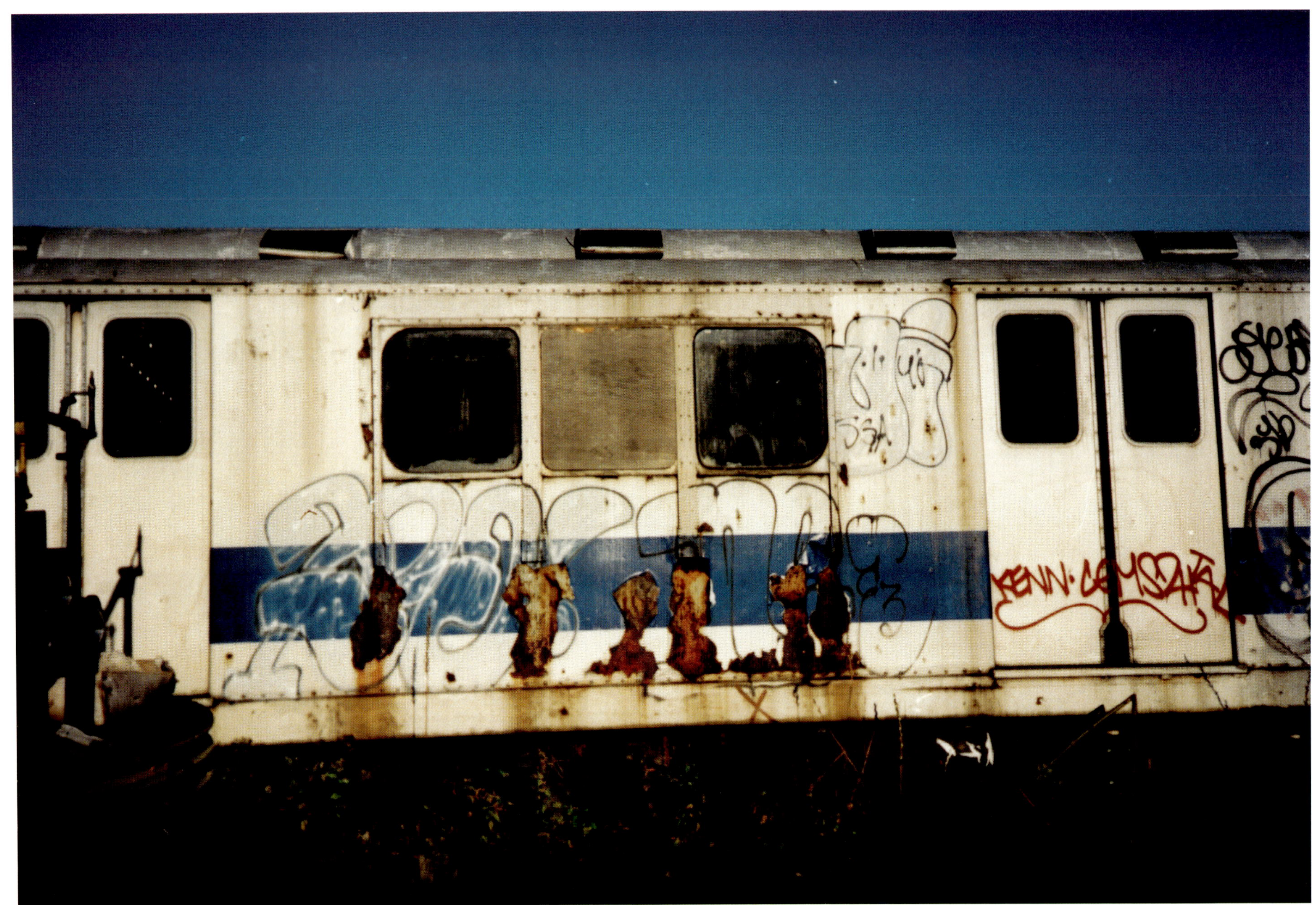

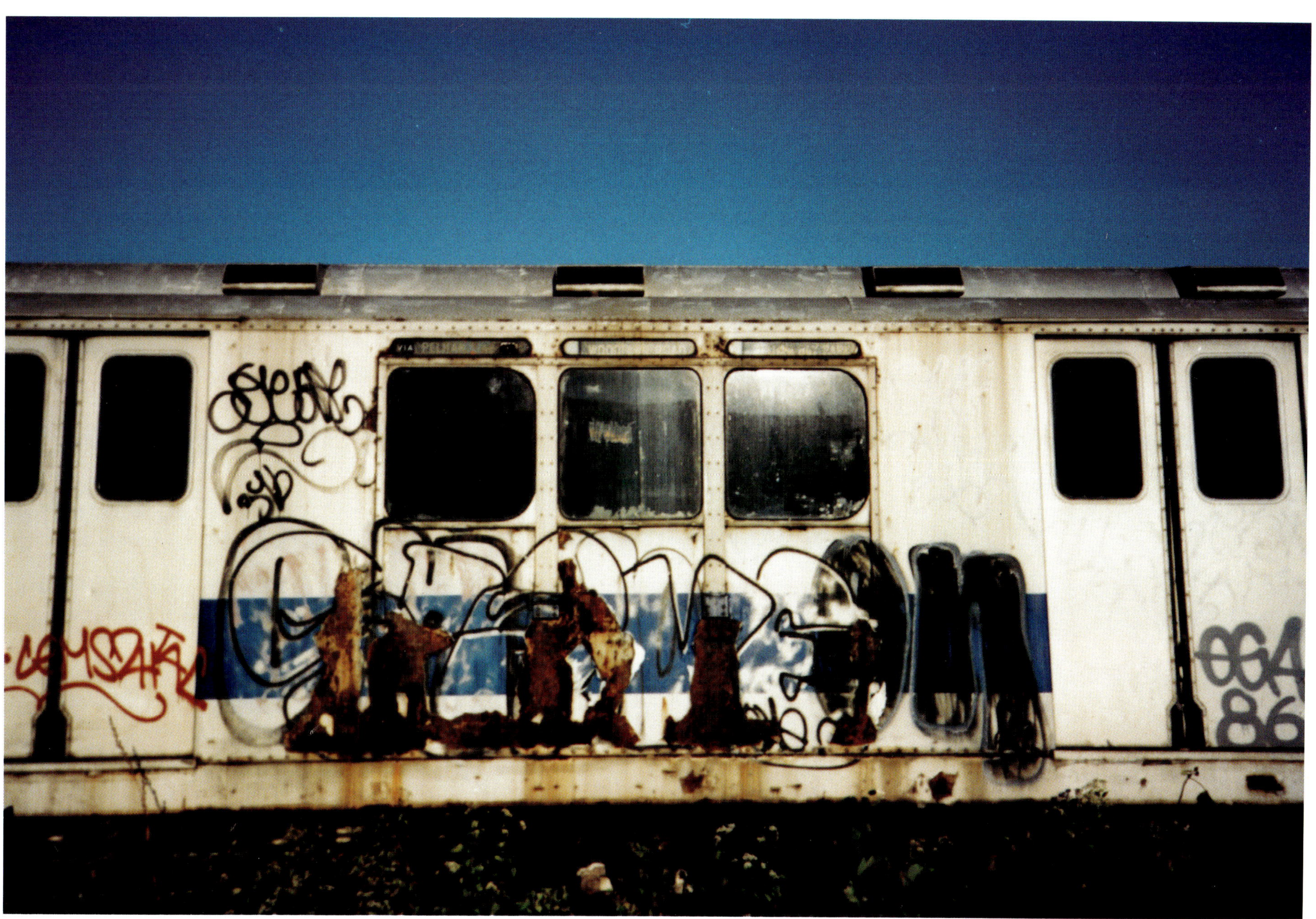

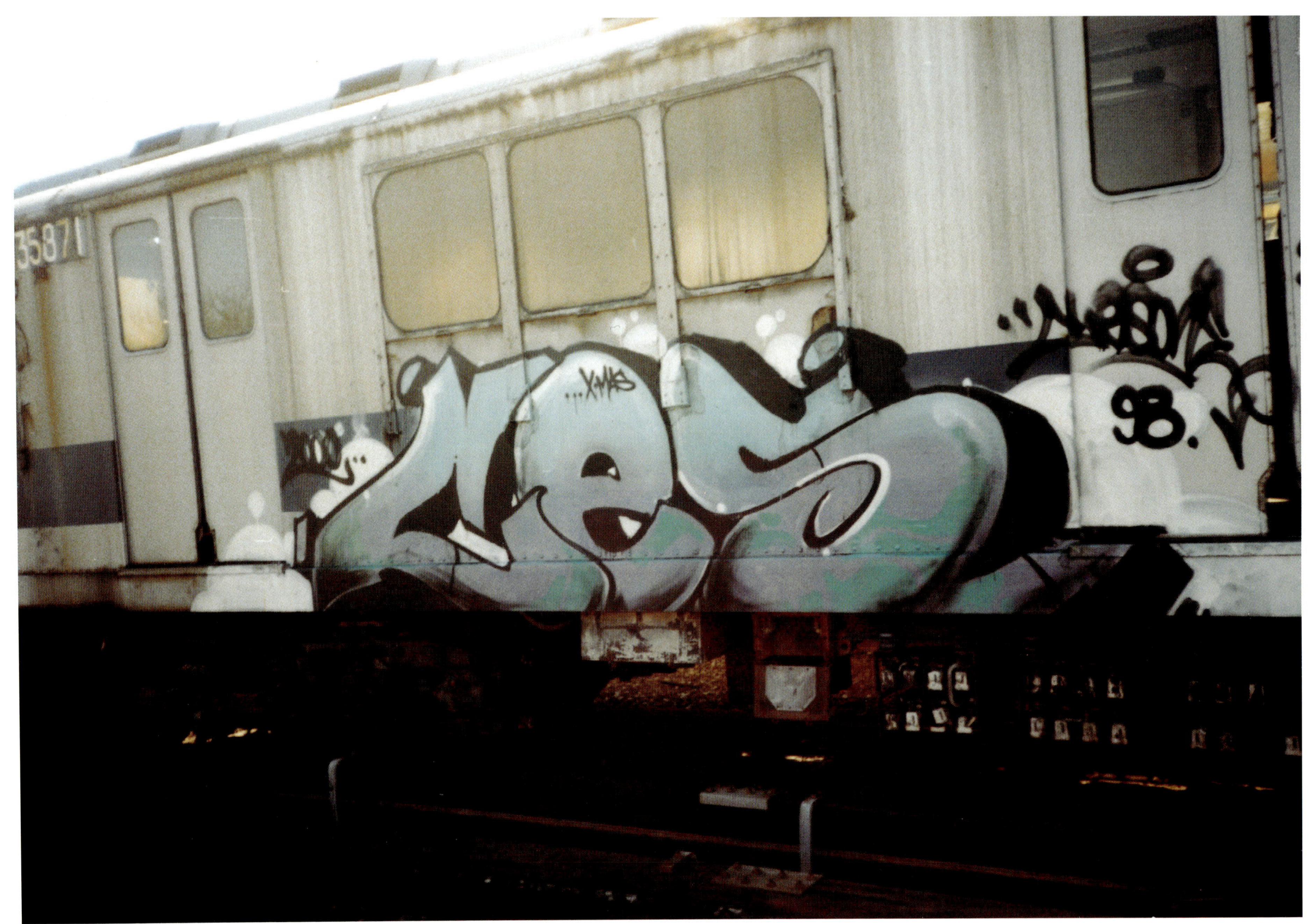

Ces

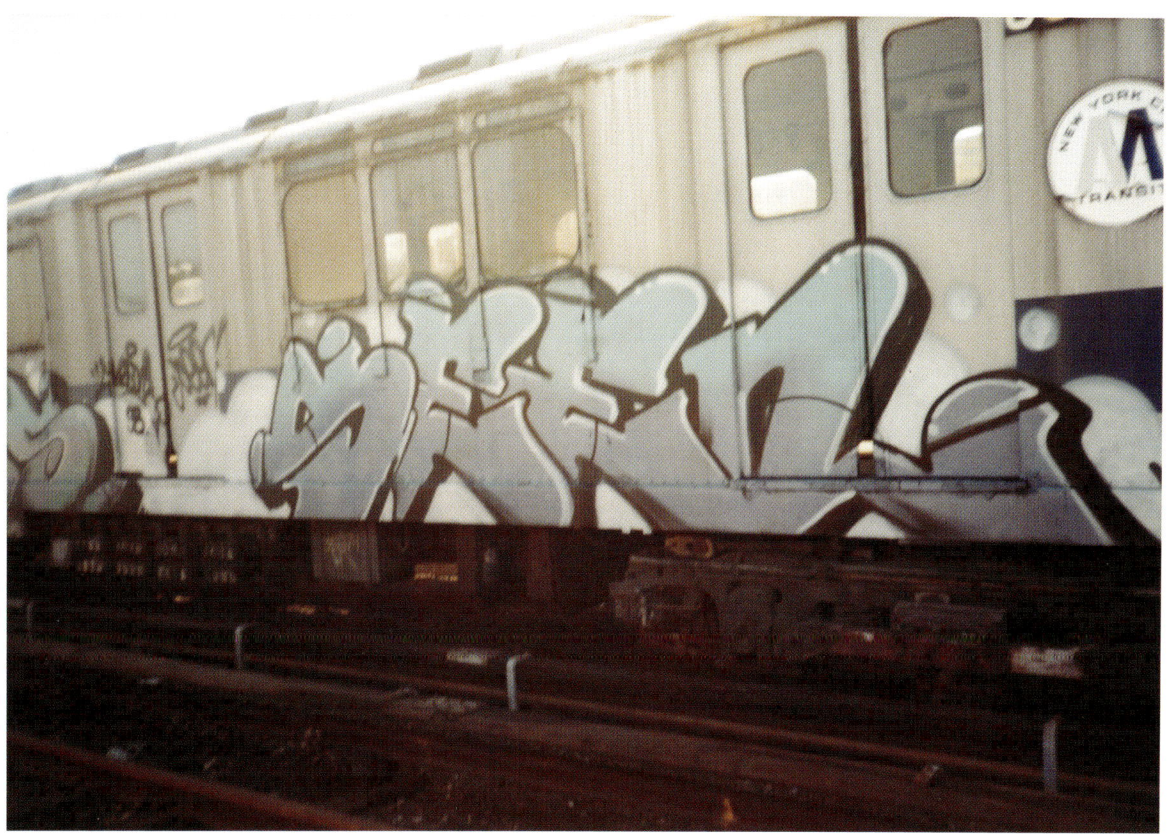

Seen (UA)

The front of the 6 yard had these two old blue -striped cars sitting there for as long as I could remember. I believe it was either Christmas day in 1998 or the day after Christmas when I drove by the 6 yard and couldn't believe my eyes. Seen and Ces had done pieces on one of the cars that were there. To see a Seen piece on a subway car in 1998 just blew my mind! I had to get into the yard to take pictures. I knew an area of the yard where I could pull the fence back and squeeze myself through. I went in, walked right up to the car and took pictures. As I finished taking them I noticed a few work bums in the same lane. They started yelling at me in the distance. I could see that one of them started talking into his walkie talkie. I left out of there the same way that I had entered. The car sat there for a while and just disappeared one day.

—Mone

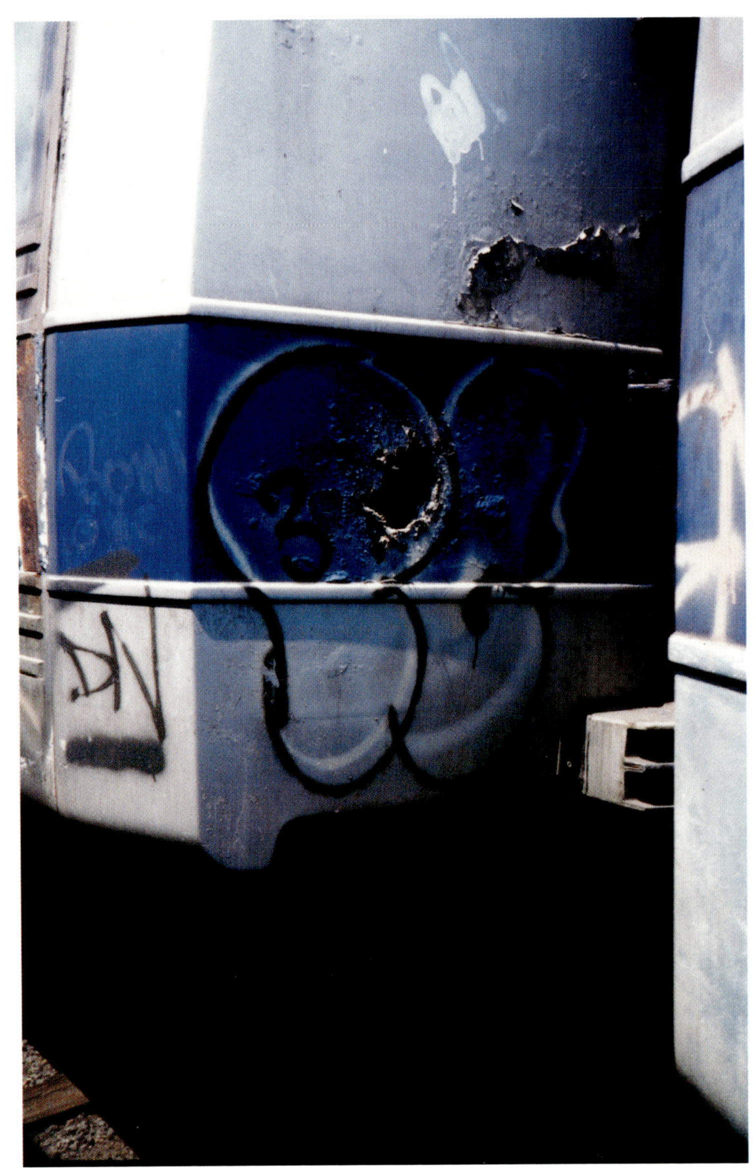

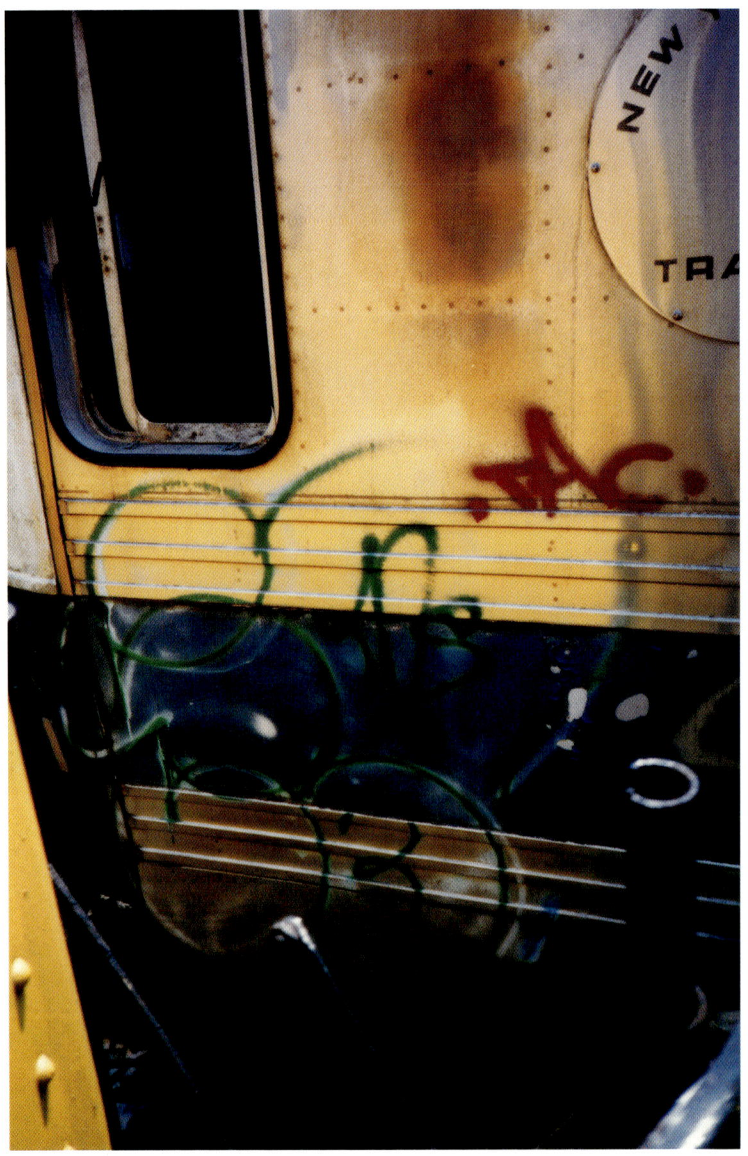

"The Ghost Yard," Left, PG3 (TPA); right, EL3 (TNS) [R.I.P.]

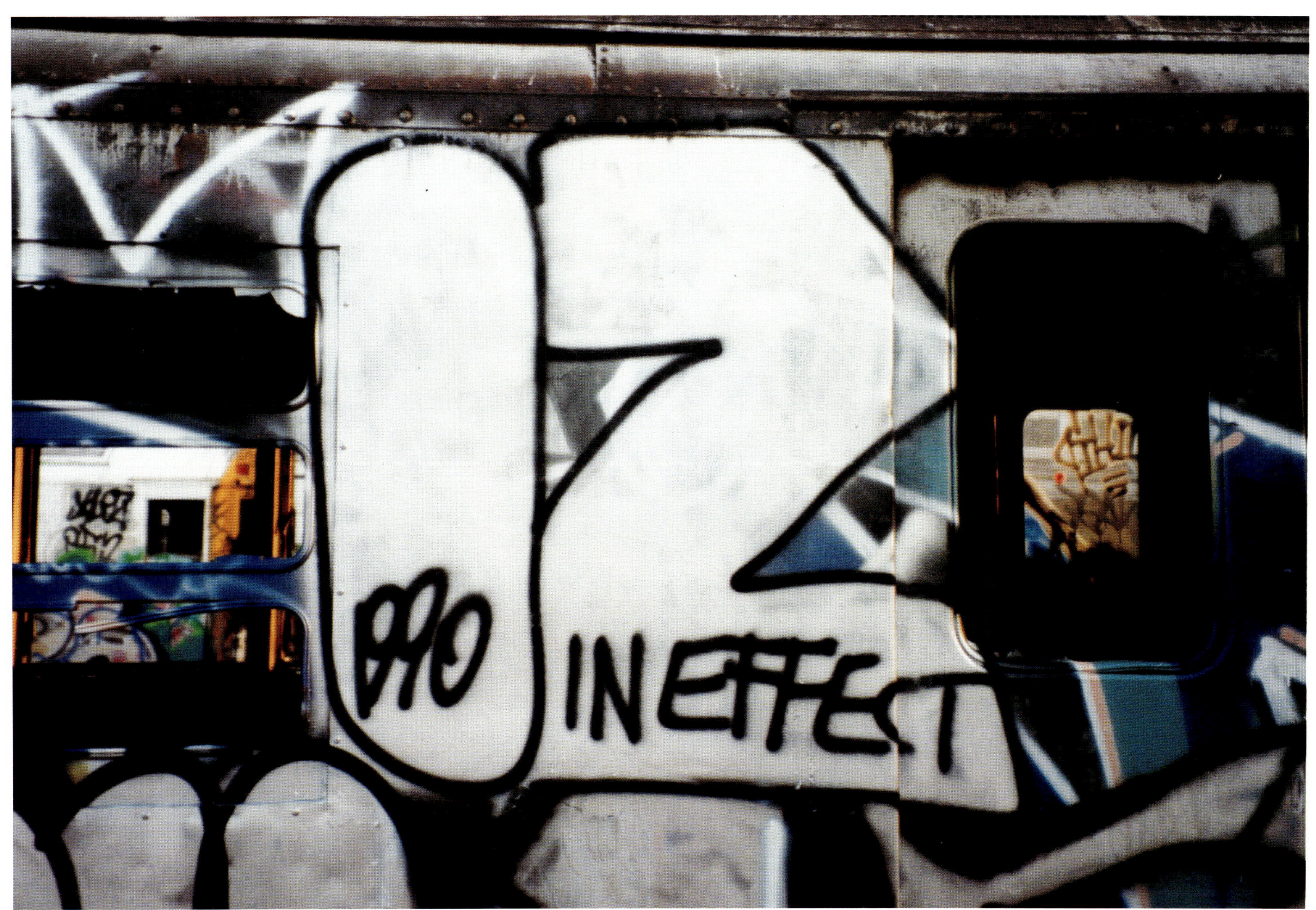

Iz the Wiz (TMB)

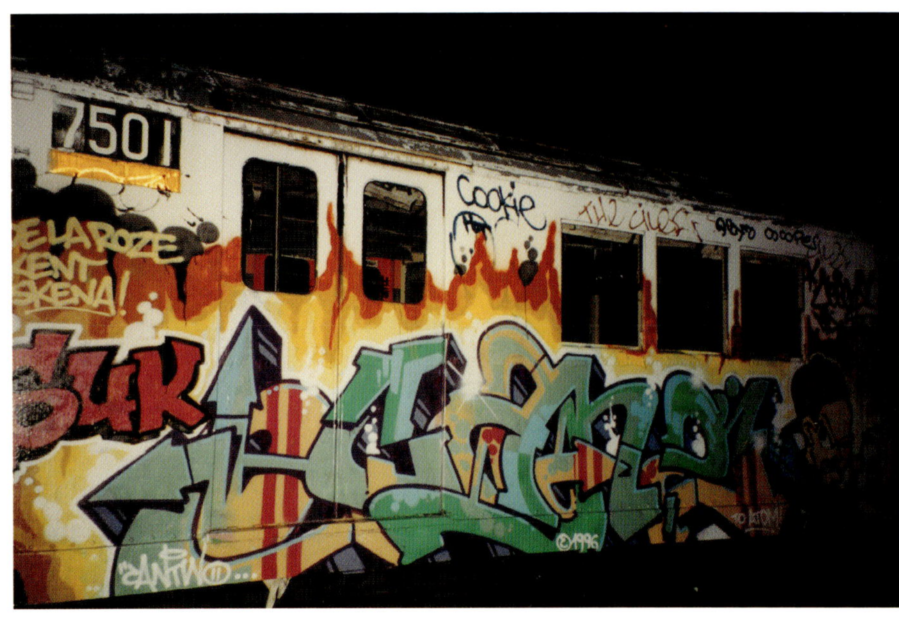

Can 2

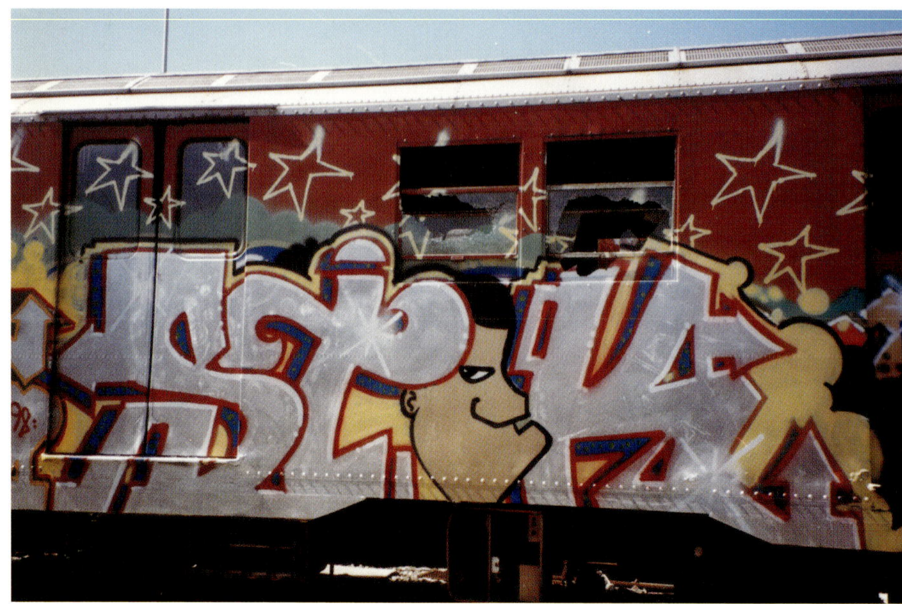

Stak (TFP)

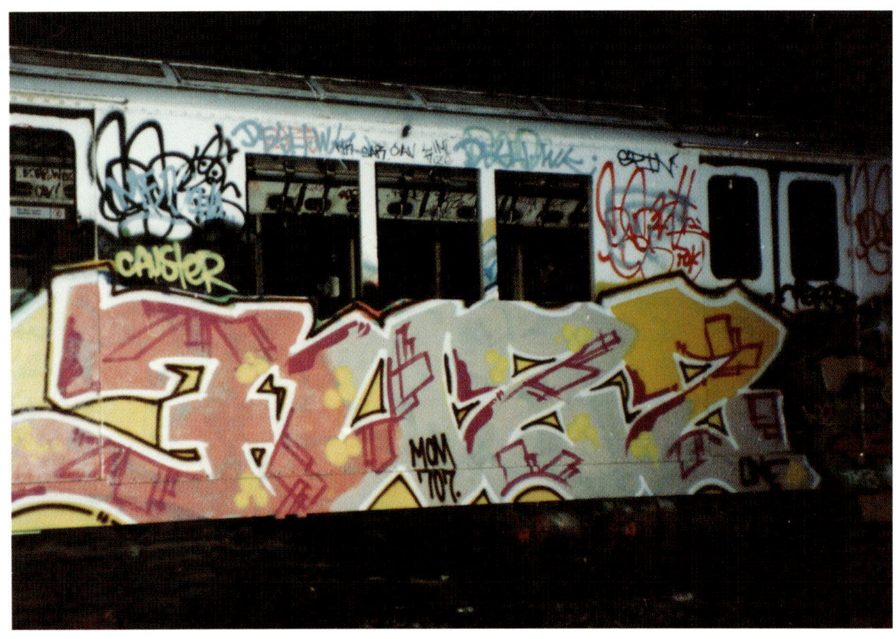

Fuzz

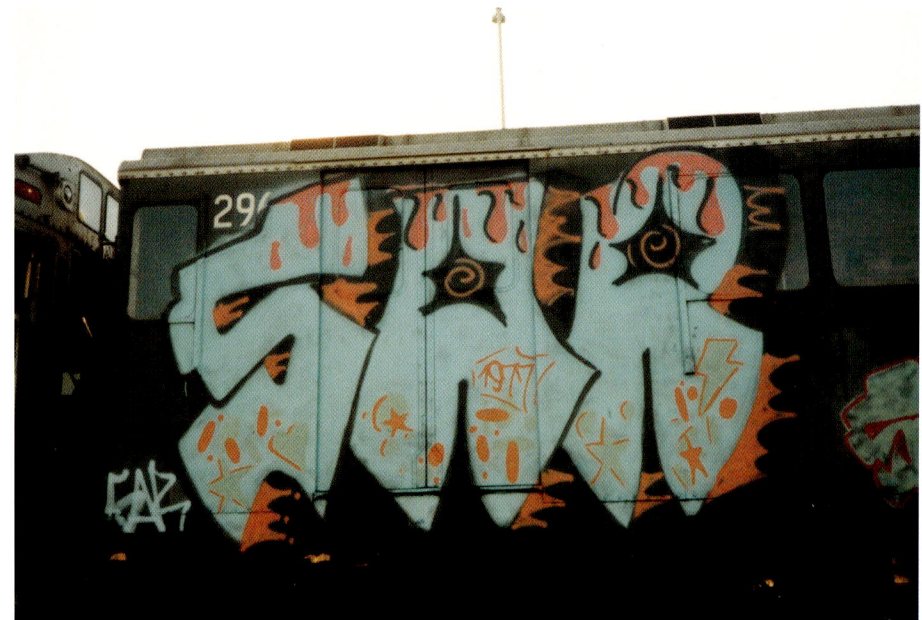

Sar (TMB)

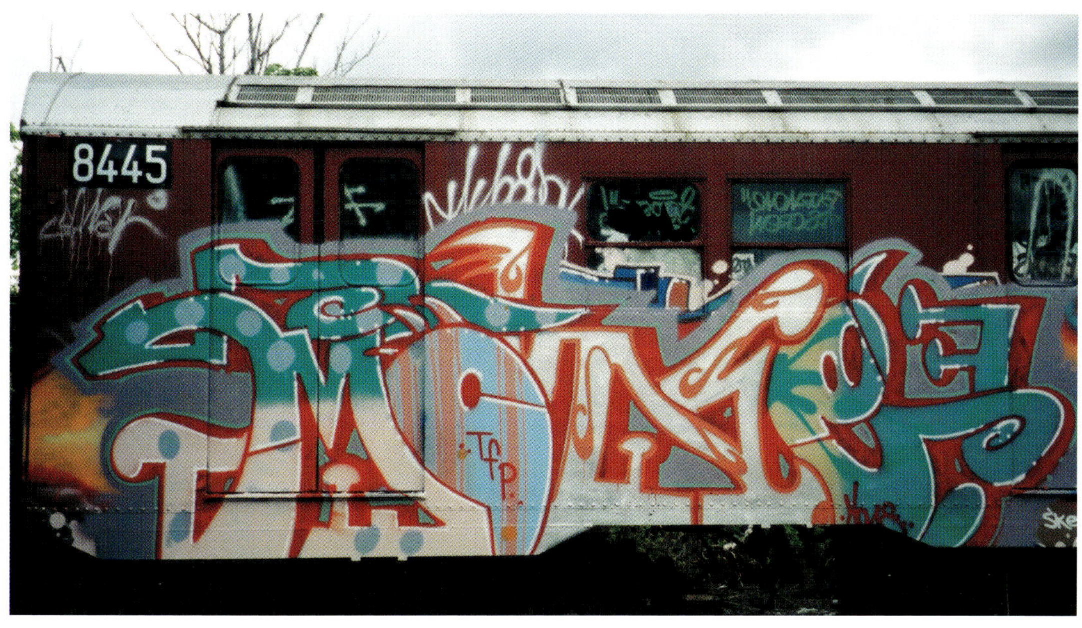

Mone (RIS)

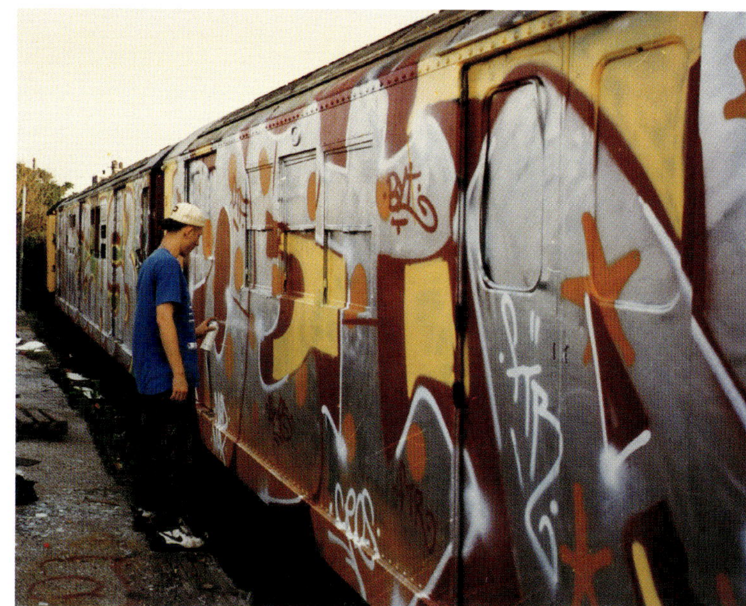

Poet (CWK)

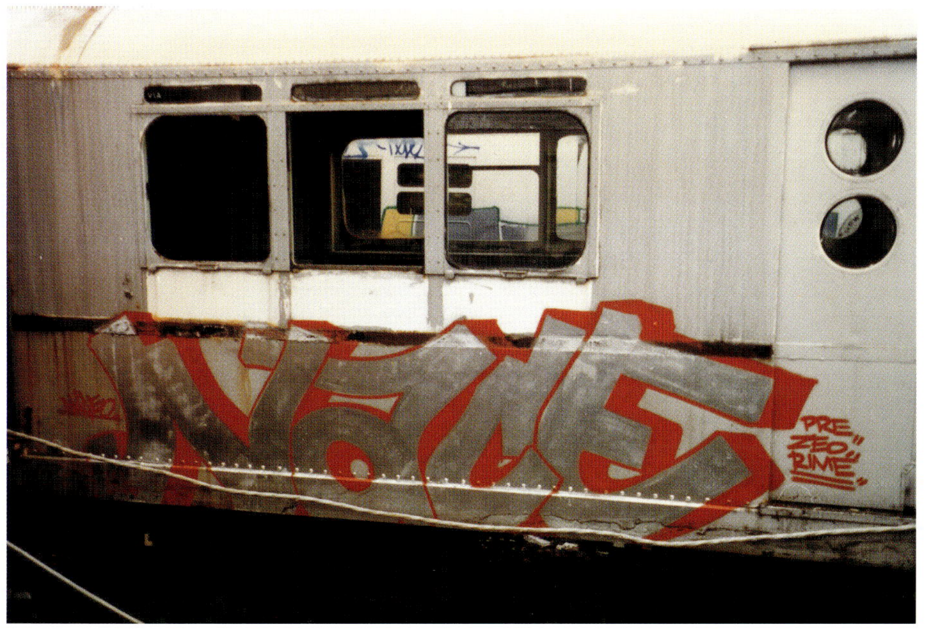

Nace [R.I.P]

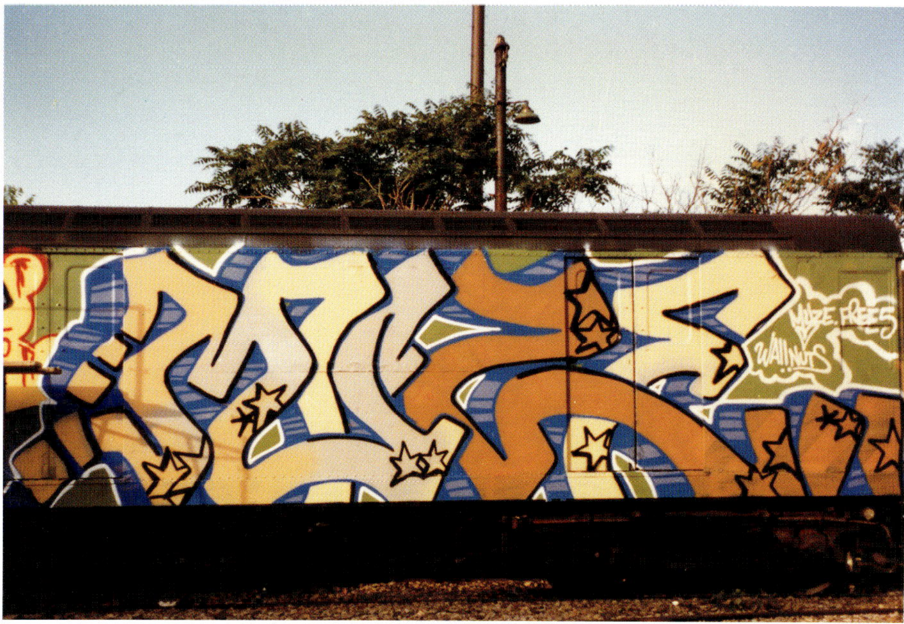

Muze

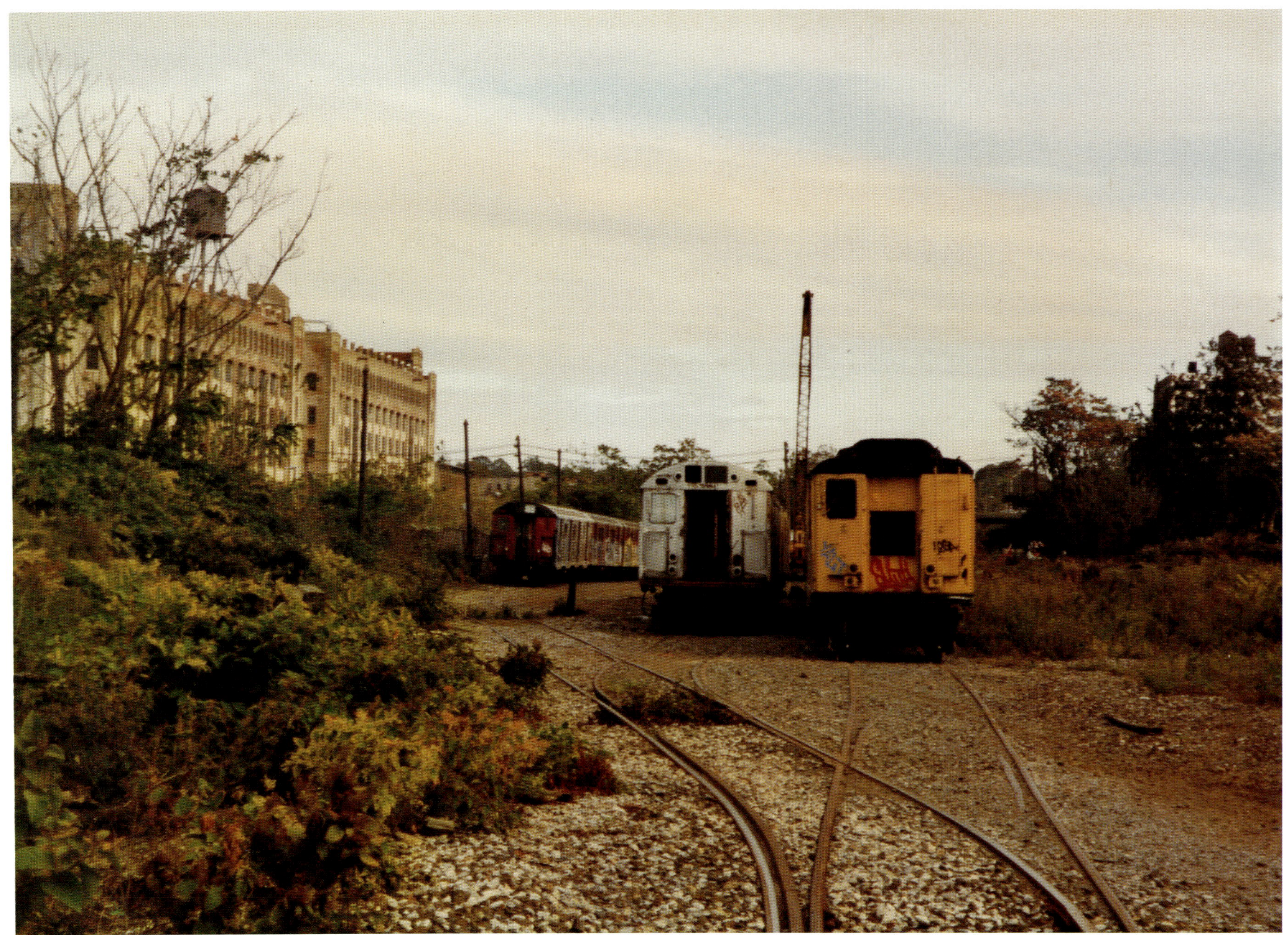

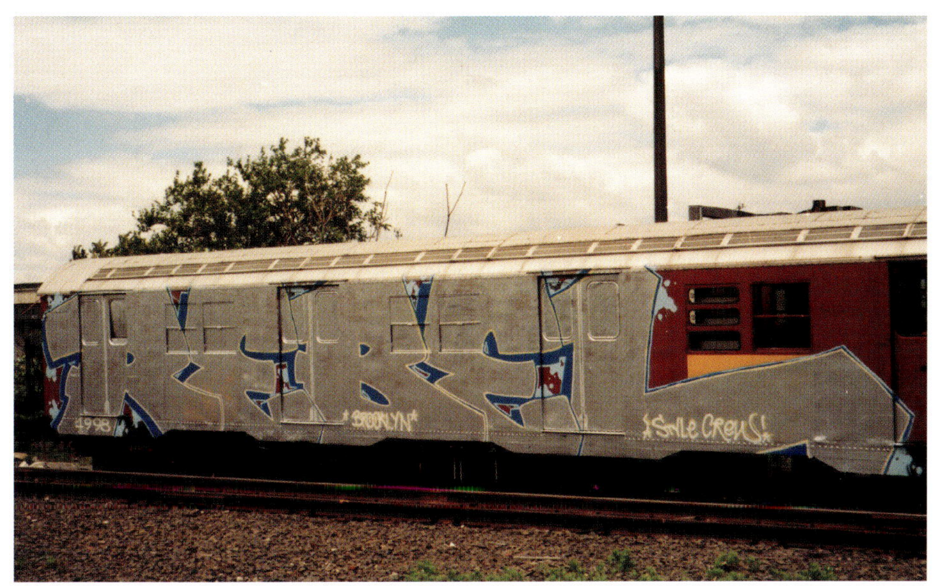

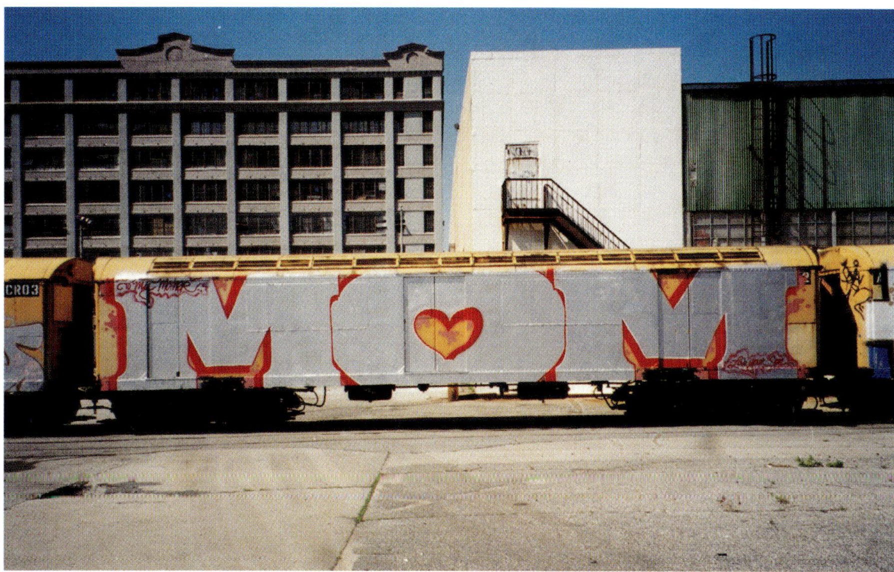

Rebel

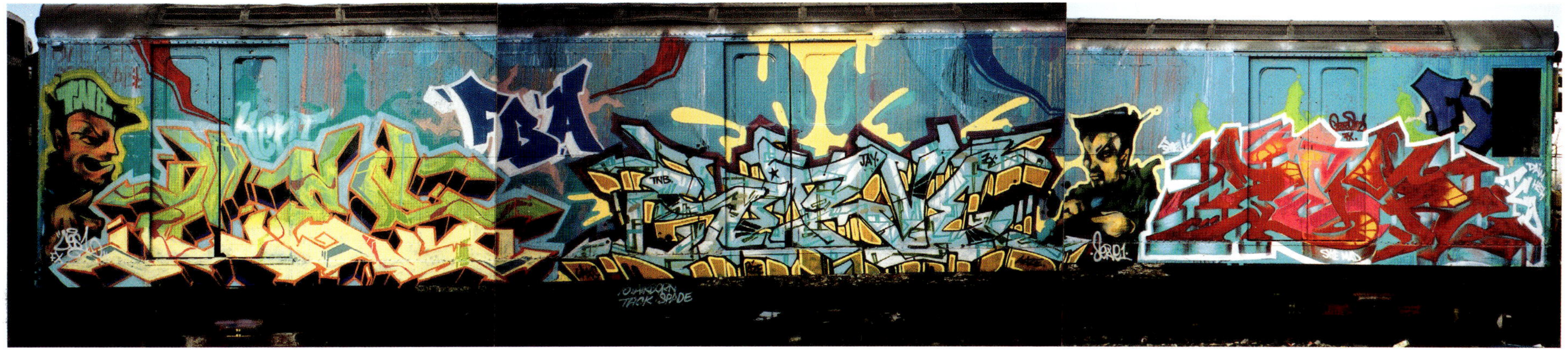

Ces, Serve, & Per

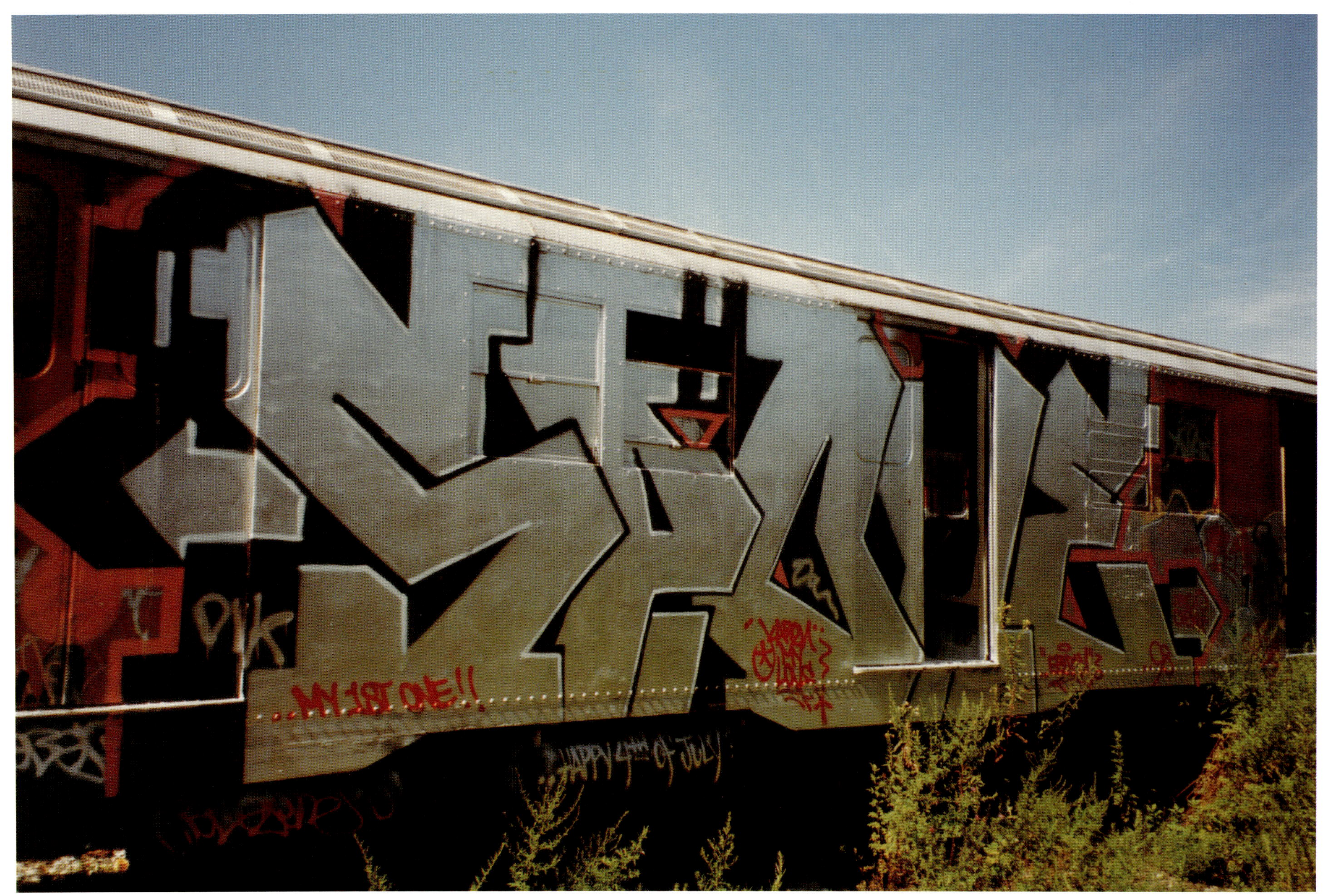

SP-one

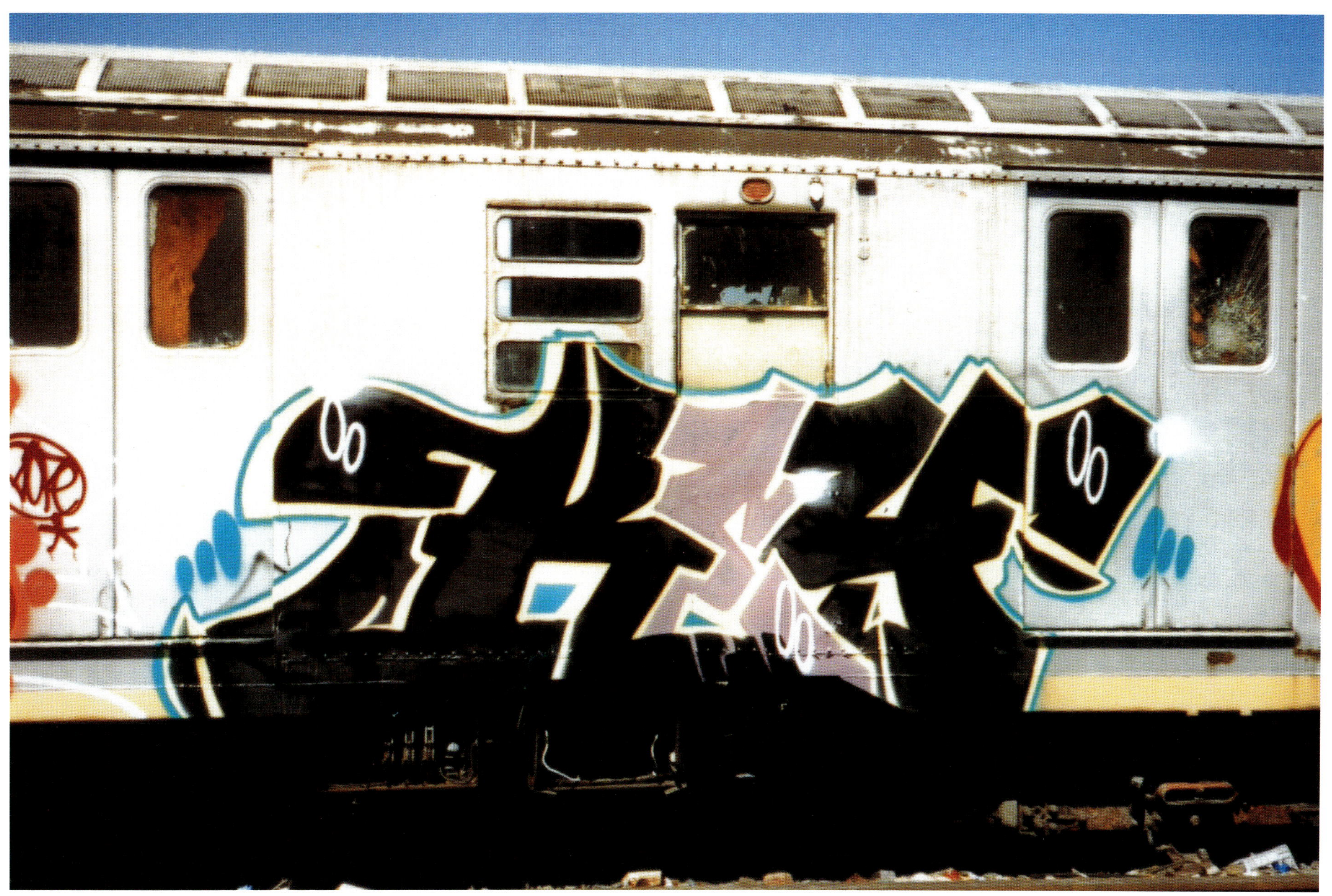

Key

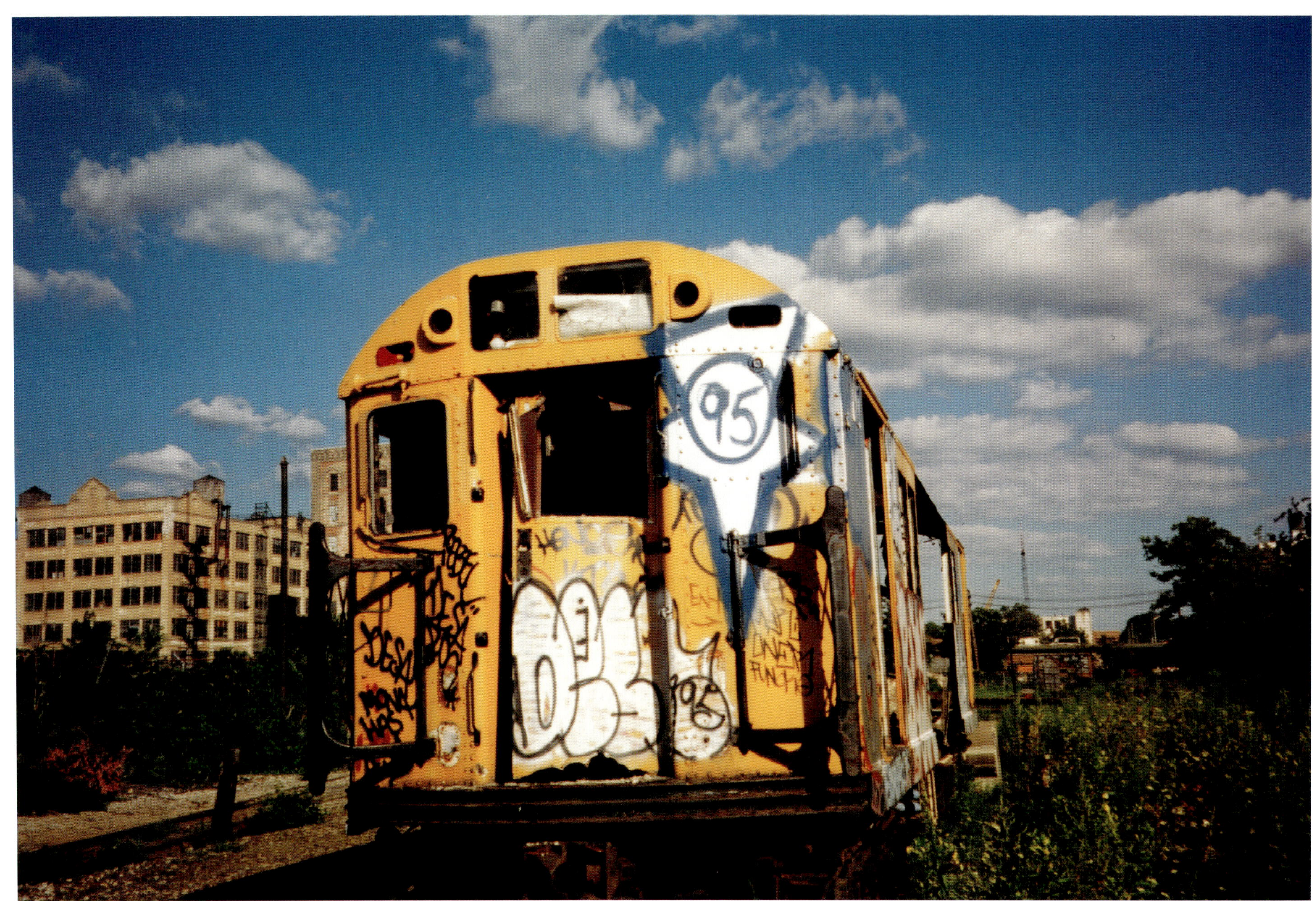
95

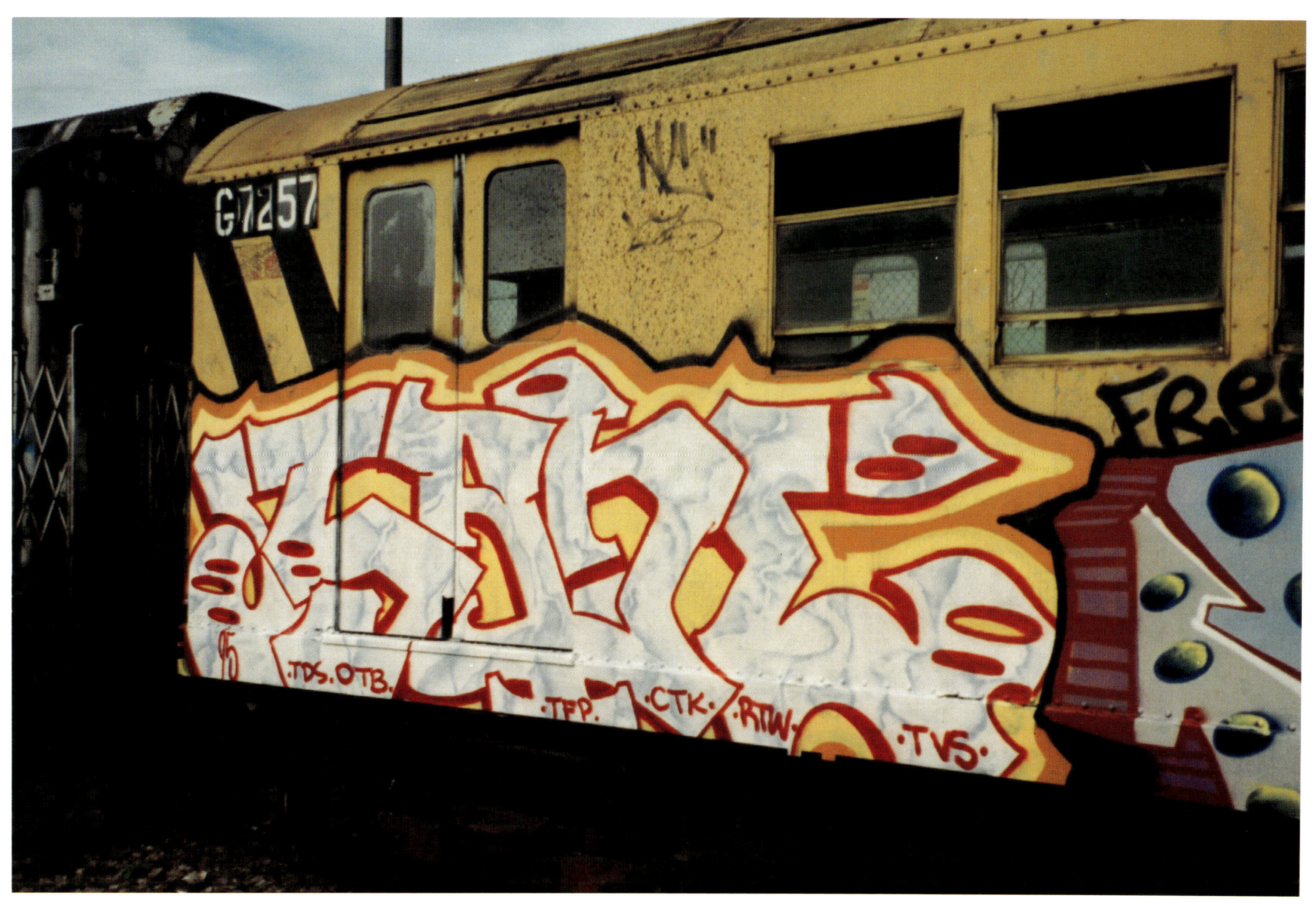

"Sane" by Smith

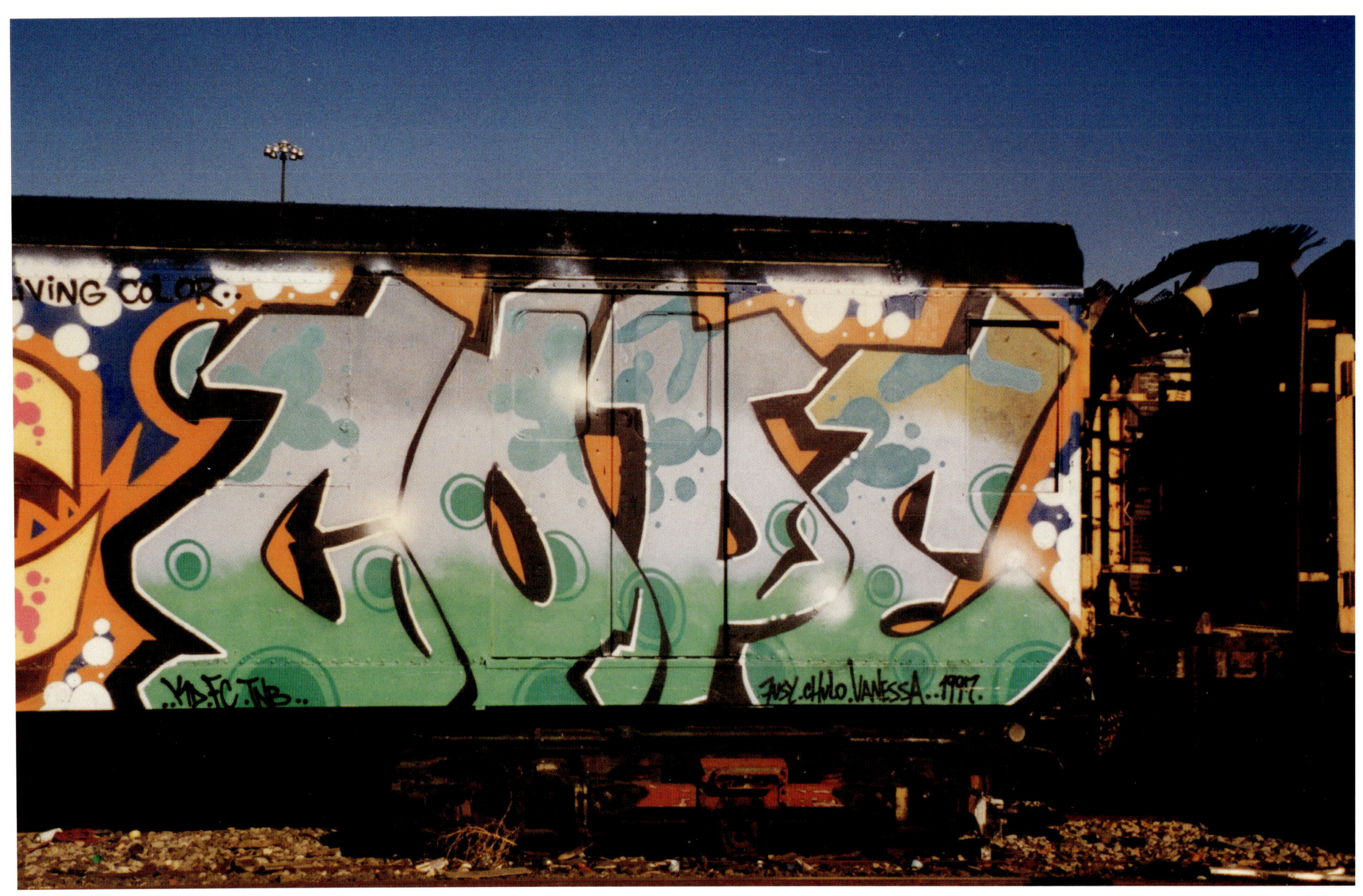

Cope II (KD)

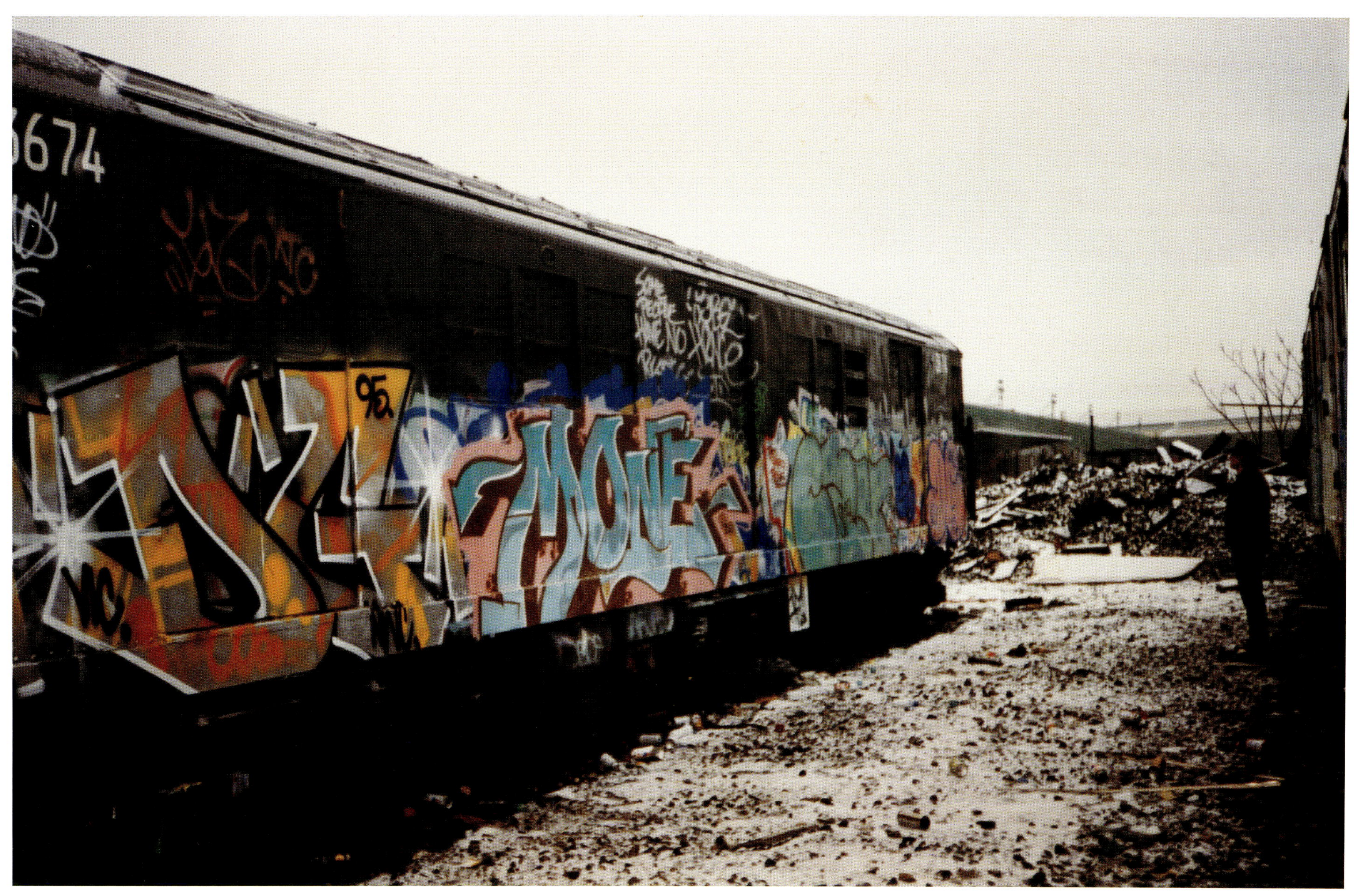

DG (NWC) & Mone (RIS)

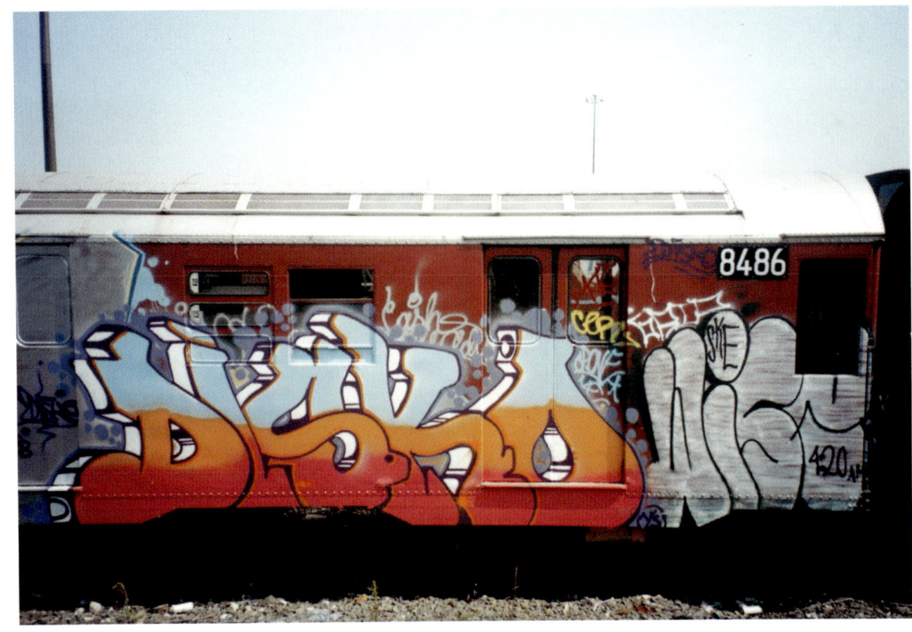

Disko (C&F)

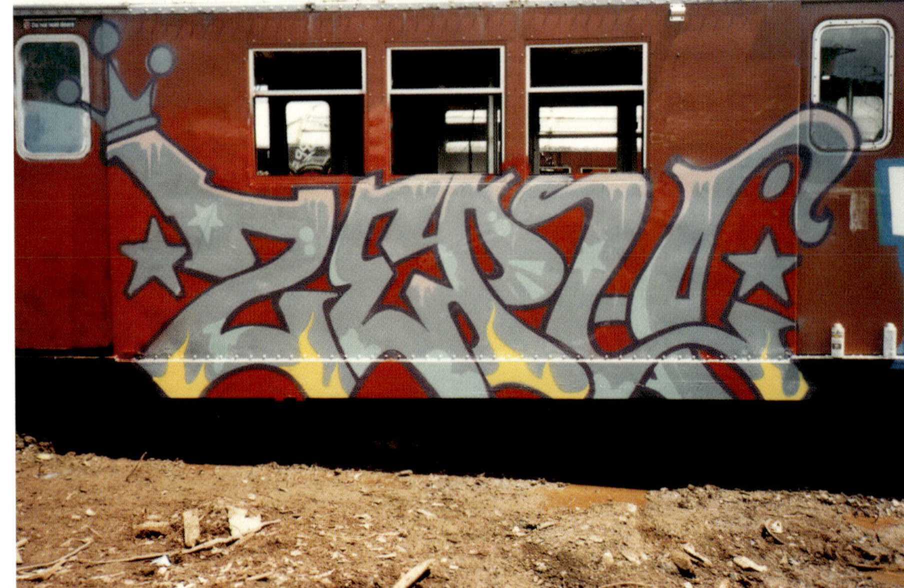

"Zeph" by Zephyr

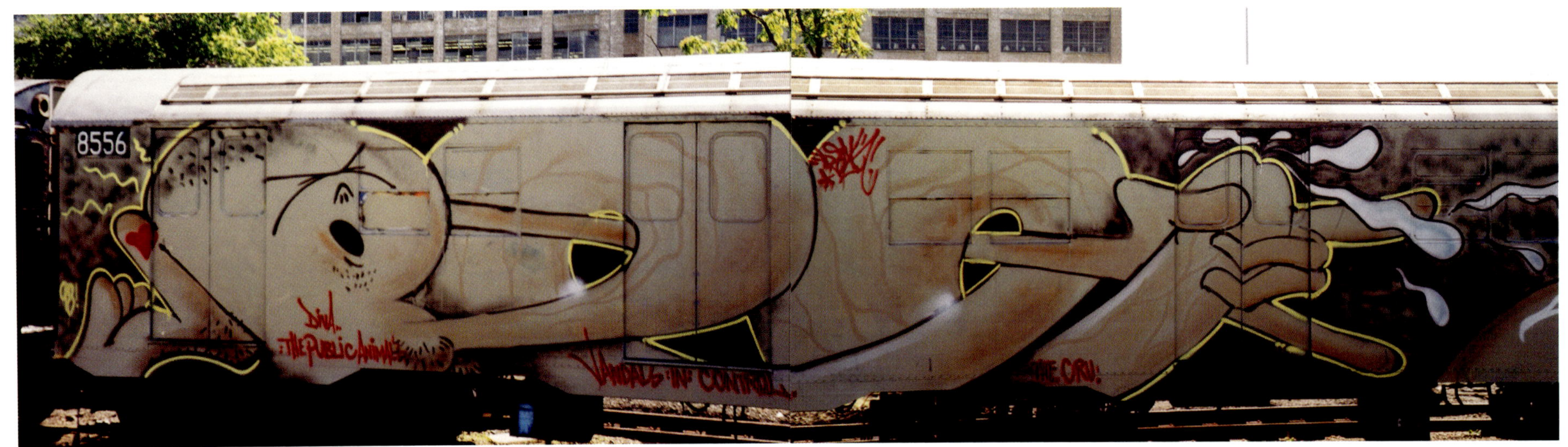

Peek (VIC)

I went to the scrap many times for the old trains. When "new" cars were brought there it was always a surprise to see if they were IRT's, BMT's, work cars, Red Birds, or White Elephants. Sometimes the cars were clean and sometimes they had bombed insides untouched since the mid-1980s. Going to the scrap yard was like traveling through time.

—Hence (C&F)

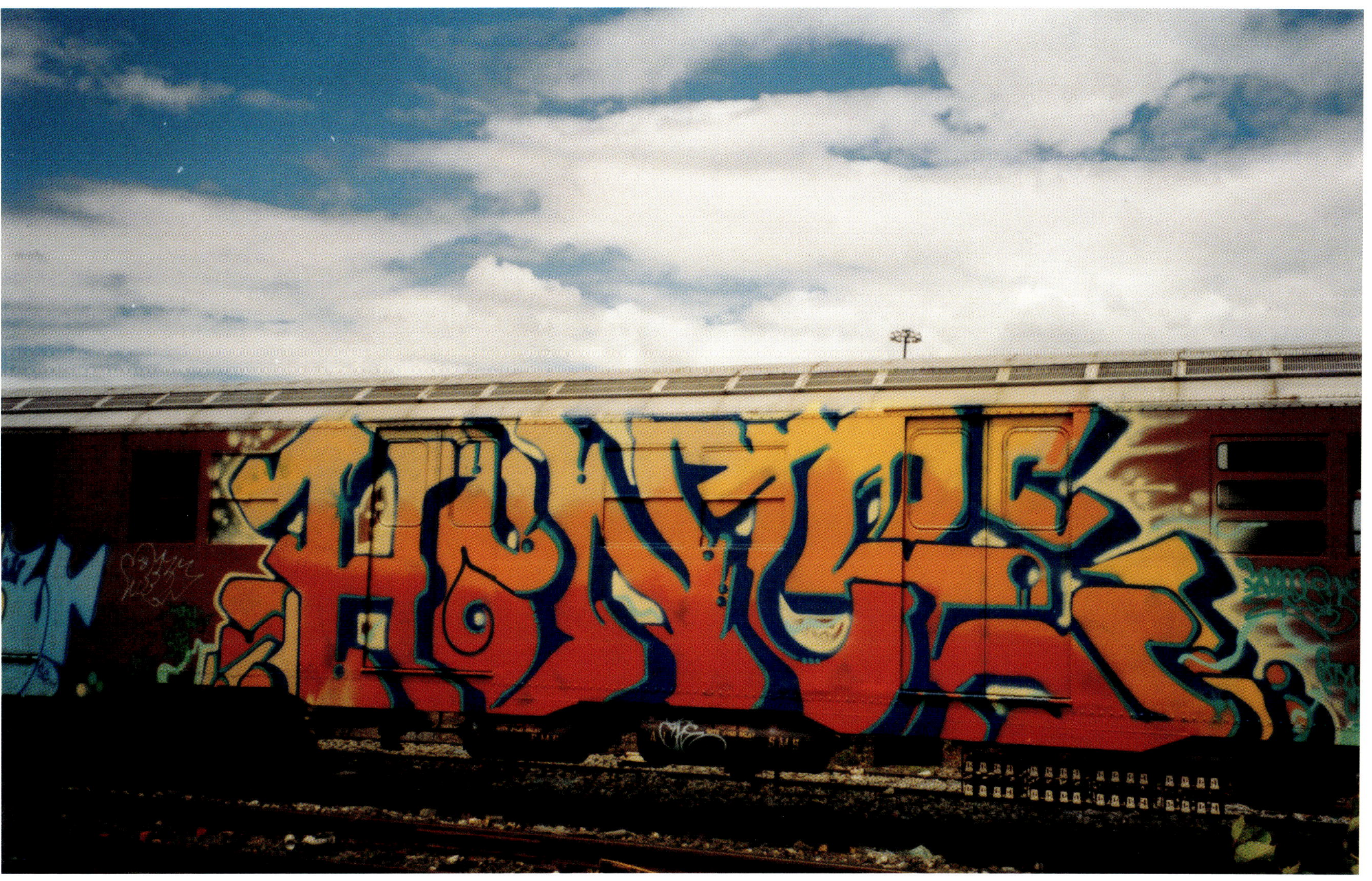

Hence (C&F)

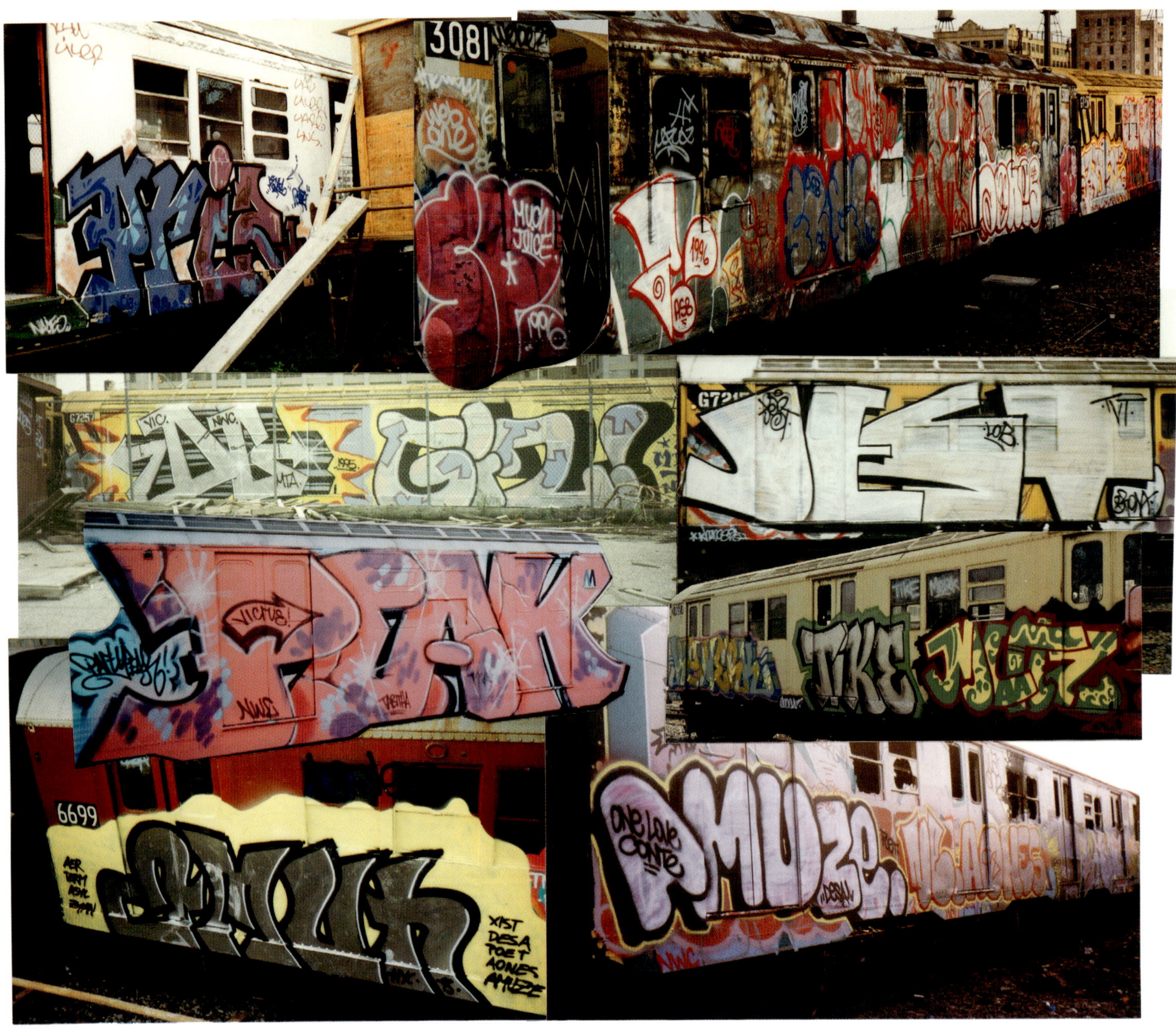
3081
MUCH JUICE
1996
6699
XIST
DESA
POET
AONES
AMUZE
ONE LOVE CONTE
TIKE

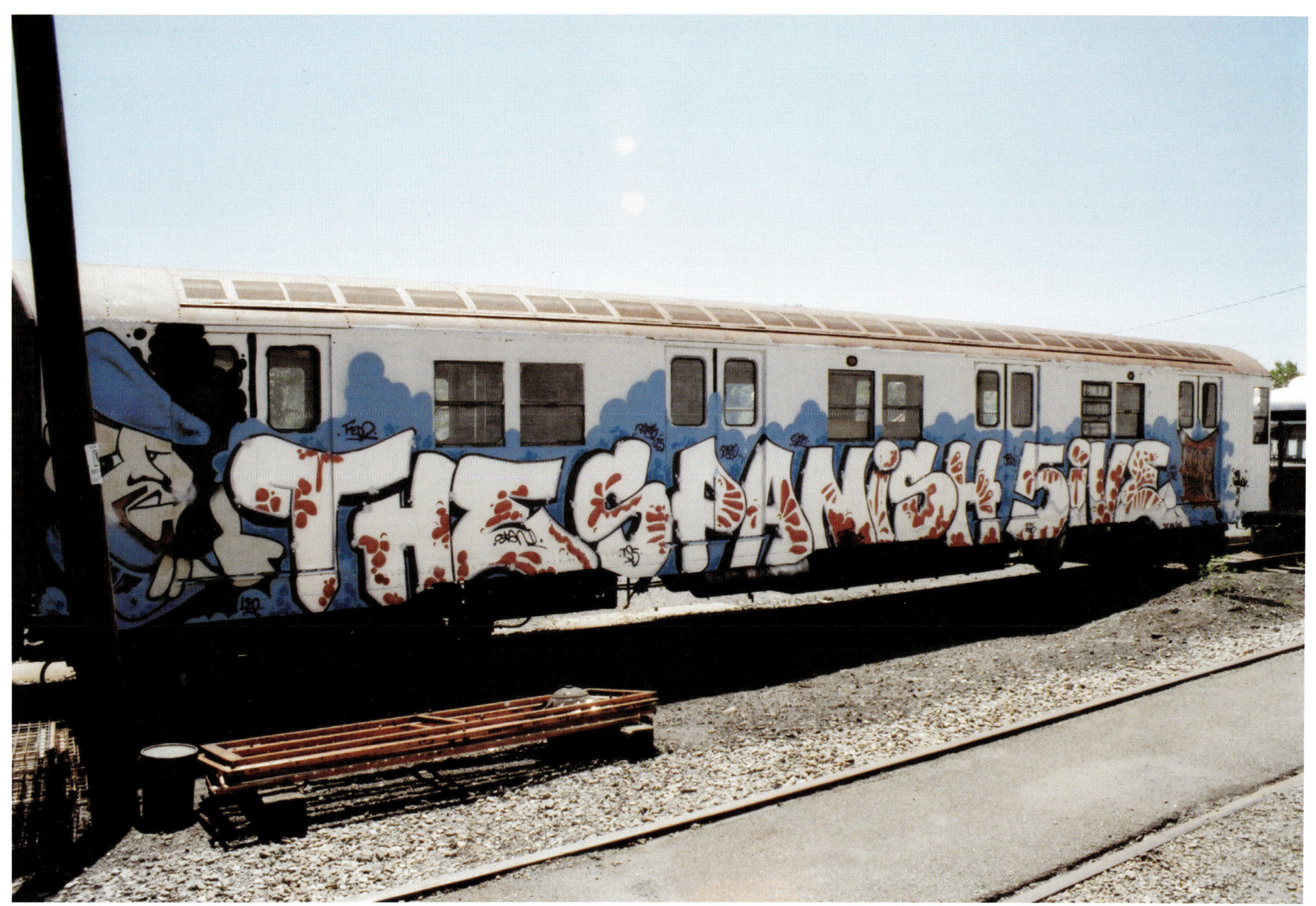

"The Spanish Five" by Stan & Priz

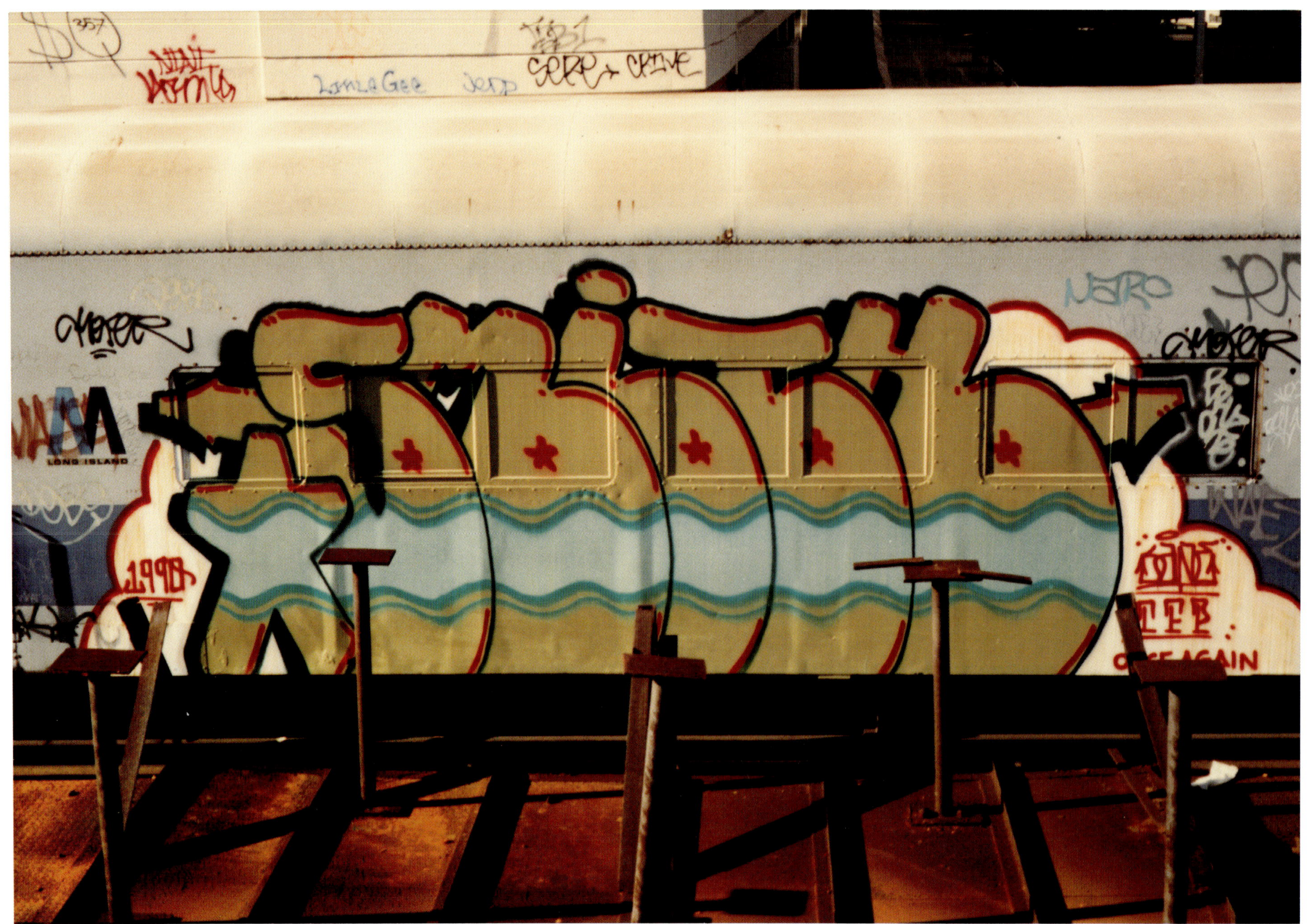

Smith

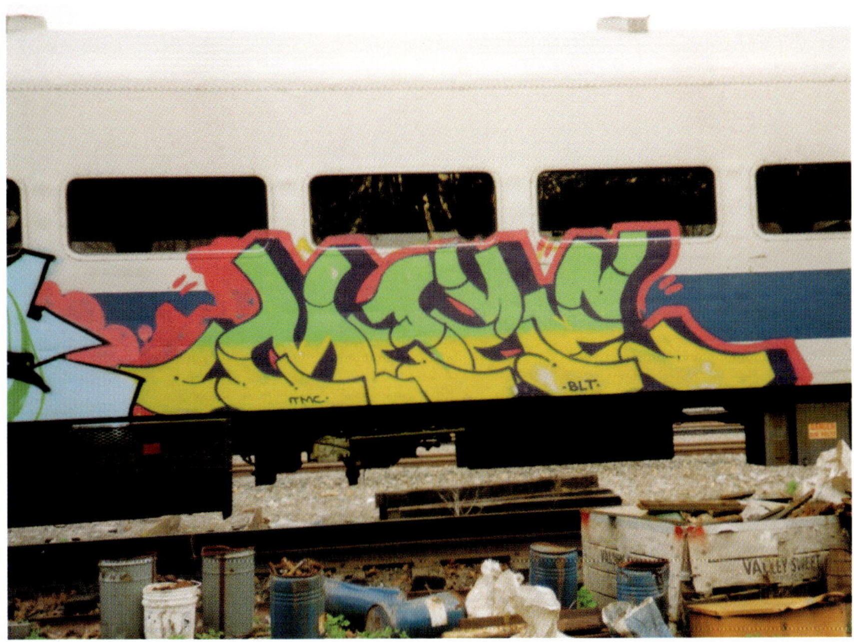

Maze (TMC)

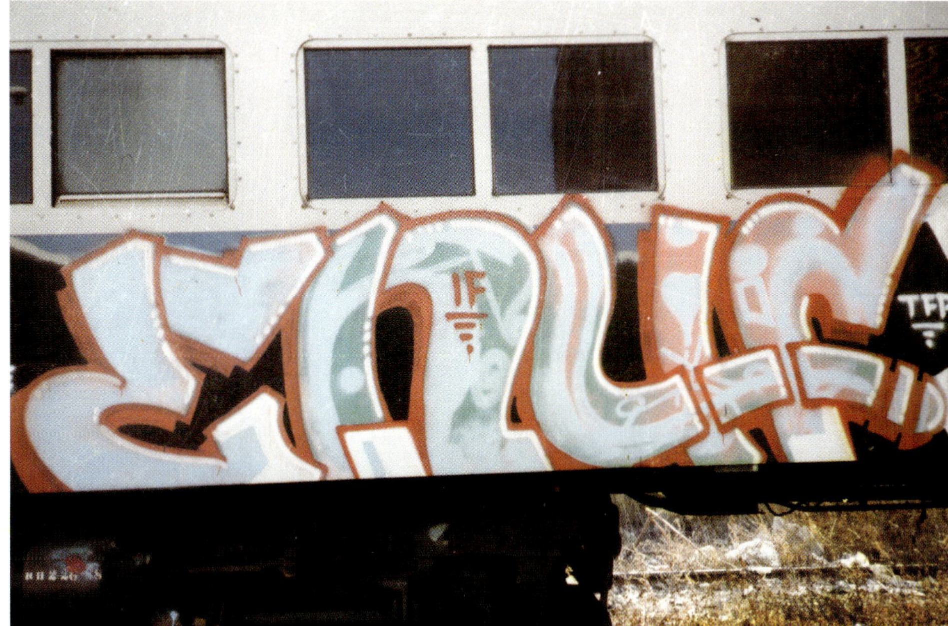

Enuf

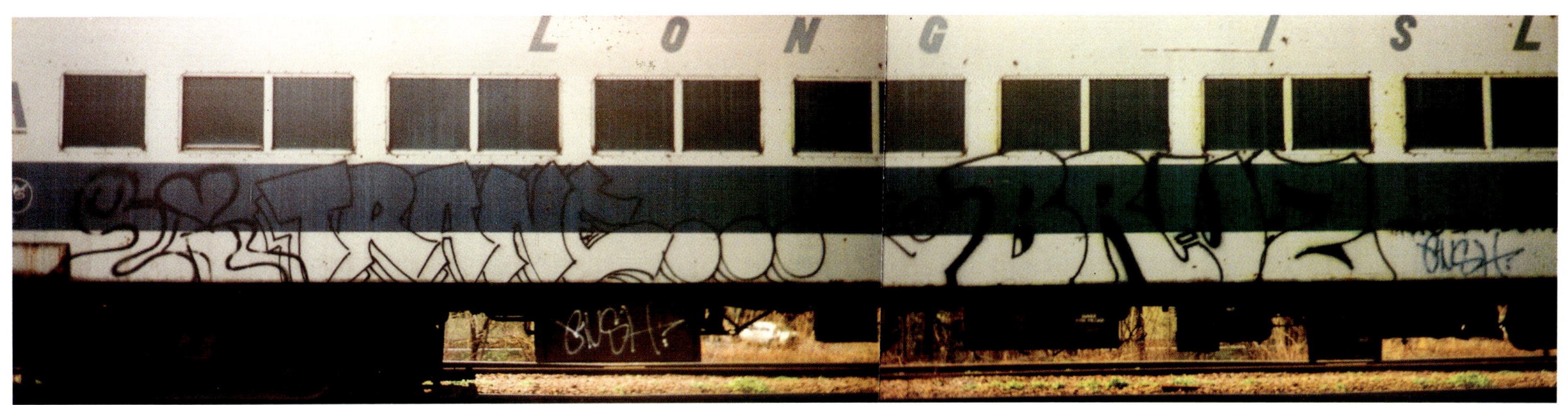

Trane & Bruz

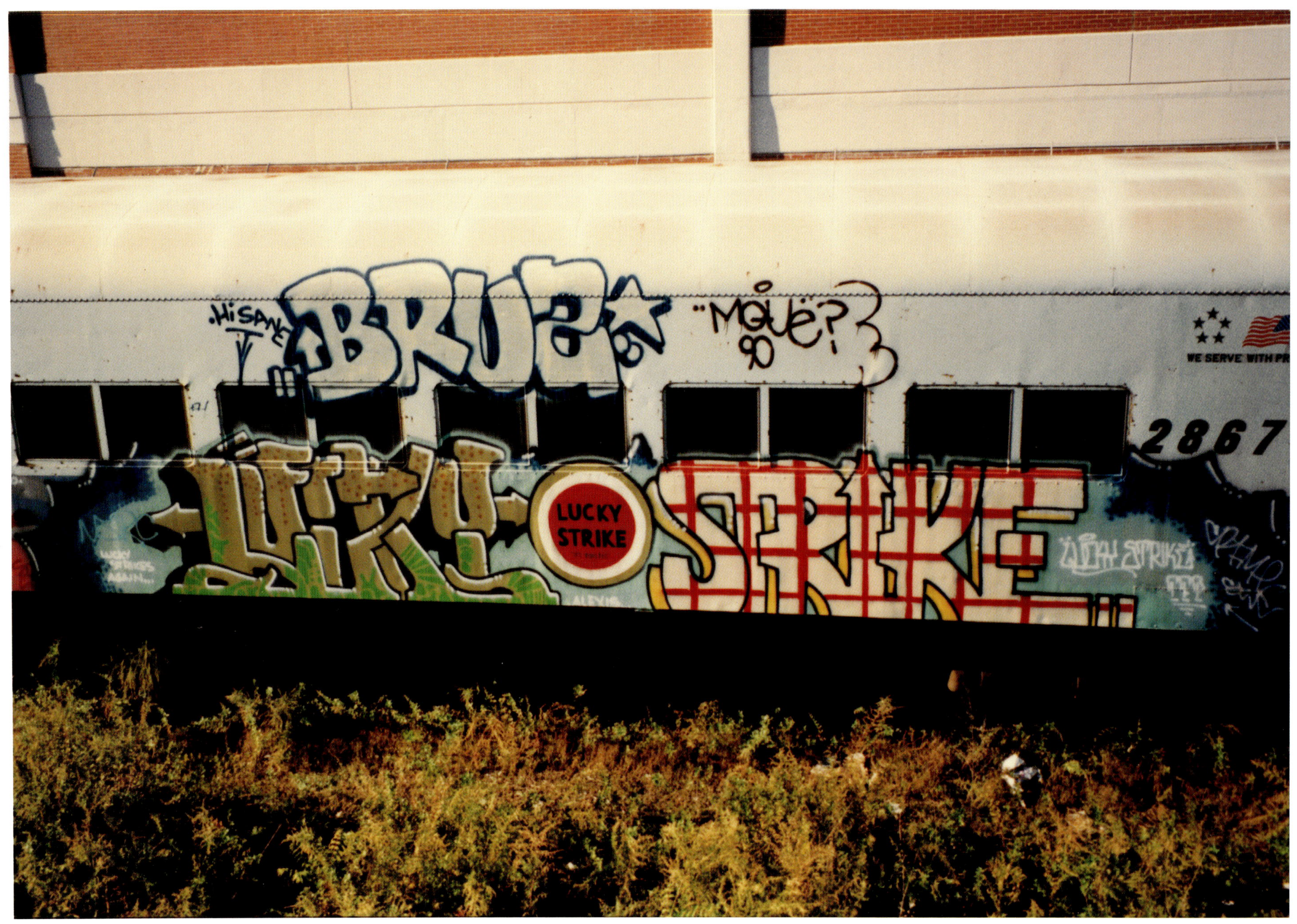

"Lucky Strike" by Smith & Sane

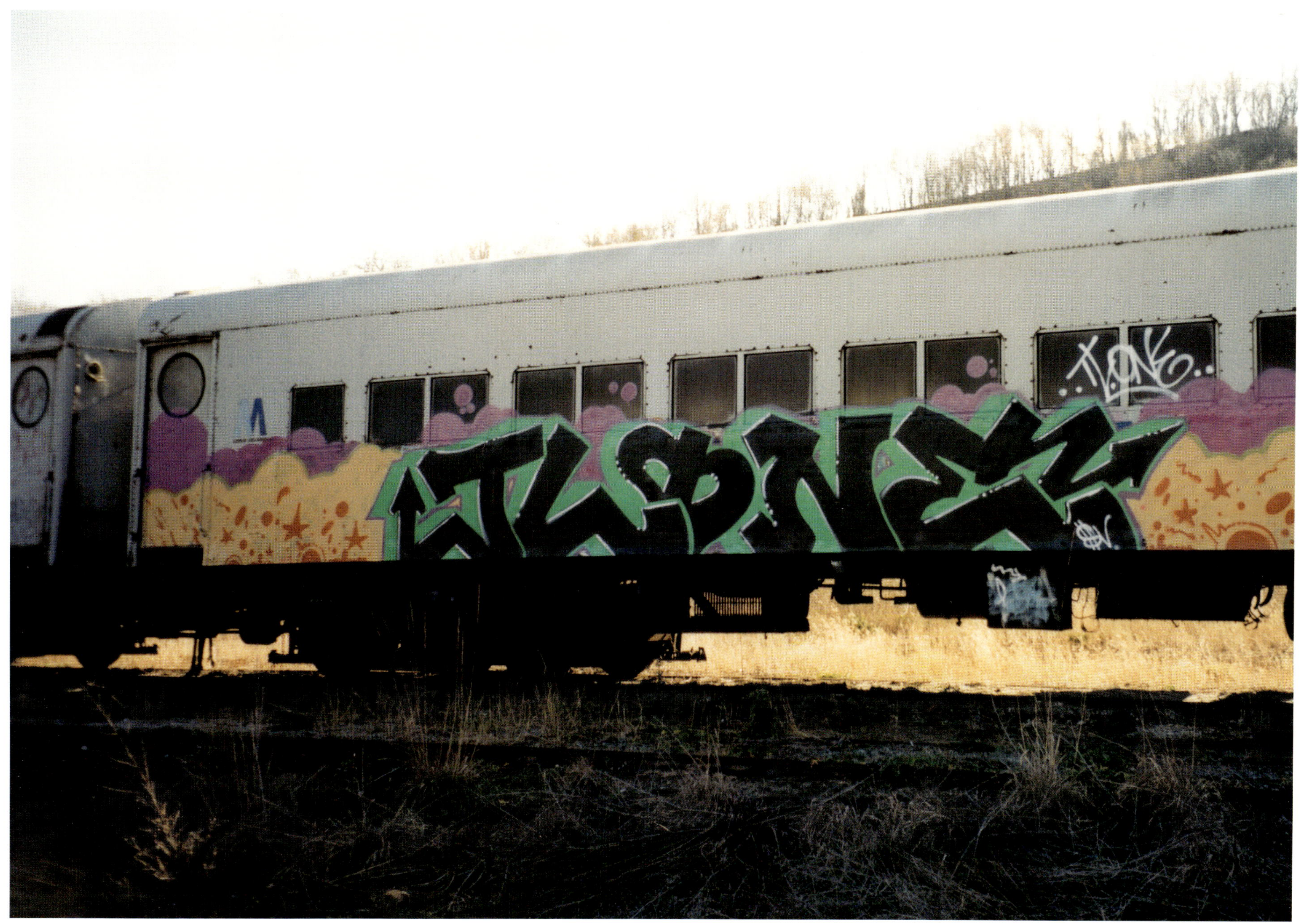

TL-one

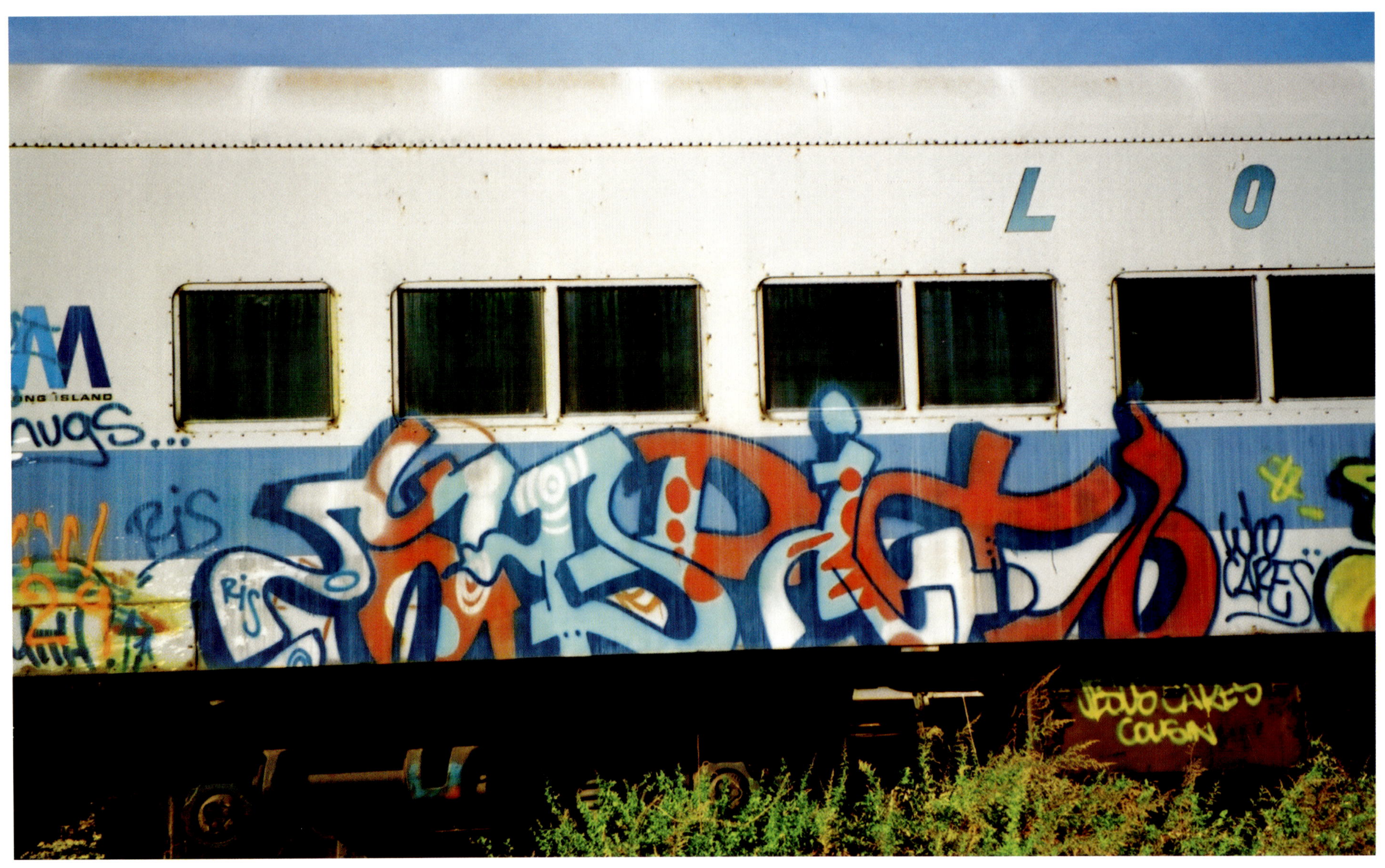

"Addict" by Ghost

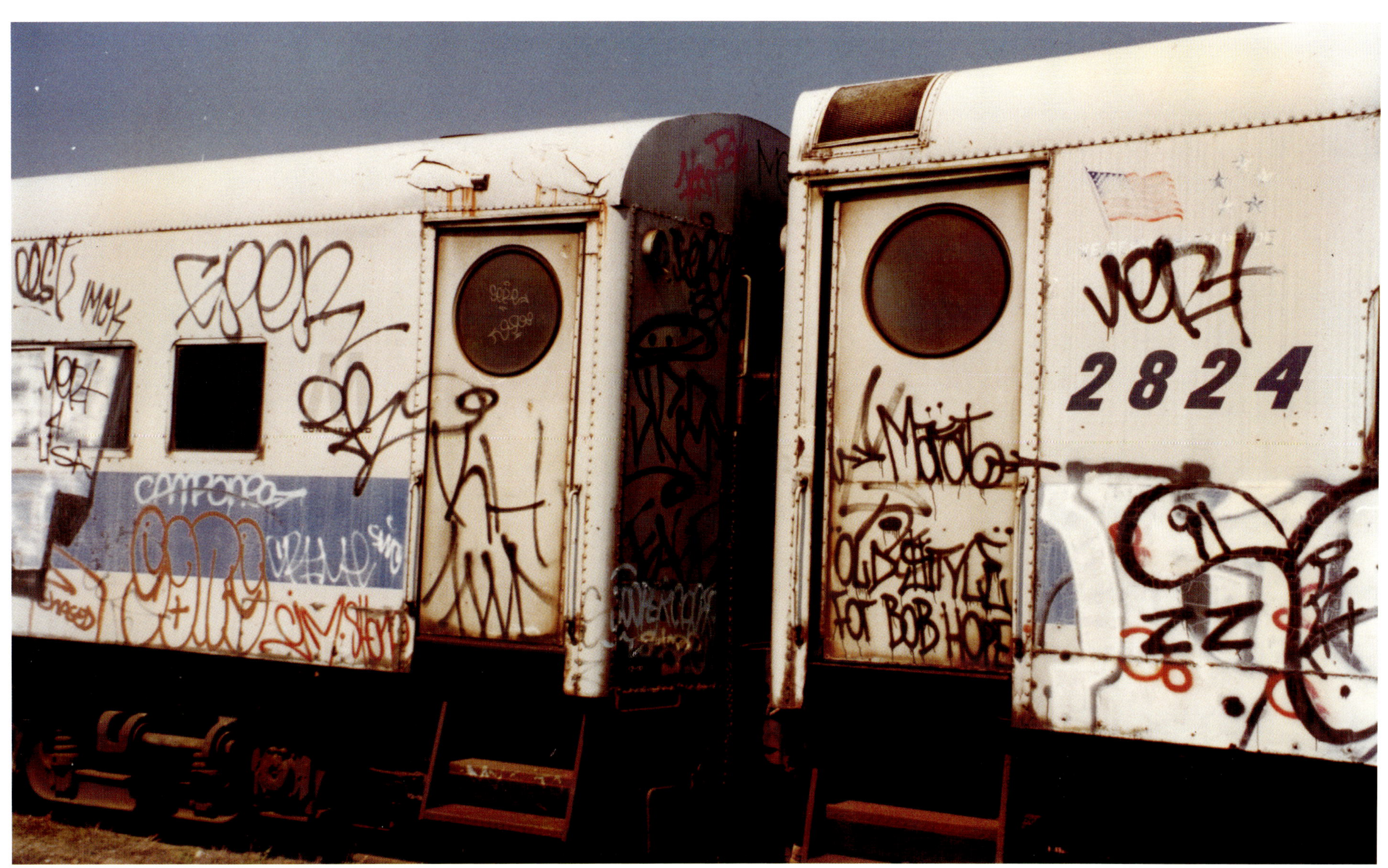
2824

Characters

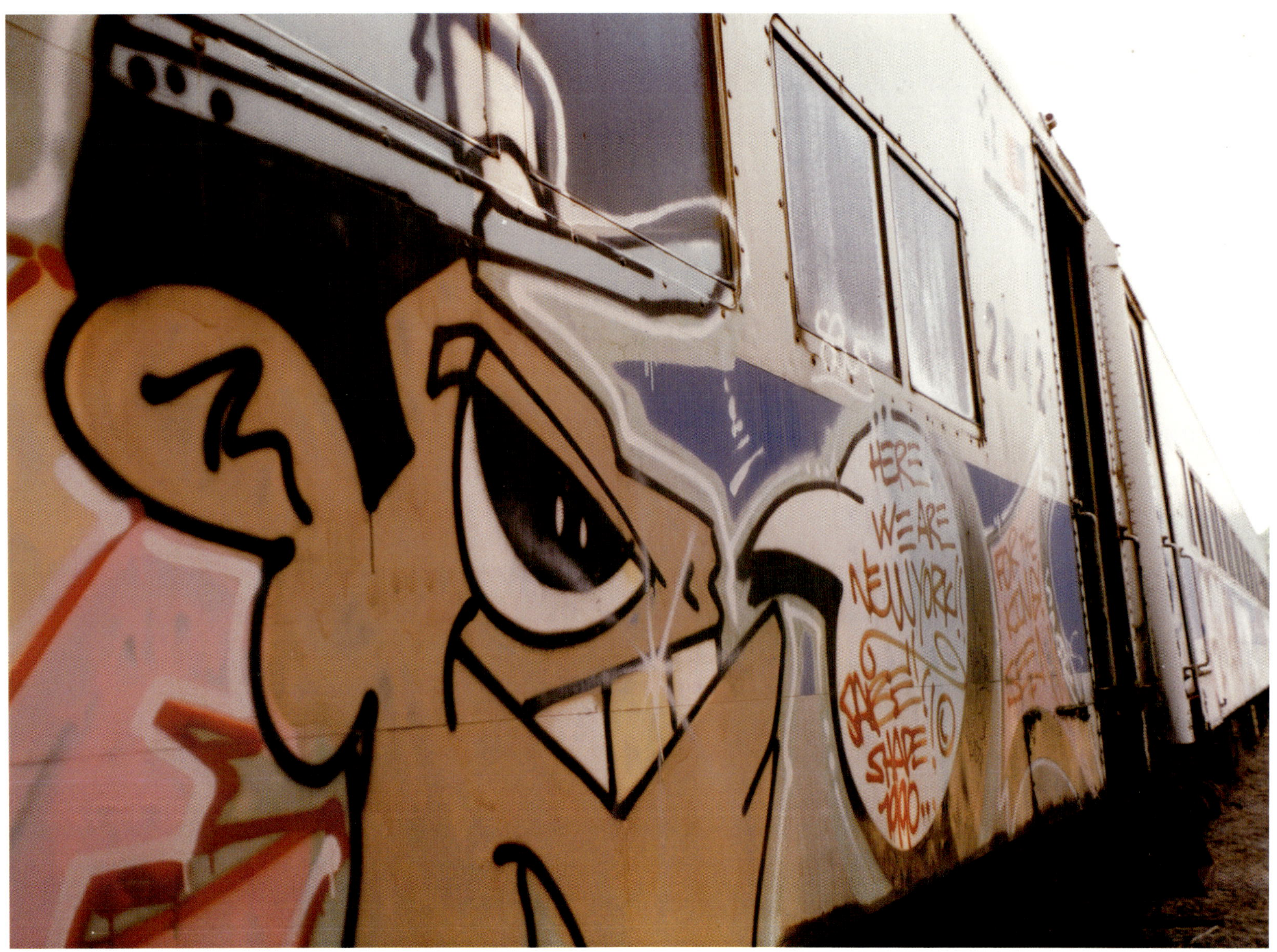

Sabe

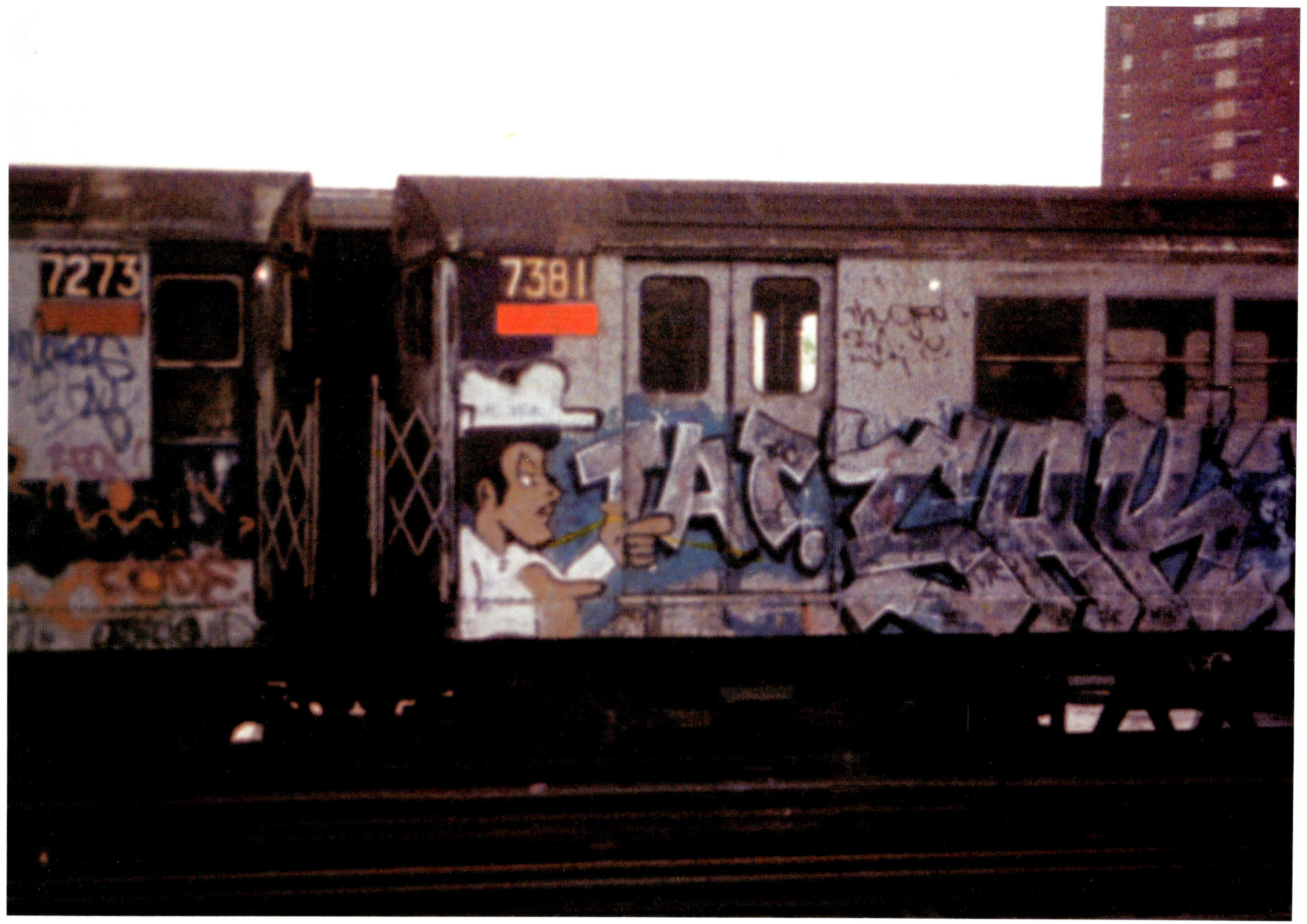

Sak

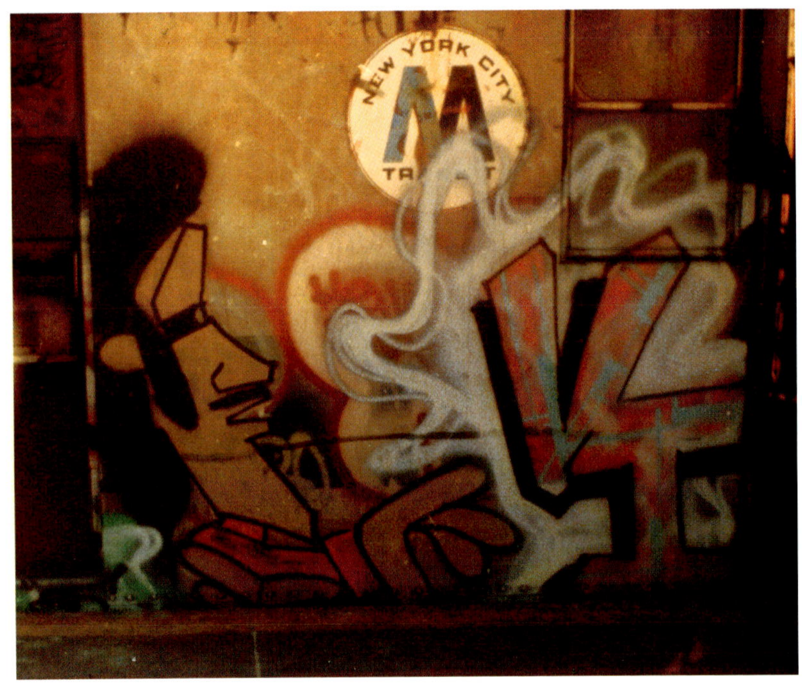

Bind

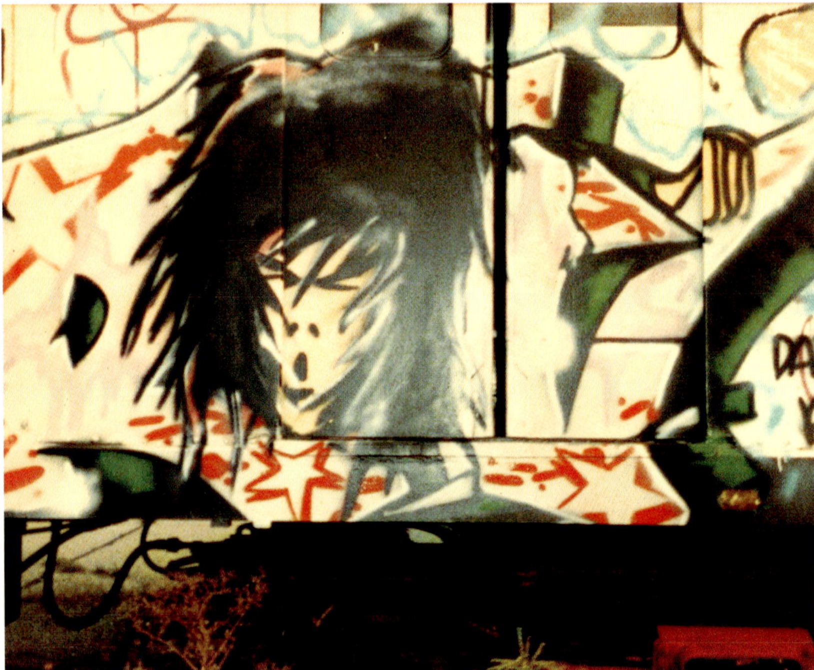

Revs

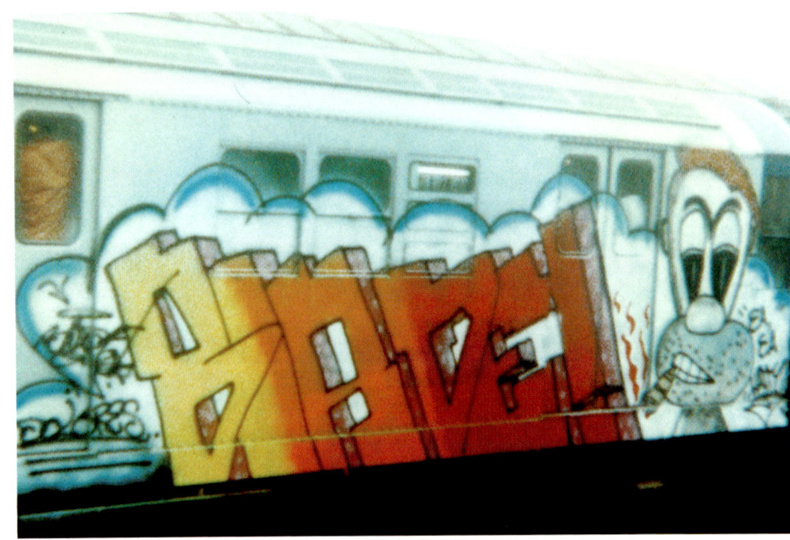

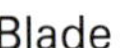

Blade

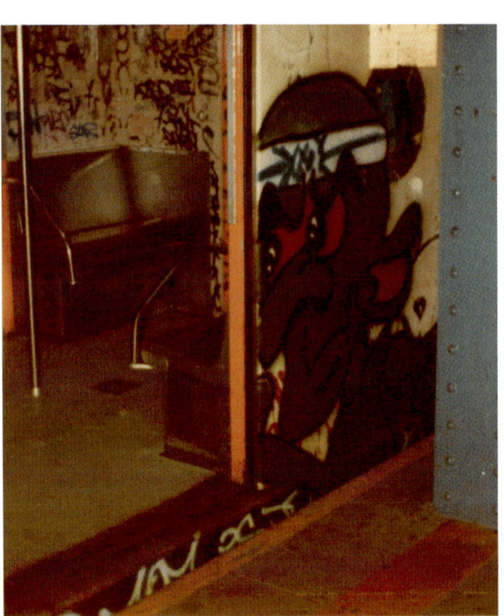

Details of a Leroy Ozzie car

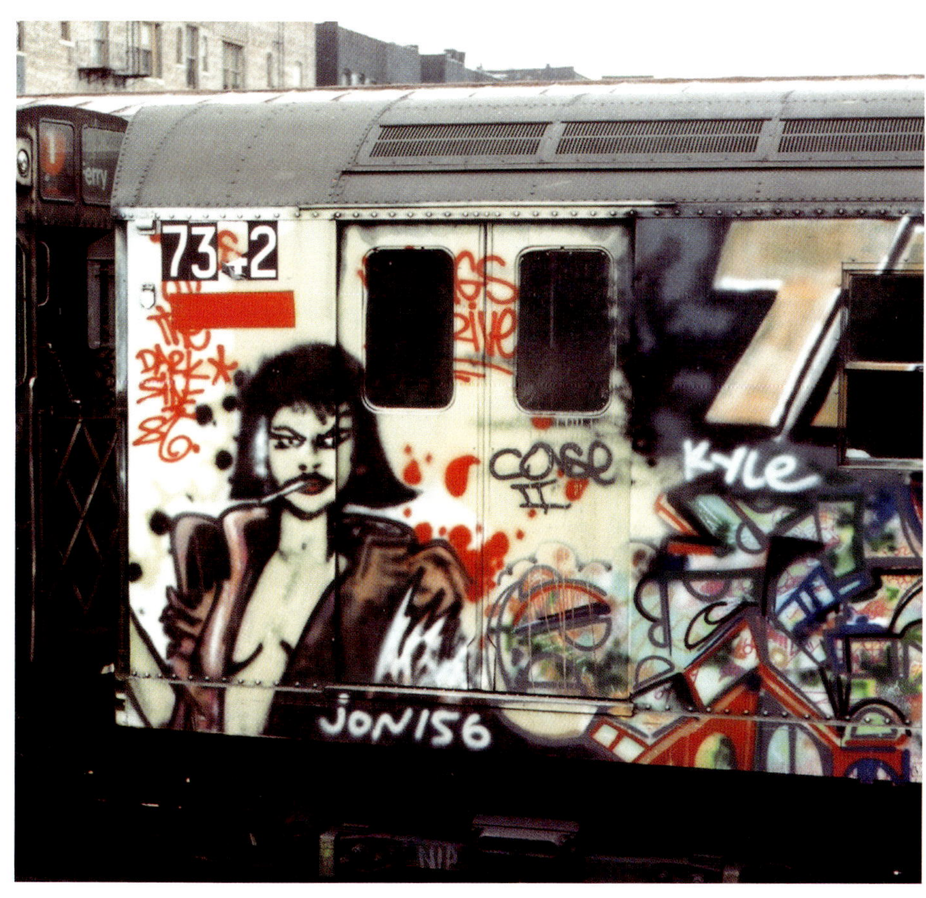

Jon 156

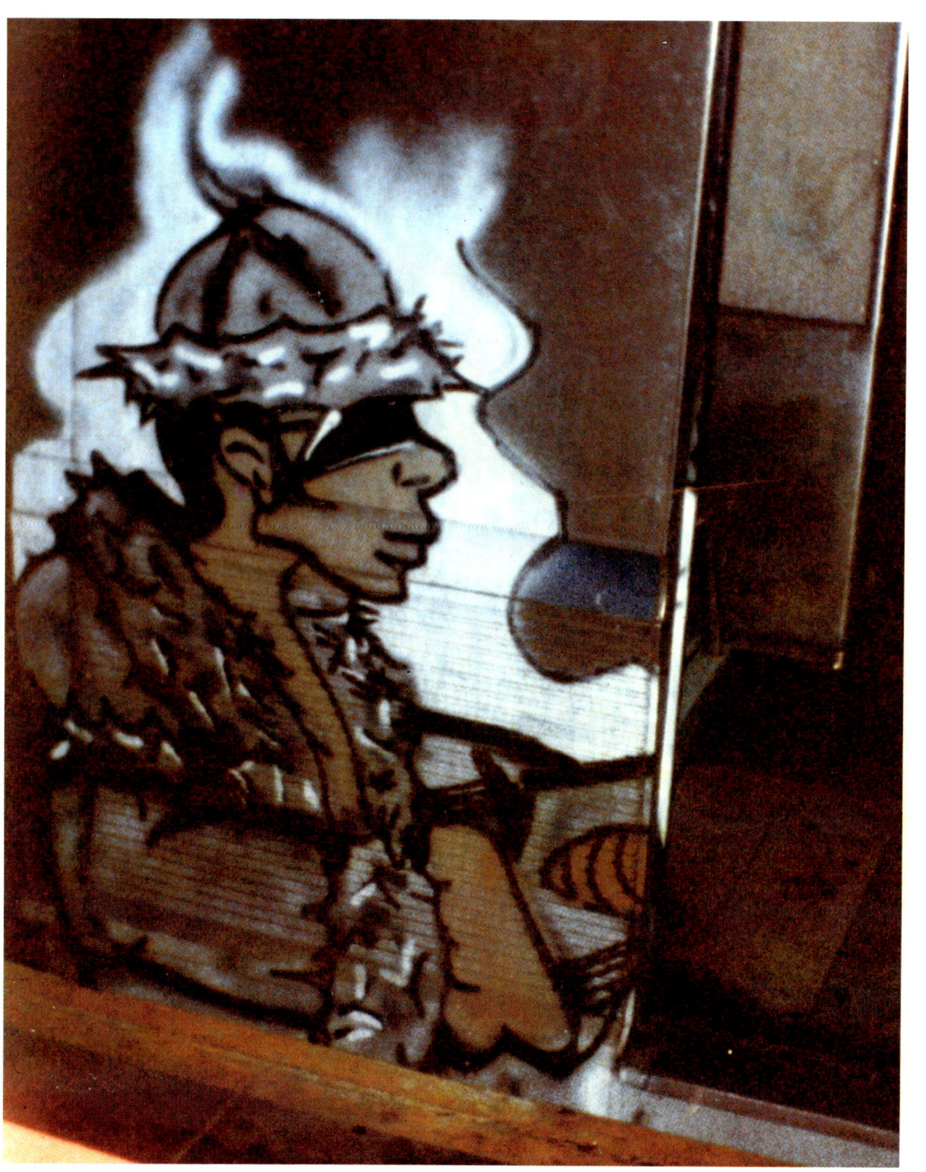

Kyle

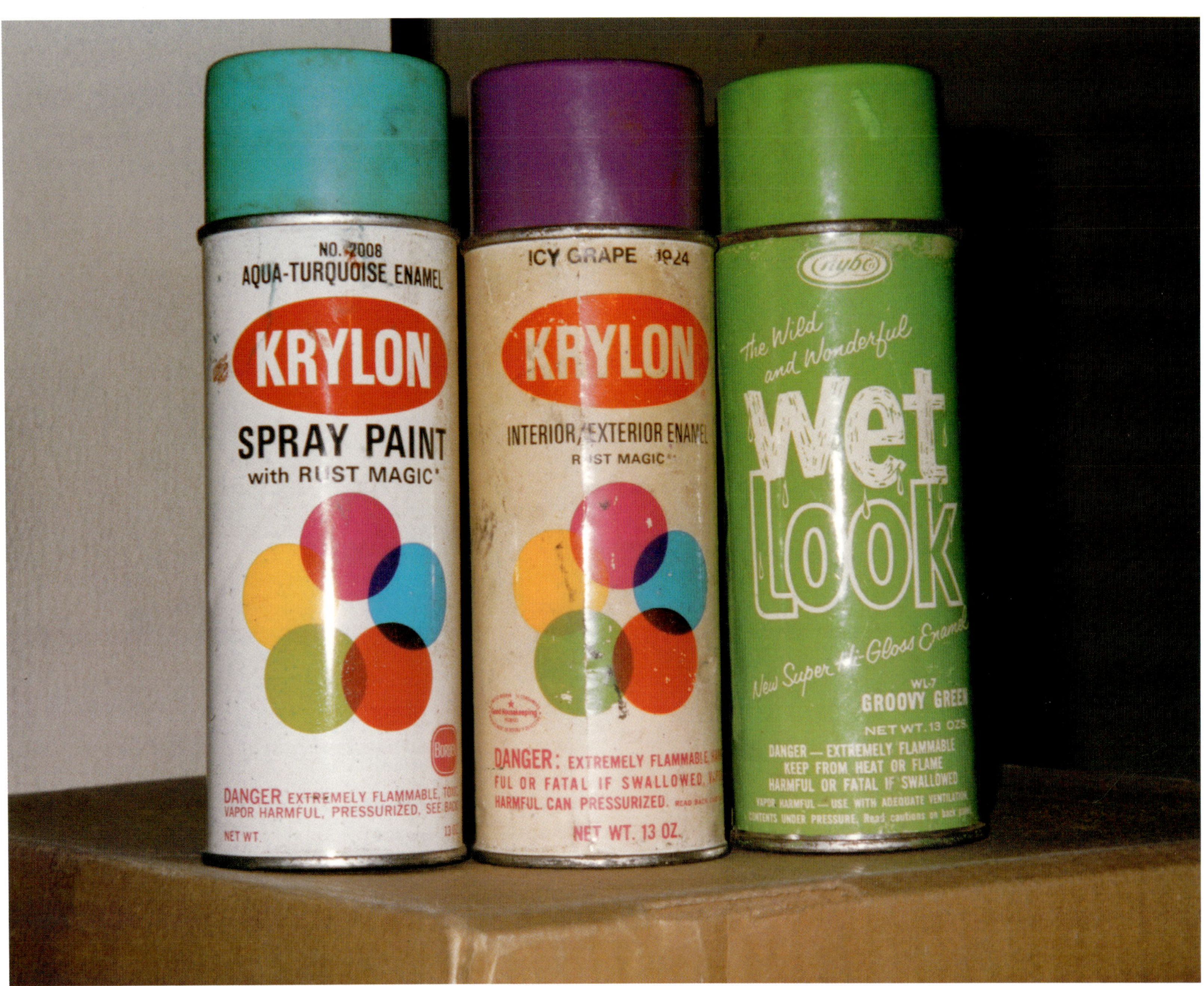

AQUA-TURQUOISE ENAMEL
KRYLON
SPRAY PAINT
with RUST MAGIC*
NET WT.
ICY GRAPE 1924
KRYLON
INTERIOR/EXTERIOR ENAMEL
NET WT. 13 OZ.
The Wild and Wonderful
Wet Look
WL-7
NET WT. 13 OZS.
DANGER — EXTREMELY FLAMMABLE
KEEP FROM HEAT OR FLAME
HARMFUL OR FATAL IF SWALLOWED

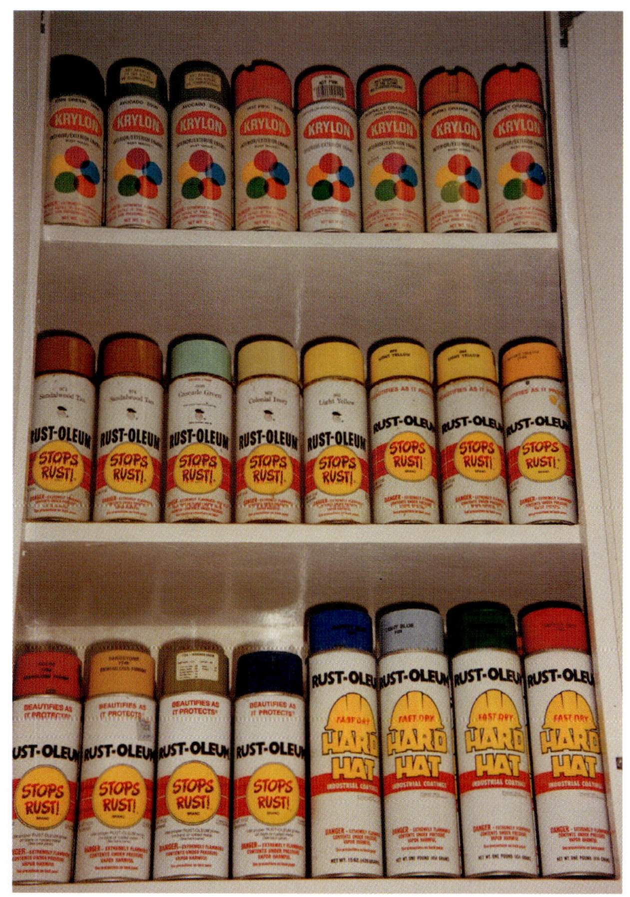
KRYLON
RUST-OLEUM
STOPS RUST!
HARD HAT

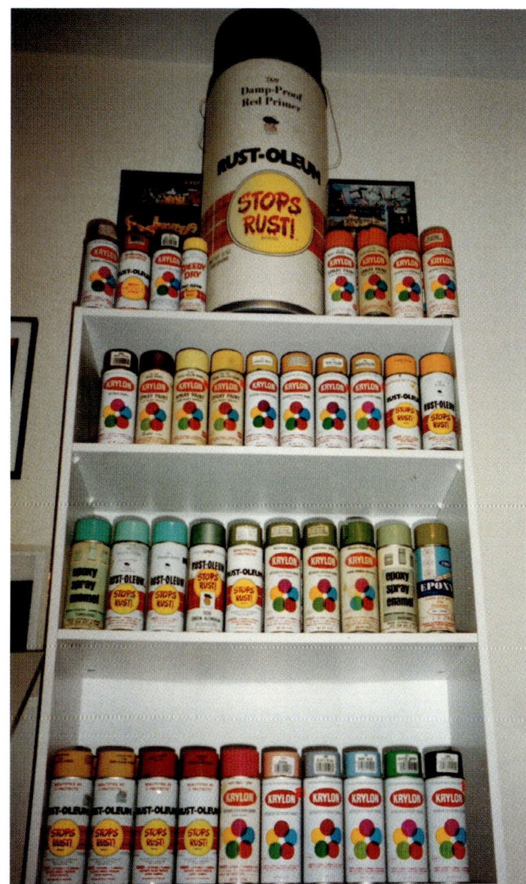
Damp-Proof Red Primer
RUST-OLEUM
STOPS RUST!
KRYLON

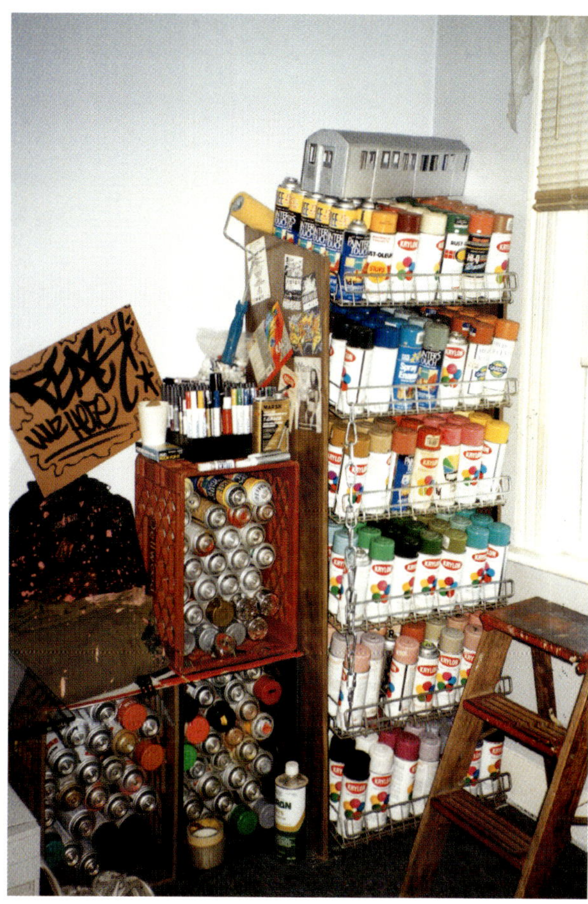

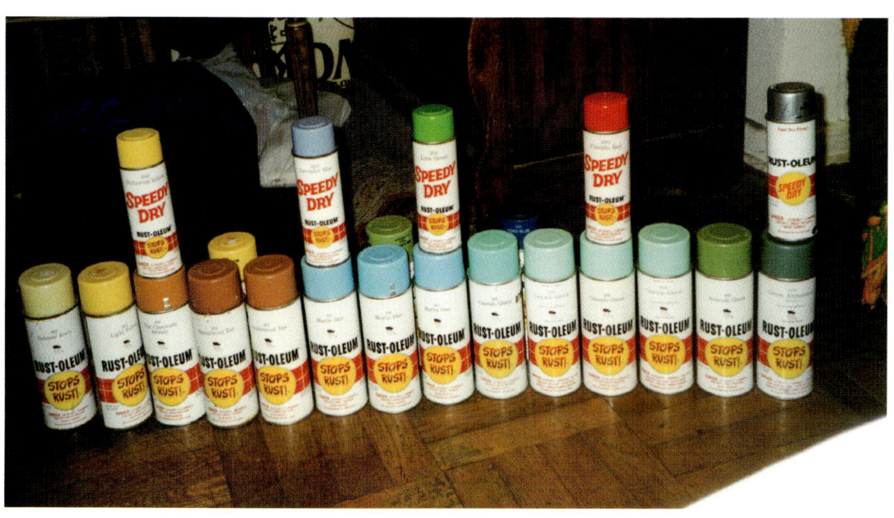
SPEEDY DRY
RUST-OLEUM
STOPS RUST!

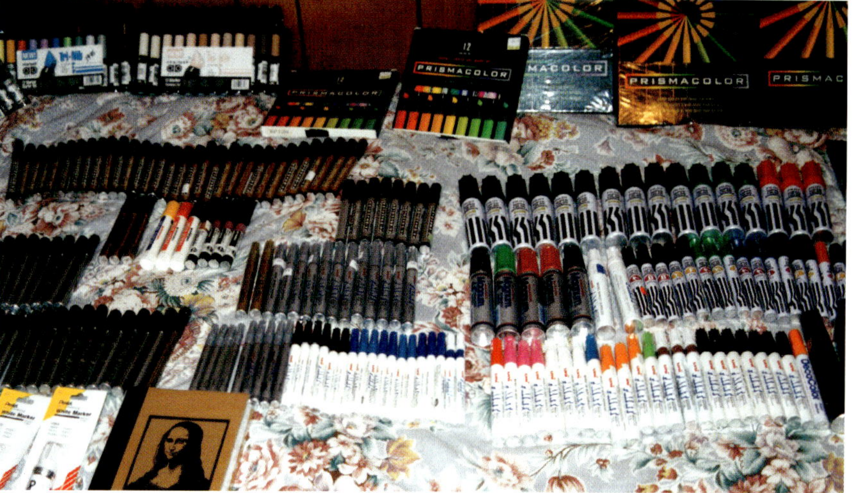
PRISMACOLOR

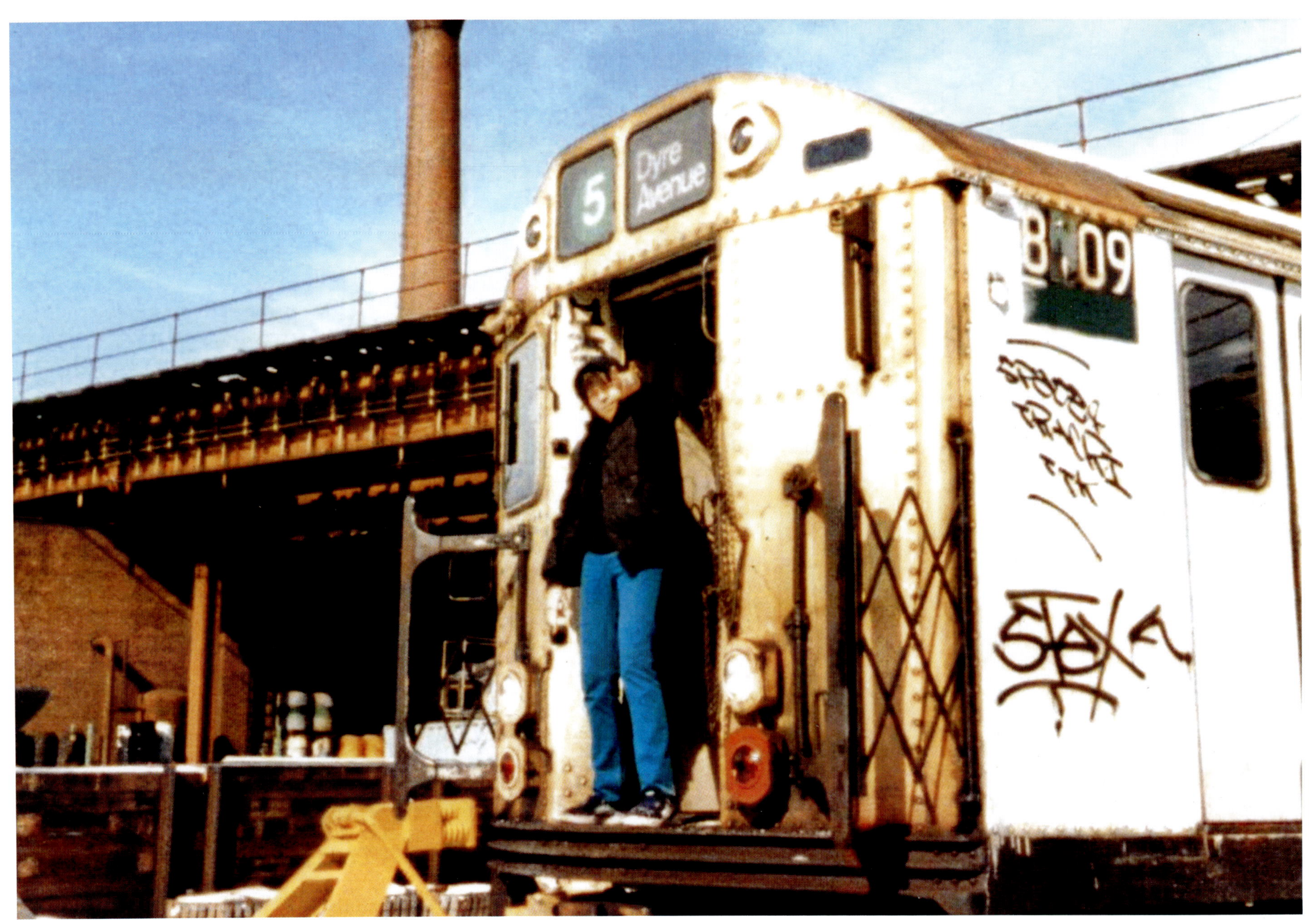

Cavs (SV), 2 Yard, 1984

Acknowledgments

I would like to thank everybody involved in the project for their time, patience, and just plain generosity.

Special thanks to:

- My wife and daughter for putting up with all this graffiti nonsense.
- Cavs for his effort in making this happen. A true freind and master photographer. The true photo king.
- Bill and Milly Myers. The best photographer I've ever seen. This book is great because of you!!!
- Joey PM, for sharing the vision and that nasty chicken place
- Mone, for rounding up the troops
- Strider. I didn't think it would take 10 years either
- Blade, for just being the king
- Poes, for meeting me in that ice storm
- Spar and Eric, two cool brothers
- Hence, rocking those T2B's
- Wolf and Team, for coming through big time
- Reas for the cool story
- Smith for the great photo and story
- Neo. Thank God for Staples
- Maze. Thanks for the flix
- Poet. 119, Farmers Oval, Good Times
- Zephyr. Great photos

I would also like to acknowledge a writer I met in junior high school in 1987. He gave me outlines, markers, and photos. He wrote Mak and introduced me to graffiti. After graduation I never saw him again.

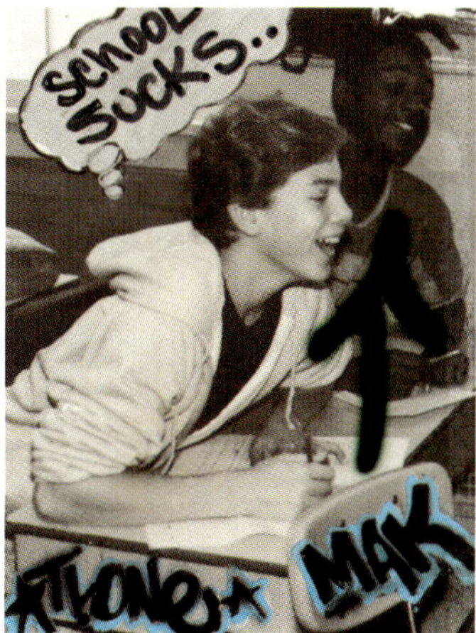

TL and MAK 1987

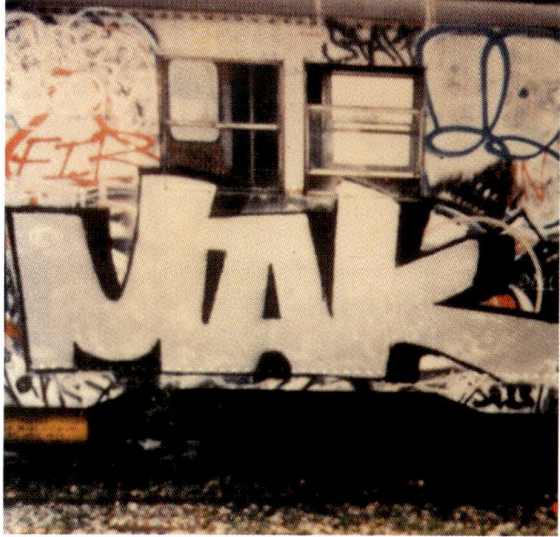

MAK 1988

Photo Credits

The photos appearing in this book are courtesy of the personal archives of the various photographers, as listed below.

Amuze, Aones: 117, 118, 121, 123, 124
Bill Myers: front & back covers, 6, 22, 42 top, 44, 51, 52, 55, 56, 57, 63, 81, 88 - 91, 93, 98, 99, 106
Bill Pollman: 73
Blade: 10, 11, 12, 138 bottom
Cavs: 24-27, 40, 42 top, 45-49, 50 top, 53, 54, 59-62, 65, 68, 69, 71, 74 -76, 77 top, 82 - 87, 94, 95 bottom, 100-103, 114, 115, 132-134, 142
Desa: 119 bottom, 122, 131 top right
DT Walker: 16, 17
Hence: 120, 126 top left, 127
Joey PM: 29-32, 33 top & bottom left, 35, 64, 77 bottom, 80, 95 TOP, 96, 97, 104, 105, 137, 138, 139 right
Maze: 42 bottom left, 50 bottom, 129, 131 top left
Mone: 112, 113, 116 top right, 117 top left, 125
Neo: 42 bottom right
Peek: 126 bottom
Poes: 28, 33 top right, 34, 58, 70
Rebel: 119 top
Smith: 43
Spar: 19 top left & bottom
Strider: 33 bottom right, 37, 38
Team: 9
Wolf: 66, 67, 108
Zephyr: 18, 23, 126 top right

All other photos are from the personal archives of the author.